Understanding and Forecasting of MONSOONS

Understanding and Forecasting of MONSOONS

Editor

P.N. Vinayachandran

CENTRE FOR SCIENCE & TECHNOLOGY OF THE NON-ALIGNED AND OTHER DEVELOPING COUNTRIES'
(NAM S&T CENTRE)

2008
DAYA PUBLISHING HOUSE
Delhi - 110 035

ISBN10 81-7035-522-2
ISBN13 978-81-7035-522-9
EAN: 9788170355229

Centre for Science and Technology of the Non-Aligned and Other Developing Countries (NAM S&T Centre)
Core-6A, 2nd Floor, India Habitat Centre, Lodhi Road,
New Delhi-110 003 (India)
Phone: +91-11-24644974, 24645134, Fax: +91-11-24644973
E-mail: namstct@gmail.com
Website: www.namstct.org

Published by : **Daya Publishing House**
1123/74, Deva Ram Park, Tri Nagar, Delhi - 110 035
Phone: 27383999, Fax: (011) 23260116
e-mail: dayabooks@vsnl.com
website: www.dayabooks.com
Showroom : 4760-61/23, Ansari Road, Darya Ganj
New Delhi - 110 002
Phone: 23245578, 23244987

Laser Typesetting : **Classic Computer Services**
Delhi - 110 035

Printed at : **Chawla Offset Printers**
Delhi - 110 052

Printed in India

Foreword

Past two decades have seen dramatic increase in the number of new findings about the causes and consequences of climate change and variability. Those are by no means the only critical issues of global environmental concern. Climate influences the local characteristics of clouds and storms, the quality and quantity of water resources, the productivity of agricultural regions, and other activities of societal concern. Agricultural productivity and economic activities are closely tied to the seasonal climate, and can be significantly affected by the extremes of floods, drought, and severe weather, as well as the steady change of average climate conditions. Developing strategies to limit adverse impacts of climate change and variability as well as to deal with various efforts related to the use of climate information to support social and economic activities (agriculture, forestry, fishery, and others) is one of the most complex and difficult tasks facing the world, including the developing nations.

El Nino Southern Oscillation (ENSO) in the Pacific has been considered as the major global phenomenon causing hydrometeorological disasters. The new findings on the Indian Ocean Dipole Mode (IODM) put much emphasis on the role of the Indian Ocean in determining the climate variability over the Asia-Africa-Pacific sectors. But the influence of the Indian Ocean on Asia-Africa-Pacific climate is less clear than that of the ENSO. It is generally felt that it must be important, but there is a lack of documentation that irrefutably demonstrates the importance of ocean – atmosphere interaction over the Indian-Ocean. There have been only a few studies that suggest the importance of Indian Ocean SST anomalies on the climate of the countries bordering the Indian Ocean.

The generation mechanism of IODM is still in an early stage of understanding. Many hypotheses postulate that this mode is forced by ENSO, but others suggest that this mode results from the air-sea interactions over the Indian Ocean itself. The correlation between the time series associated with the IODM and the Southern Oscillation Index is still unclear. Both IODM and ENSO strongly influence the monsoon systems in various regions over the Asia-Africa-Pacific sectors. Extensive and detailed investigations on the extreme climate conditions related to IODM, ENSO, and monsoon interactions, including the development of global and regional forecast systems, are necessary in order to be able to cope with their negative impacts and gain maximum benefits from their positive impacts.

In pursuance of an ongoing dialogue between the NAM S&T Centre and the Indonesian National Meteorological and Geophysical Agency (BMG) a meeting was held in New Delhi on 26-27 May 2005 with participation of Indonesian and Indian experts and the officials of the NAM S&T Centre to explore the possibility of furthering the bi- and multilateral cooperation in the field of atmospheric sciences. A delegation from BMG, Indonesia, and Indian scientists from leading organisations such as India Meteorological Department (IMD), Indian Institute of Science (IISc, Bangalore) and NCMRWF participated in the meeting. The experts discussed major areas in meteorology like El Nino - Southern Oscillation (ENSO), Indian Ocean Dipole Mode (IODM), Monsoon and Weather prediction, Ocean-Atmosphere-Land Interaction, etc. As recommended in this meeting, an international roundtable on 'Understanding and Prediction of Summer and Winter Monsoons' was organized in Jakarta/Bandung, Indonesia jointly by the NAM S&T Centre and BMG, Indonesia during 21-24 November 2005.

Thirty six scientists and professionals from Australia, India, Indonesia, Myanmar, Pakistan, Singapore, Sri Lanka, and Tanzania participated in the Roundtable. The participants deliberated on various issues such as variability, predictability & prediction, ocean-atmosphere-land interactions and monsoon, applications of extended climate prediction and climate change and monsoons; and geophysical instrumentation: design and production. The deliberations provided an opportunity to all the participants to share information and ideas on the subject, and as the co-organizer of the meeting, I am definite that it served the purpose for which it was organized.

This publication being brought out by the NAM S&T Centre is based on the presentations made at the Roundtable and is the meaningful outcome of the same. Having been associated with the subject for so many years, particularly in Indonesia, I am sure that this book will prove to be an excellent reference for those in both the developed and the developing countries engaged in policy planning and implementation of schemes and programmes on weather forecasting, modelling and related issues.

Ir. Sri Woro B. Harijono
Director General,
National Meteorological and Geophysical Agency (BMG),
Jakarta Pusat - 10720, INDONESIA
E-mail: sriworo@bmg.go.id

Preface

Monsoons modulate the rhythm of life in several countries spread across Asia, Africa and Australia. The amount of rain received during monsoons critically controls the way of life, culture and economy. Therefore, prediction of the monsoons has been considered an unavoidable endeavour. The basis and skill of forecasting monsoons is heavily dependent on understanding its intricate structure as well as variability and consequently, every data set and its analyses and each attempt to simulate monsoons claims a significant place in science.

This volume presents a collection of papers on various aspects of monsoons. These papers are selected from an "International Roundtable on Understanding and Prediction of Summer and Winter Monsoons' held at Jakarta/Bandung, Indonesia during 21-24 November, 2005. The topics covered in this volume include, observed aspects of monsoons in several countries, analyses of model simulations and forecasts, survey of instrumentation and analysis techniques, and projections of monsoon in the future climate. I hope that the different snapshots presented in this volume will provide useful information on monsoons to students and researchers.

The editor is thankful to all the authors who have painstakingly gone through the process of writing the paper and revising them according to the suggestions. The service of several reviewers is also gratefully acknowledged. The reviewers involved in examining the papers were: S. K. Satheesh, V. Venugopal, J. Kurian, P. A. Francis, K. Rajendran, S. Janakiraman, K. V. Vinu, B. Chakrapani and S. Bhattacharya. I am thankful to Dr. Arun P. Kulshreshtha for encouraging me to take up the responsibility of editing this book. It would not have been possible to co-ordinate the review process without the support from Mr. M. Bandyopadhyay and I am extremely grateful to him.

P. N. Vinayachandran
Centre for Atmospheric and Oceanic Sciences,
Indian Institute of Science, Bangalore – 560 012, India
E-mail: vinay@caos.iisc.ernet.in

About this Volume

Monsoons are the lifelines of the countries in South Asia, Southeast Asia and East Africa. This also happens to be a vast geographical region comprising developing countries with large (and growing) population. Monsoons impact the economies of these nations not only in fiscal terms but more importantly in terms of health, food security and water availability.

Monsoons are complex meteorological phenomena of global dimensions and are not yet fully understood. Yet the fact remains that they are people-friendly to a very large extent in the sense that they do arrive around the dates that they have been arriving all along. While there are large inter-seasonal and intra-seasonal variations in the amount and geographical distribution of the associated rainfall, monsoons do not entirely fail the area that they serve. But it will certainly be helpful if the vagaries of the monsoons could be predicted with some precision both in terms of timing and rainfall. This quest has been engaging the attention of scientists for over three centuries now. The scientific contributions of Edmond Halley in the 17th Century, Henry Blanford and John Eliot in the 19th Century, and Sir Gilbert Walker in the first quarter of the 20th Century are very well known. Blanford, Eliot and Walker had the privilege of heading the India Meteorological Department, which was established in 1875 with the specific mandate to study and 'foreshadow' the monsoon rainfall over India.

Monsoons are now an active area of research all over the world and some of the most talented researchers are engaged in understanding their various facets the world over. Newer approaches are being attempted assisted by new technologies – both observational and computational. Scientists in developing countries are also active in this field. What is all the more encouraging is the fact that monsoon research is being pursued as institutional programmes with substantial initiative and support from government agencies, academic bodies and international organisations. The Roundtable on 'Understanding and Prediction of Summer and Winter Monsoons' organised in Jakarta and Bandung in Indonesia by the Centre for Science and Technology of the Non-aligned and Other Developing Countries (NAM S&T Centre) in November 2005, was a worthy attempt to further monsoon research and to upgrade awareness for enhanced effort in this field.

This event was all the more noteworthy because this was a meeting point of researchers and decision makers from developing countries, dealt with a subject (Monsoon Research) of great concern to developing countries, was held in a developing country, and was organised by an international body of developing countries (NAM S&T Centre). The Roundtable was attended by the representatives of eight developing countries (India, Indonesia, Myanmar, Pakistan, Singapore, Sri Lanka, Tanzania and Uganda) and also had the benefit of participation of a distinguished atmospheric scientist from Australia.

NAM S&T Centre, under the initiative of its Director, Professor Arun P. Kulshreshtha, has seen it fit to document the presentations made by the scientists at the Roundtable so that the review and research work presented at the sessions remain on record and serve as reference and impetus for further work especially by the scientists in the countries affected directly by monsoons. Professor P. N. Vinayachandran has critically edited the papers which are presented in this volume titled 'Understanding and Forecasting of Monsoons'.

The book contains 16 research / review papers which may be categorized under five groups as follows:

(a) Country Reviews – 4 papers
(b) Observational Network – 1 paper
(c) Technique Development and Validation – 3 papers
(d) Monsoon Variability – 3 papers, and
(e) Monsoon Indicators – 5 papers

The papers presenting country reviews deal with the status of short range, medium range, long range and extended range forecasting in India including long range high resolution forecast of monsoon rainfall. The paper from Tanzania records the impact of monsoons on the largely agrarian economy of the country. The paper on observational network provides an overview of present status and future modernisation plans of the national meteorological service in India. The three papers on development and validation of techniques deal with diverse topics such as data assimilation, development of statistical dynamical models for predicting location-specific weather during monsoon and prediction of local rainfall from GCM output using projection pursuit technique. The three papers on monsoon climate variability relate to the monsoonal climate profile of Sri Lanka, characteristics of the Indian summer monsoon in the global warming scenario and the decadal to inter-decadal time-scale climate variability in the context of Asian/Indian monsoon system. The five papers that bring out the possibility of using certain climatic indicators to assess the behaviour of the monsoon system research parameters such as Eurasian and

Tibetan snowfall, ENSO, decomposition of Madden Julian Oscillation, Indian Ocean Dipole Mode and sunspot numbers. All the authors have presented their material well and most of the papers have provided ample references to assist further studies.

One does not expect path breaking research results in a presentation of this type but these do indicate the variety and spread of the efforts that are currently afoot in the developing countries of the premier monsoon region of South/Southeast Asia and East Africa. These should serve to spur further effort and synergy with bilateral or international support.

This has been a very good beginning by the NAM S&T Centre. It is hoped that the Centre would be able to organise similar 'Monsoon Meets' once in about two years in different parts of the Monsoon World which, as said earlier, comprises mostly the developing countries. The series of proceedings emerging from such biennial conferences should go a long way to accelerate monsoon research in developing countries.

S.M. Kulshrestha
Former Director General of Meteorology (India)

Contents

Introduction

The word 'Monsoon' indicates a rainy season but the domain of monsoon encompasses seasonal changes in prevailing surface wind direction especially between summer and winter. The ability to anticipate how monsoon, and the resultant climate, will behave from one year to the next will lead to better management of agriculture, water supplies, fisheries and other resources. Prediction of monsoon however is one of the major challenges of climate research as it is an extremely complex phenomenon involving variabilities over a wide range of spatial and temporal scales. Recent studies have suggested that the El Niño – Southern Oscillation (ENSO) may have an influence on the year-to-year variability of the Asian Summer Monsoon. The term El Niño was originally used by fishermen along the coasts of Ecuador and Peru to refer to a warm ocean event that typically appears around Christmas time and once begun, it lasts for several months. Fish are less abundant during these warm intervals, so fishermen often take a break to repair their equipment and spend time with their families. Peru is one of the several countries that are already successfully using predictions of El Niño in connection with agricultural planning. Countries those have taken similar initiatives include Australia, Brazil, Ethiopia, India and Indonesia among others.

A recently devised method for forecasting monsoon-season weather in Bangladesh could improve agricultural production in south Asia and equatorial Africa. The new technique produced 20- to 25-day forecasts of rainfall in the 1 million-square-kilometer area of Bangladesh during the summer of 2002. In the future, such forecasts could guide farmers in choosing optimal planting times and making other decisions, such as better water management, that affect crop production.

In India, the scientists have developed a new monsoon forecast model that is claimed to be more accurate giving better advance warning about possible drought - a knowledge that is crucial for the country's agriculture and economy. Developed by the India Meteorological Department (IMD), this model uses eight land, ocean and wind parameters to predict the extent of the monsoon replacing an earlier 16-parameter model developed in 1988 and is claimed to be ~95 per cent accurate. The new model enables a long range seasonal forecast to be made 40 days earlier than before and allows scientists to update their predictions halfway through the June-September monsoon season, a time that is crucial for Indian summer crops.

The impact of climate change is felt more severely in the majority of developing countries because of resource and infrastructure constraints. As such they must develop and implement incremental policies and more accurate prediction systems. The governments have always acutely felt the need for accurate monsoon predictions in the wake of major droughts with adverse impact on the economy. Keeping the same under consideration the Centre for Science and Technology of the Non-Aligned and Other Developing Countries (NAM S&T Centre) has identified this topic as one of its priority areas and organised an international Roundtable on 'Understanding and Prediction of Summer and Winter Monsoons' in Jakarta/Bandung, Indonesia during 21-24 November 2005 in association with the Indonesian National Agency of Meteorology and Geophysics (BMG), Government of Indonesia and the National Centre for Medium Range Weather Forecasting (NCMRWF), Department of Science & Technology, Government of India. This event was designed as a step to formulate collaborative programmes aimed at strengthening the capability of the non-aligned and other developing countries in climate prediction and modelling areas, including their application in various efforts to cope with the impact of climate variability with particular focus on the impact of interactions between monsoons, ENSO and the Indian Ocean Dipole Mode, and to define a firm ground for joint projects, the best path to be taken up as well as the best ways to achieve the objectives and accomplish the mission.

36 scientists and professionals from eight countries, including Dr. John McBride from the Bureau of Meteorology, Australia; 10 scientists from India, namely, Dr. A. K. Bohra, Dr. Akhilesh Gupta, Dr. P. Maini and Ms. Munmun Das Gupta from NCMRWF; Mr. S. R. Kalsi and Mr. S. K. Banerjee from India Meteorological Department, New Delhi; Prof. S. K. Dash from the Centre for Atmospheric Sciences, Indian Institute of Technology (IIT), Delhi; Mrs. S. K. Patwardhan from Indian Institute of Tropical Meteorology (IITM), Pune; Mr. Gopal Krishna Patra from the CSIR Centre for Mathematical Modelling and Computer Simulation, Bangalore; and Prof. P. N. Vinayachandran from the Centre for Atmospheric & Oceanic Sciences, Indian Institute of Science, Bangalore; Dr. Ko Ko Oo, Director General, Ministry of Science & Technology, Myanmar; Dr. Tariq Masood Ali Khan, Research Officer in the National Institute of Oceanography, Karachi, Pakistan; Mr. Chien Wan Tham, Head R&D, Meteorological Services Division, National Environment Agency (NEA), Singapore; Dr. Chandima Gomes, Senior Lecturer in Physics, University of Colombo, Sri Lanka; Mr. Eliakim E. Matari, Manager, Central Forecast Office (CFO), Tanzania

Meteorological Agency; and several participants from the host country Indonesia attended the technical sessions of the Roundtable and presented their papers.

The Roundtable started with an opening speech by Ir. Sri Woro B. Harijono, Director General of the National Meteorological and Geophysical Agency (BMG), Indonesia and a keynote speech by Prof. Kusmayanto Kadiman, Minister of Research for Science and Technology, Indonesia, which was followed by three technical sessions.

The first technical session was on Monsoon Science and had two sub-sessions, namely on Variability, Predictability & Prediction and Ocean-Atmosphere-Land Interactions & Monsoon. In this session it was proposed to organise the second International Roundtable in India in the year 2007 with the scientific themes of monsoons: Variability, Predictability and Prediction, Ocean-Atmosphere-Land Interactions & Monsoon, and Monsoon Processes: Cloud Interaction.

The second technical session was on Applications, which again had two sub-sessions, namely, on Extended Climate Prediction: Status and Challenge and Climate Change and Monsoons. The recommendations made during this session were (a) to exchange the data and organise a short-term training programme in 2006 related to the weather prediction on topics, viz. data assimilation programme, sectoral application of medium range weather forecast and statistical and dynamical downscaling techniques, (b) to exchange the data and organise a short period training programme in 2006 on extended climate prediction with the statistical and dynamical downscaling techniques, and (c) undertake joint operational activities in 2007 related to climate change and monsoons with the topics of monsoons in the warming scenario.

Discussion in the third technical session on Geophysical Instrumentation: Design and Production resulted in the planning of joint design and production, development of radiosonde transmitter and the advanced instrumentation and network.

Besides the above, a special session was organised on the first day of the Roundtable, in which Dr. P.S. Goel (Secretary, Department of Ocean Development, India) and Dr. Prih Harjadi (BMG-Indonesia) delivered scientific lectures on Tsunami. Also the lectures by Prof. Vinayachandran of the Indian Institute of Science, India and Dr. John Mc Bride of Australia were held in Bandung Institute of Technology on 23rd November which were attended by ~100 persons, including the Roundtable participants, students and faculty members of the Institute. A visit to the venue of the Afro-Asian Conference was also organised in Bandung.

On behalf of the Centre, I would like to express sincere gratitude to Ir. Sri Woro B. Harijono, DG, BMG, Dr. Mezak A. Ratag, Research Professor and Director, R&D Centre, BMG and other members of the organising committee of the Roundtable for excellent planning. I am especially thankful to Mr. Urip Haryoko of BMG who had been the real force behind the successful management of this event at the Indonesian end. I am also grateful to the generous support of the Department of Science & Technology (DST), Government of India for sponsoring the international travel of the Indian participants.

I would like to acknowledge the dynamic involvement and untiring efforts of Prof. P. N. Vinayachandran for technical editing of the proceedings, and acknowledge my gratitude to Dr. S. M. Kulshrestha, former Director General, India Meteorological Department for reviewing the contents of this publication and suggesting future course of action. Last, but not the least, the valuable services provided by the entire team of the NAM S&T Centre, particularly by Mr. M. Bandyopadhyay, Mr. Gaurav Gaur and Mr. Pankaj Buttan, which culminated in compiling the presented papers and giving a shape to the volume, are deeply appreciated.

I hope that the volume would serve as a useful reference material for the meteorologists and experts working in the area of monsoon prediction and will help the developing countries in working out appropriate plans and programmes on understanding and prediction of monsoons.

Arun P. Kulshreshtha
Director, NAM S&T Centre

1

Short and Long Range Forecasting in India

S.R. Kalsi
India Meteorological Department,
New Delhi, India
Phone: +91-11-24623210; Fax: +91-11-24643128
E-mail: imdsrk@yahoo.com

ABSTRACT

A wide range of weather events affect India. A huge infrastructure for monitoring these events as well as forecasting their development on short and long range time scales has been established in India Meteorological Department (IMD). This paper reviews the efforts made by IMD in this regard. A major initiative to effect overall improvements in observing and forecasting systems has also been undertaken by IMD to improve the quality of service. This is included as Vision-2015 in this paper.

Introduction

There are a wide range of meteorological, hydrological and climate phenomena which pose a threat to life, property and the environment in India. The local range of potentially dangerous and frequently occurring hydrometeorological phenomena are the following:

- Floods/flash floods by heavy precipitation and cloud bursts
- Tropical Cyclones and storm surges

- Droughts
- Severe convective storms–thunderstorms, hailstorms, lightning
- Heat wave and cold wave
- Snow avalanches

The spatial and temporal scales of these hazards vary widely from short-lived, violent phenomena of limited extent (*e.g.* severe thunderstorms), through large systems such as Tropical Cyclones (TCs) and monsoon lows and depressions. India is affected by disturbances originating in the west particularly during winter. These are also large scale disturbances known as Western Disturbances (WDs). These events can subject large areas to disastrous weather phenomena like strong winds, heavy flood producing rains, heavy snowfall and extreme hot or cold temperature conditions for period of several days. At the largest scale there are widespread droughts that affect huge sub-continental areas for months to years, causing famine and loss of life, mass exodus of population from the drought hit areas, along with increased risk of wildfires which are experienced in the Himalayas. The forecasting requirements can range from very short range forecasts of less than one hour in the case of severe thunderstorms and flash floods; through short and medium range forecasts from a few hours to days for intense TCs, WDs, heavy rains, extreme temperatures and high winds; up to seasonal and inter-annual time scale forecasts for phenomena like droughts. IMD has the mandate to provide weather and climate related information to support developmental activities in weather sensitive sectors such as agriculture, aviation, shipping, water resources management etc. As far as forecasting is concerned, weather events such as TCs, Monsoon and WDs are handled best through short range forecast. Long range forecast for southwest monsoon is also issued but drought is only dynamically monitored. India has been issuing long range forecast of summer rains for over hundred years. In fact, India was the first country in the world to start seasonal prediction. Some details of the short and long range forecast system are detailed in the subsequent two paragraphs. The infrastructure available in IMD at present is not adequate to monitor and provide realistic forecasts of high impact weather events. IMD is undertaking major initiatives to modernize its infrastructure and improve the forecasting services. Some details of this proposed scheme are also included in this paper.

Observing Systems

IMD has established a huge infrastructure in the form of Surface and Upper Air observatories, Radars and Satellite systems for acquisition of meteorological observations which are transmitted over fast telecom channels for submission to analysis and forecast centres that produce a variety of user specific products. Since there are logistic problems in manning observatories to provide coverage to the entire area of responsibility Automatic Weather Stations (AWSs) are likely to replace some of the observatories which are being run on co-operative basis. AWSs would augment the existing synoptic network and may also be valuable even in mesoscale monitoring. Data from ships of opportunity have been used since time immemorial for analysis of tropical cyclones and monsoons developing over sea areas. It has been supplemented with data from a set of buoys that have been installed under National Data Buoy Programme of Department of Ocean Development, Govt. of India.

Our ability to detect many meteorological and hydrological hazards has been revolutionized by the development of remote sensing techniques which are used judiciously in conjunction with other available information mostly from synoptic weather charts. Satellite imagery has added precision to the location and tracking of all types of weather disturbances. It has been exhaustively used for analysis and forecasting of TCs (Kalsi, 2002). Satellite data is also used for determining the aerial extent and intensity of rainfall and snowfall, define the extent of flooded and snow covered areas and in tracking squall lines and other hazardous convective phenomena. Arrangements are made during events of intense storms to receive and process INSAT data at hourly intervals. Based on the satellite image interpretation, advisories for heavy rainfall are also provided. It is also being increasingly used in monitoring drought conditions through vegetation indices and other approaches. Satellite numerical products such as cloud motion vectors, sea surface temperatures, vertical temperature and humidity profiles etc are of immense importance for Numerical Weather Prediction (NWP) techniques. Some of these parameters are being retrieved and used in the analysis and forecast system in IMD. Similarly, weather radars which are being planned for the areas unravelled by them until now provide enhanced capability to identify and track violent phenomena such as TCs thunderstorms and even tornadoes. There are a number of products which are now available from Doppler Weather Radars deployed at couple of stations. These are very useful not only in nowcasting but also in short range forecasting.

Short-range Forecasting

IMD forecast centres rely on conventional synoptic techniques for short range forecasting. In the absence of suitable mesoscale network of automatic weather stations emphasis for small-scale weather phenomenon like violent thunderstorms is laid mostly on suitable synoptic settings identified through the synoptic charts. The prediction of small or mesoscale hazards such as severe thunderstorms, squalls and flashfloods which are experienced in some parts of India in certain seasons is attempted on a nowcast/very short range time scale. Forecast techniques for these hazards are still largely extrapolative, being heavily dependent on continuously updated observational information on storm movement, rainfall intensity from real-time networks of satellites, rain gauges and radar stations. Useful forecasts of the behaviour of larger, synoptic/near synoptic scale weather systems usually seen as TCs, WDs and depressions are being prepared couple of days in advance. Synoptic models for the development of these systems are available and are used in their analysis and forecasting. Surface pressure analysis, changes in humidity, temperature and pressure at the mean sea level and the upper air charts provide useful tools for forecast.

Dvorak (1984) technique is used for TC intensity analysis. When combined with ship, buoy and surface and upper air data collected from land-based stations, Dvorak technique provides a very good tool for TC forecasting. Intensity prediction of TCs using NWP technique is still problematic but satellite imagery gives good indications both for track and intensity forecast for TCs. When the TCs approach the coast and are within the reconnaissance range of Cyclone Detection Radar (CDR), greater reliance is made on the use of CDRs that provide better insight into structural evolution of TC (Raghavan, 1997). The information on radius of maximum reflectivity from CDRs and maximum estimated winds from satellite imagery go a long way in meeting requirements of storm surge models (Dube *et al.*, 1997; Ghosh *et al.*, 1983; IMD, 2004)

The monsoon is the presiding deity so far as Indian agriculture is concerned. The issues related to its onset, advance, strengthening and weakening leading to wet and dry spells continue to be very important. These issues have been reviewed in Rao (1976). Despite the tremendous global efforts on the onset of monsoon (Krishnamurti *et al.*, 1979; Fasullo & Webster, 2003), the issue continues to be somewhat unresolved. The onset occurs initially near the southern tip of the Indian Peninsula. The northward progression of monsoon is symptomatic of a large scale transition of deep convection from the equatorial to continental regions (Rao 1976; Sikka and Gadgil 1980; Webster 1983). A lot of useful knowledge has been obtained on the anatomy of monsoon circulation and this is quite important in short range forecasting (Rao, 1976).

IMD runs a Limited Area Analysis and Forecast System (LAFS) to provide numerical guidance for short range forecasting. It consists of real time processing of data received on Global Telecommunication System, decoding and quality control procedure and a multivariable optimum interpolation system. The system uses both conventional as well as non-conventional data in the data assimilation scheme. The first guess for preparing the analysis is taken from the Global Model Forecast System (T-80/18L) run at National Centre for Medium Range Weather Forecasting (NCMRWF). Analysis is carried out at 12 sigma levels for the RSMC, New Delhi area of responsibility. The limited area model is adapted from Florida State University and is run twice a day using 00UTC and 12 UTC initial conditions. The lateral boundary conditions are taken form global model forecasts of T-80 model of NCMRWF. The details of IMD limited area model can be found in Krishnamurti *et al.* (1989). The performance of the model is well documented in Kalsi (1999) and has been used to forecast TCs, monsoon systems and WDs.

A Quasi- Lagrangian Model (QLM) adapted from NCEP, USA (Mathur, 1991) has also been running in IMD for last couple of years. QLM is a multilevel primitive equation fine-mesh model cast in the σ (= p/p_s) coordinate system (Mathur 1991). The numerical integration of the model is carried out by using the so-called quasi-Lagrangian method. The model has a limited domain in a Cartesian grid system. The horizontal grid spacing is 40 km and the integration domain consists of 111x111 grid points in a 4400x4400 Km^2 area that is centred on the initial position of the cyclone. The QLM uses 16 σ layers (17 σ levels) in the vertical. The model incorporates physical processes which include surface frictional effects, sea air exchange of sensible and latent heat, convective release of latent heat, divergence damping, horizontal diffusion, and isobaric condensation of water vapour. Radiation and turbulent processes, which have only marginal impact in the development, are excluded to minimise computational time.

A special feature of the QLM is prescription of an idealised vortex and a steering current. The idealised vortex is created from the three dimensional structure of a cyclone via empirical functions. The construction of idealised vortex is done from the current observed structure of the storm and needs information like the present location of the storm, the central pressure, the value of the outermost closed isobar, size of the storm etc. which are gathered from the preliminary synoptic analysis and satellite imagery. This idealised vortex is merged with the analysis on the QLM grid to obtain the final initial analysis for running the model. The steering current is generated via a circulation that resembles a dipole. The current storm speed and direction are utilised in calculation of the steering current. This model is now integrated upto 72 hours to provide cyclone track. TC track forecast with this model is found to be more reliable. However, the average track forecast error for 24 hour is of the order of 140 km. Model outputs are being generated by successful runs of QLM model for TCs at IMD. This model is also run with boundary conditions from T80 global model of NCMRWF.

MM5 model at NCMRWF has been used for real-time mesoscale predictions (Das, 2002a) and has been applied for a vide range of weather phenomenon (Das, 2002b). Eta model of NCMRWF is also used for short to medium range forecasts (Rajgopal & Iyengar, 2003). IMD has also deployed MM5 that runs on initial and boundary conditions of NCEP, USA. Though forecasting skill for larger weather systems has been improving steadily over the years, it is still inadequate to provide optimal early warning for even larger scale severe events. Ongoing world wide research efforts aimed at increasing forecast accuracy for these systems have the potential to make a significant contribution to upgrading future early warning capabilities.

Widespread drought evolves relatively slowly when compared with other hazards and may persist for months or years and it can be difficult, if not impossible, to predict its end. During drought situations, it is difficult to implement many remedial actions and those measures which can be taken are often site and situation specific. Developing predictive skill for large geographic regions on monthly and seasonal time scales (using Global Circulation Models and similar statistical techniques), however, offers promise for increasingly useful forecasts of the onset, severity and duration of drought. Efforts are being made for providing realistic forecasts on these time scales.

Long Range Forecasting in IMD

The India Meteorological Department (IMD) has been issuing long-range forecasts of the southwest monsoon rainfall since 1886. Sir Gilbert Walker who was the Director General of IMD from 1904 to 1924 led to the development of the first objective model based on statistical correlations between monsoon rainfall and antecedent global atmosphere, land and ocean parameters.

The 16 Parameter Power Regression and parametric model developed by Gowariker *et al.* (1991) were introduced operationally by IMD in 1988. Initially, the model showed high success even in quantitative terms, but subsequently the forecast considerably deviated from the actual. The average error in the period 1990-2002 was 9% more than twice the model error. The difference between the forecast and realised rainfall was 19% in 1994, an excess monsoon year and 20%, in the drought monsoon year 2002.

The year 2002 turned out to be an All-India drought year with an overall rainfall deficiency of 19%, while IMD had predicted a normal monsoon, resulting in a lot of attention getting focused on IMD's prediction methodology. In addition, over the recent series of successive normal monsoons over the country as a whole but with drought situations prevailing over many parts of the country, user demand had been building up for an earlier forecast of the monsoon, a mid-season update and for month-wise rainfall forecasts. This motivated IMD in 2003 to review the operational long range forecast models. In 2003 several new models were introduced by IMD for LRF purposes. New 8 and 10 parameters models replaced the 16 parameters models for operational use. The details of these models are discussed in Rajeevan *et al.* (2004).

IMD has also developed a probabilistic model using statistical discriminate analysis techniques applied to the same 8/10 parameters. These models provide the probability of rainfall for the whole country in five broad rainfall categories. An 8-parameter power regression model for July rainfall has also been developed on the same lines as well as for the model the seasonal rainfall.

All the models developed by IMD for the long range forecast on the southwest monsoon rainfall and adopted for operational purposes in 2003 stood the test of verification in real time but failed again in 2004. Therefore, IMD has further refined its models; number of parameters in the new models is reduced to 5 to 6. Best 5 models are selected from cluster of all possible models. The ensemble made out of them is the weighted average of all the 5 models. IMD also developed new experimental statistical models. Two new methods have been explored. One is ensemble regression method, in which we select the best five models from cluster of all possible models with a predictor set. Another method is non-parametric regression based on projection pursuit regression. This method can account for the non-linearity of the predictor-rainfall relationship. Both these models have shown satisfactory performance in 2002 and 2004 drought years, in which IMD's operational forecast failed.

Dynamical models have also been utilised to simulate seasonal monsoon rainfall. Seasonal simulations of the Indian summer rainfall have been carried out using NCMRWF global model at T80 resolution. The model was able to reproduce some of the essential features of the Indian monsoon and its intra-seasonal variability satisfactorily (Kar *et al.*, 2003). A number of modelling groups have utilised similar initial and boundary conditions to simulate contrasting monsoons such as 1987 and 1988. Most models are seen to have systematic bias in simulating regional features of monsoon. 30 Atmospheric General Circulation Models (AGCMs) have also been integrated over 10 year period to simulate mean monsoon during 1979-88 with identical specified SSTs. Gadgil and Sajani (1998) have validated the monsoon precipitation over Africa and India in Atmospheric Model Intercomparison Project (AMIP) runs of these 30 AGCMs. Their study revealed that (i) some models simulate the observed seasonal migration of the primary rain belt over the Asian West Pacific region, in several other models, this rain belt remains over the equatorial oceans in all the seasons, (ii) very few models are able to capture all fluctuations between good and poor monsoon seasons observed in the AMIP decade and (iii) a good rainfall climatology and proper simulation of the inter-annual variation are associated.

European Centre for Medium Range Weather Forecasting (ECMWF) has carried out a model integration for the 15-year period 1979-93. The Bay of Bengal monsoon was simulated well by the model but over estimated rainfall over northeast India and the southern equatorial trough region. On the other hand model could not simulate the precipitation pattern on the West Coast. So far as inter-annual variability is concerned, anomaly in seasonal rainfall was picked up well only in some years. The seasonal mean rainfall is sensitive to slowly varying boundary condition but this sensitivity breaks down in years like 1997(a major ENSO year). This is attributed to intra-seasonal fluctuations and also to weak Boundary Forcing Indian Summer Monsoon Rainfall coupling. Since the coupling is showing weakening during the recent years, sensitivity of monsoon on initial conditions warrant ensemble prediction techniques using operational dynamical models.

IMD has also installed a dynamical prediction system at National Climate Centre, Pune for preparing seasonal forecasts. For this purpose, the dynamical model of Experimental Climate Prediction Centre (ECPC) was adopted. This model is considered to be one of the models with good skill for the monsoon prediction. For preparing the model climatology, seasonal simulations from 1979-2003 with observed SST data have been prepared. For the 2005 monsoon season, IMD prepared experimental forecast based on this dynamical model. Indian Institute of Science (IISc), Bangalore is collaborating with IMD to implement this system.

Vision – 2015

IMD has a vision in improving the data collection, analysis and forecasting system for the country, which is being actively pursued. The new infrastructure that is being proposed would augment the overall observing systems to monitor developments of severe weather events. It is proposed to have a network of 1000 AWSs, 4000 Automatic Raingauges, 5 additional RS/RW stations, 5 wind profilers and Doppler radars. Though a large number of highly useful data products are available over GTS from a variety of non-conventional *in situ* and remote sensing systems being operated internationally, India is also planning to launch INSAT-3D system in 2006 which will provide both imaging and sounding missions. This will further improve the analysis and forecast capabilities particularly in region of sparse data.

A case for a versatile computer system is being processed for deployment in the Regional Specialized Meteorological Centre, New Delhi in which it is proposed to run a variety of global, regional and mesoscale models. This will boost development in data assimilation and forecasting techniques. High resolution mesoscale models with much better representation of orography should enable us to foreshadow high impact weather events on short to medium range time scales. A requirement of extended range weather prediction with a lead-time of one month has come from the Ministry of Agriculture. IMD is already working in collaboration with IISc, Bangalore on Long Range Forecast front and it is in close contact with Indian Institute of Technology, Delhi (IIT)-to pursue this proposal after acquisition of a High Power Computer System.

Further, telecom system of the department is being overhauled to phase out age-old teleprinter lines by high-speed data circuits. Even the smallest observatories would be provided with much better telecom facilities for expeditious transmission of weather data to the nearest data collecting centres. IMD is currently pursuing the scheme of establishment of district level Information Centres in which satellite based data reception and analysis facility will be provided. This will improve utilisation of IMD forecast and other products at district level and would also go a long way in improving early warning systems as it will facilitate and strengthen the closer interaction with disaster management agencies at the State and District level. The internet capability has been strengthened in which data bandwidth is increased to 2Mbps. This would enable easy accessibility to website by a wide variety of users including IMD's field officers.

References

1. Das, Someshwar, 2002a: Real Time mesoscale weather forecasting over Indian region using MM5 modeling system, NCMRWF Research Report No. NMRF/RR/3/2002, 77.
2. Das, Someshwar, 2002b: Evaluation and verification of MM5 forecasts over the Indian region. Twelfth PSU/NCAR Mesoscale Model User's Workshop, 24-25 June, 2002, Boulder, CO, USA, 77.
3. Dube, S.K., Rao, A.D., Sinha, P.C., Murty T.S. and A. Babulayan, 1997: Storm surges in the Bay of Bengal and its prediction, Mausam, 48, 283-304.
4. Dvorak, V.F., 1984: Tropical Cyclone Intensity Analysis using satellite data, NOAA, Tech. Rep.,
5. Fasullo, J., and Webster, P.J., 2002, A Hydrological Definition of Indian Monsoon Onset and Withdrawal, Journal of Climate, American Meteorological Society, Vol. 16, 3200-3211.
6. Gadgil, S., Sajani, S., 1998, Monsoon precipitation in AMIP runs, Climate Dynamics, 14, 659-689.
7. Ghosh, S.K., Diwan, B.N. and Singh, V.C., 1983: Numerical simulation of storm surge envelopes associated with the recent severe cyclonic storms impinging on the east and west coast of India, Mausam 34, 399-404
8. Gowariker, V., Thapliyal, V., Kulshrestha, S.M. Mandal, G.S., Sen Roy, N., and Sikka, D.R., 1991, A Power regression model for long range forecast for SW monsoon rainfall over India, Mausam, 42, 125-130.
9. Kalsi, S.R, R. Zehr, Mark DeMaria and John Knaff, 2002: An Indo-US Joint Study of Intense Tropical Cyclones of North Indian Ocean. Report available with India Meteorological Department and NOAA/NESDIS.
10. Kalsi, S.R., 1999: Some aspects of Gujarat cyclone of June 1998, proceedings of National Symposium, Tropmet, 1999 published as Meteorology beyond 2000, pp302-308.

11. Kalsi, S.R., 2002: Use of Satellite Imagery in Tropical Cyclone Intensity Analysis and Forecasting, Meteorological Monograph, Cyclone Warning Division No.1/ 2002, India Meteorological Department, New Delhi-110003, India.

12. Kar, S.C., Iyengar, G.R., Das, Swati Basu, Jeorge, J.P. and Mitra, A.K. 2003: Improvements in the NCMRWF Global Atmospheric Modeling System in Weather & Climate Modelling, Ed. By S.V. Singh, Swati Basu, T.N. Krishnamurti, New Age International Publishers, 5-22.

13. Krishnamurti, T.N., Arun Kumar, Yap, K.S. Ashu, P., Dastoor, Noels Davidson and Jian Sheng, 1990: "Performance of a high-resolution mesoscale tropical prediction model" Advances in Geophysics, 32, Academic Press INC, 133-286.

14. Mathur, M.B., 1991: The National Meteorological Centre's Quasi-Langrangian Model for Hurricane Prediction, Mon. Wea. Rev., 119,6,1419-1447.

15. Raghvan, S., 1997: Radar observations of tropical cyclones over the Indian Seas, Mausam 48. 2, 169-188.

16. Rajeevan, M., 2001: Prediction of Indian summer monsoon: Status, problems and prospects, Current Science, Vol. 81, No. 11, 1451-1457.

17. Rajeevan, M., D.S. Pai, Dikshit, S., and Kelkar, R.R., 2004, IMD's new operational model for long range forecast of southwest monsoon rainfall over India and their verification for 2003, Current Science, 86, 422-431.

18. Rajagopal, E.N. and Iyangar G.R., 2003: Proceeding of Workshop, New Delhi during 7-9 Feb. 2002 under the aegis of Indo-US Science and Technology Forum.

19. Rao, Y.P., 1976: Southwest monsoon: Synoptic Meteorology, Meteor, Monogr., No. 1/1976, India Meteorological Department, 376.

20. Sikka, D.R., and Gadgil, S., 1980: On the maximum cloud zone and the ITCZ over Indian longitudes during the southwest monsoon. Mon. Wea. Rev. 108, 1840-1853.

21. Webster, P.J., 1983: Mechanism of monsoon transition: Surface hydrology effects, J. Atmos. Sci., 40, 2110-2124.

2

Medium and Extended Range Forecasting of Indian Monsoon

A.K. Bohra*, G. Iyengar, E.N. Rajagopal, M. Dasgupta, R. Ashrit, S. Basu and A.K. Mitra

National Centre of Medium Range Weather Forecasting, Ministry of Earth Science, Govt. of India, A-50, Sec-62, Noida, U.P., India

Phone: +91-120-2403611; Fax: +91-120-2400062

**E-mail: akbohra@ncmrwf.gov.in*

ABSTRACT

Monsoon is a kind of climatic phenomena in which the dominant wind system changes with seasons. The need to provide accurate weather forecasts during the monsoon arises from various user interests. Agriculture is one such very highly weather sensitive sector where stakes for reliable weather forecasts are very high. In India, because of various constraints, farmers and planners need relatively longer lead time as compared to their counterparts in developed world to take necessary actions on the basis of weather forecasts. In India, monsoon forecasts are generated for three time-scales viz. short range (1-2 days ahead), medium range (3-7 days ahead) and long range forecasts for monthly and seasonal scales. India Meteorological Department (IMD) generates short and long range predictions. National Centre for Medium Range Weather Forecasting (NCMRWF) is responsible for the medium range predictions. For the last 3-monsoon season NCMRWF is issuing experimental dynamical extended range prediction in collaboration with SAC/ISRO. Given the very complex nature of monsoon, it is not possible to generate reliable forecasts beyond a day or two ahead using the conventional synoptic methods. Efforts have been made to implement forecasting systems based on numerical weather prediction (NWP) techniques to generate forecast on short, medium and even monthly scales on routine basis for all seasons including the monsoon.

Introduction

The Asian monsoon is an active component of the northern hemispheric circulation. It brings large amount of water vapour from the Indian and Pacific Oceans to the mainland. As a consequence, a large amount of rainfall is formed in the monsoon region. Because of close relationship between monsoon and rainfall, monsoon variability influences economy, industry, agriculture and daily life of the people of this region. The Indian monsoon is a sub-system of the Asian monsoon and governs the very pulse of life in India as about 65% of the population of the country is engaged in agriculture or agriculture related activities. During the monsoon season, there are periods of dry and wet spells caused by distinct epochs of flow patterns. The need to provide accurate weather forecasts during the monsoon arises from various user interests. Agriculture is one such very highly weather sensitive sector where stakes for reliable weather forecasts are very high. In India, because of various constraints, farmers and planners need relatively longer lead time as compared to their counterparts in developed world to take necessary actions on the basis of weather forecasts, hence the need for medium and extended/seasonal scale prediction.

Using conventional synoptic forecast techniques it is not realistically possible to predict the weather beyond a day or two. India has, therefore, tried to keep pace with development of numerical weather prediction (NWP) techniques and for last decade or so has been employing these techniques for generating short and medium range weather forecasts for a large number of user agencies, particularly for the agriculture, planning and defence sectors. In this study, forecasting systems for generating medium and extended range forecasts for monsoons are described. The use of meso-scale regional models for dynamical downscaling of details during high impact weather is also presented.

Global Medium Range Assimilation and Forecasting

Medium Range Forecasting (MRF) is a classical initial value, boundary condition problem. The usual approach is to start from an initial global analysis, based on data, and proceed to integrate numerically, by a step-by-step procedure, a set of equations that are to describe the hydrodynamics and thermodynamics of the atmosphere. The practical limit of predictability of weather is about seven to ten days because the atmosphere is a chaotic system. The limit reduces further in tropical and monsoon regions because of the complex nature of many physical processes and feedback mechanisms operating in the region.

Since June 1, 1994 an end-to-end global assimilation forecast system is being run for generating medium range forecasts based on 00 UTC initial conditions in operational mode with special emphasis on providing location specific forecasts for farmers. This forecast system runs on Cray SV1 (24 processor; 8 GB of memory) computer system at NCMRWF.

The medium range analysis forecast system of the NCMRWF consists of the following sub-systems:

1. Data reception, processing, and quality control
2. Data Assimilation

3. Model integration
4. Post-processing and diagnostic studies
5. Preparation of location specific forecasts for agro-meteorological advisories.

The data used in the system is mainly extracted from the GTS raw data. Non-conventional data, particularly from satellites, is also received on near real time basis using ftp facility from various sources. The operational global data assimilation system comprises of global spectral model of T80/L18 resolution and a three dimensional variational data assimilation system. Both, the model and the analysis scheme have adapted from NCEP (Parrish *et al.*, 1997; Das Gupta *et al.*, 2003). An intermittent data assimilation scheme in 6-hour cycle is run. 6-hour forecasts of the T80/L18 model are utilised to serve as the first guess for the subsequent analysis. The model is integrated daily up to seven days starting from 00 UTC analyses on real time basis. However, the forecasts up to 5 days are disseminated to various user agencies.

The present version of operational model is being run at T80 resolution in the horizontal and has 18 vertical layers in sigma coordinate system. The model incorporates a number of physical processes that are of direct relevance for monsoon regime. These are: surface fluxes are computed using Monin-Obukhove Similarity theory; Turbulent Diffusion in boundary layer using non-local closure; Lacis and Hansen, and Harshvardhan schemes for shortwave radiation; Fels and Schwarzkopf Scheme for longwave radiation; Modified Kuo scheme for deep convection; Tiedtke Scheme for shallow convection; Manabe's scheme for Large Scale condensation; Slingo scheme for clouds; Kessler's scheme for rain evaporation. We have conducted experiments by making changes to the different parameterisation schemes of convection, boundary layer etc. (George and Begum 1997; Basu *et al.*, 2002; Das *et al.*, 2001 and 2002).

The MRF system provides several products of basic flow variables, derived fields and accumulated precipitation. These products are provided to various user agencies as NWP guidance in their forecasting activities. Location specific analysis and forecast products are provided to agriculture sector. The feedback from user agencies shows that the products have been found useful. Constant research and development efforts are made to improve the products (George and Begum 1997; Basu *et al.*, 2002; Das *et al.*, 2001 and 2002). The features of monsoon such as monsoon trough and Mascarene High are well simulated in the analysis. The day 5 forecast is also able to maintain these features. The low-level jet, the tropical easterly jet, the Tibetan High etc. are well simulated. The operational system has been found to predict reasonably well the monsoon systems such as lows, depressions, off shore troughs, fluctuations of monsoon trough position, monsoon-extra-tropic interaction etc. Figures 1 and 2 shows the mean and the systematic errors at 850 hPa and 200 hPa levels respectively.

Understanding, and as a result prediction of monsoon has been hampered by the limited physical and dynamical information around the vast mountains in Asia and the oceanic regions. Availability of observational data over these regions is expected to improve the understanding and prediction. Of late, there has been a spurt in various kinds of satellite data that can be ingested into the assimilation forecast systems. The use of satellite data in NWP has advanced substantially in the last decade. It has shown clear positive impact in northern hemisphere, southern hemisphere, and tropics (Derber *et al.*, 1997). The forecast impact of satellite data now equals or exceeds impact of radiosonde in both the hemispheres. At NCMRWF concerted effort is made to download satellite data from various sources. Impact and sensitivity studies are carried out before including the data in operational system. Figure 3 shows the improvements in the analysis and the forecast of a monsoon rain giving system during September 2005. By including high-resolution METEOSAT satellite winds, we see improvements in both the analysis and forecasts of the said system.

The performance of assimilation forecast systems over monsoon region and tropics suffers from spin up problem. The conventional data is inadequate to define adequately the initial moisture and heating fields over this region. At NCMRWF recently the model resolution of the global model and corresponding assimilation scheme has been increased to T170 (about 70 km) in horizontal and 28 levels in vertical. Forecasts from operational (T80/L18) and T170/L28 model have been compared (Kar, 2002). The details brought about and the associated positive impact by the increased resolution is noted. However, the forecast of the rainfall for the monsoon regime is still a difficult issue (Basu, 2005). The case of exceptional heavy rainfall during 26-27 July 2005 at Mumbai was analysed at NCMRWF (Bohra *et al.*, 2005). From the preliminary studies, we feel that model resolution (horizontal/vertical) and assimilation of satellite direct radiances play an important role in the rainfall forecasts. Figure 4 shows poor performance of global models even with higher resolution. A more in depth study is required to find the deficiencies in the global models to capture heavy rainfall events.

Ensemble prediction techniques give some hope to get an idea of the uncertainties involved in these forecasts. At NCMRWF a 10-member ensemble technique has been tested, and the results are encouraging. Figure 5 shows the improvements in the skill of tropical wind prediction during monsoon 2005 month. We have compared the performance of the NCMRWF global system with another global model (UKMO) in capturing the progress and onset of the summer monsoon over the south Asia part (Indian region). Figure 6 shows the evolution of kinetic energy at 850 hPa and the total perceptible water over the Arabian Sea region. The large-scale pattern of evolution agrees well. However, the UKMO being a much higher resolution model, as expected shows more intra-seasonal variability.

Regional Meso-Scale Assimilation and Models

Since January 1, 2002, Eta Model at horizontal resolution of 32 km and 38 vertical levels is being run operationally for 48 hours daily based on 00 UTC analysis. The model is cast on semi-staggered Arakawa E-grid. It is run on the domain 60-100E and 5-45N. It uses silhouette step topography. The aim has been to improve delineation of the structure of the rainfall forecasts better. Recently a PC based version of this model has been developed on request of one of the BIMSTEC countries. A 22 km horizontal resolution version is also being tested to capture very tropical systems. Figure 7 shows the wind and rainfall prediction for the Mumbai heavy rainfall event of 26-27 July 2005. The mesoscale model Eta is able to capture the intense circulation and associated enhanced rainfall. By using improved analysis (initial condition) from UKMO we find further improvements in intensity and rainfall. Recently MM5 model has been implemented at NCMRWF with the aim of testing various cloud convective parameterisation schemes and improving the parameterisation in global model, to simulate meso-scale convective system over Indian monsoon region, and generate cloud scale parameters etc. The Forecasts are generated using this model on real time basis. At present the model is nested at three resolutions of 90, 30, and 10 km for mesoscale forecasting. The model successfully depicted the meso-scale features of heavy rainfall events that are not captured by the operational global model. Some results from MM5 are shown in Figure 8. By using the initial analysis from UKMO, we saw a tremendous improvement in rainfall quantity along the west coast of India during the Mumbai heavy rainfall event of 26-27 July 2005. This clearly shows the impact of initial analysis on a mesoscale modelling system. Realizing the importance of assimilation we have recently implemented a 3-D variational mesoscale data assimilation system at NCMRWF. The initial results are very encouraging. The upcoming mesoscale observation network and the high resolution satellite data can now be readily assimilated in our mesoscale analysis/prediction system.

Extended Range Monsoon Forecasting

Long periods of drought or flood during any summer monsoon season can have a devastating effect on human life and the country's economy. Reliable seasonal to inter-annual prediction of summer monsoon rainfall is required for the Indian subcontinent. Apart from agriculture, interest in seasonal prediction has grown from the commerce and industry related sectors also. Traditionally in India statistical methods are used for operational extended range seasonal forecasting of summer monsoon rainfall. During the last three years (2002-2005) experimental attempts have been made to use NCMRWF dynamical model for extended range monsoon rainfall forecasting. For each monsoon month (June to September) ensemble integration of 10 members are performed of the NCMRWF Global Model (T80L18) from five initial conditions and two SST predictions for each initial data. The predicted SSTs are by analogue method and persistence method (prepared at MOG/SAC) is generally used for changing the boundary condition during the model integration. Anomalies in the model predicted rainfalls are computed using the model climate. Probability of occurrence of excess, normal or deficient rainfall (% chance) in homogenous zones is prepared. Figure 9 shows the sample probability forecasts from monsoon 2005 season. With availability of observed rainfall anomalies the extended range forecasts are being verified. The air-sea interaction plays a greater role in the evolution of seasonal monsoon. The Equatorial Indian Ocean particularly is very important (Gadgil *et al.*, 2003) to be included in the seasonal forecast model. For this at NCMRWF a coupled ocean-atmosphere model with assimilation is being developed.

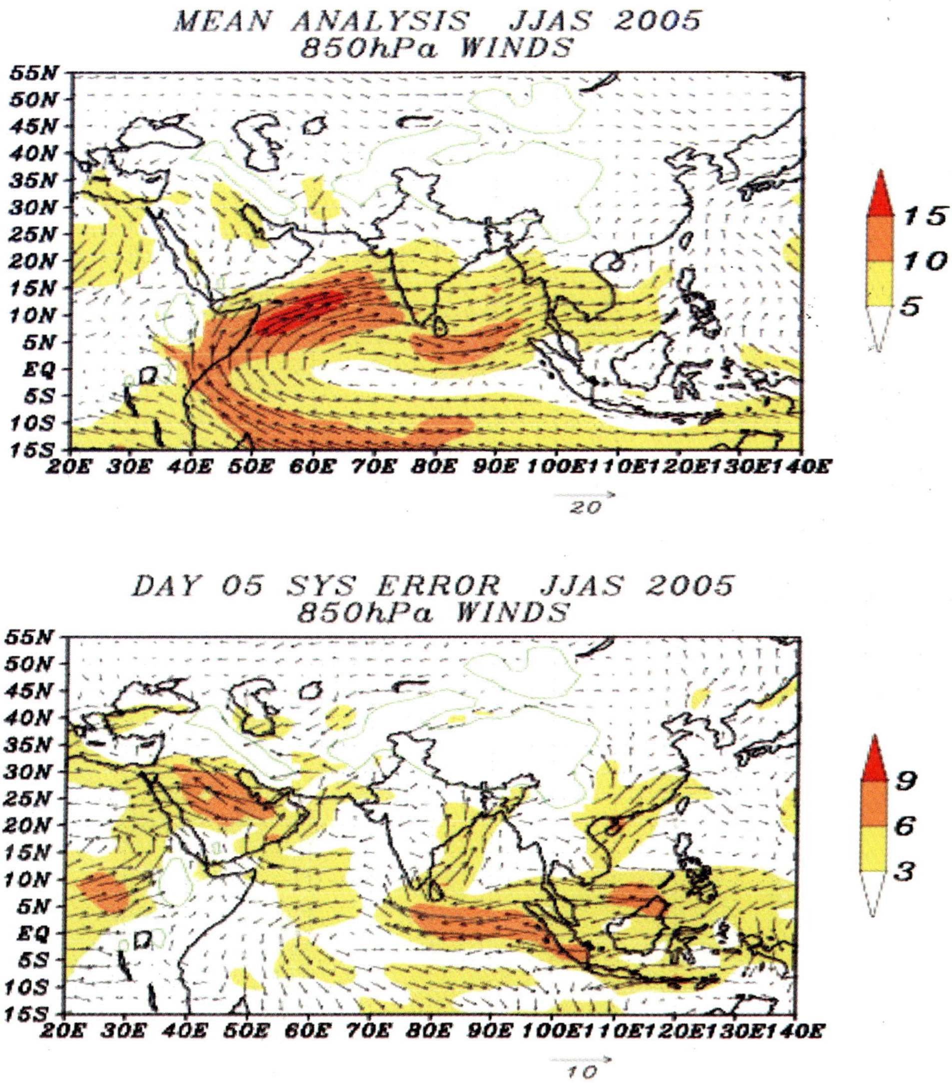

Figure 1: Mean and Systematic Error for the Monsoon Period of 2005 from NCMRWF Global Operational Analysis/Forecast System at 850 hPa

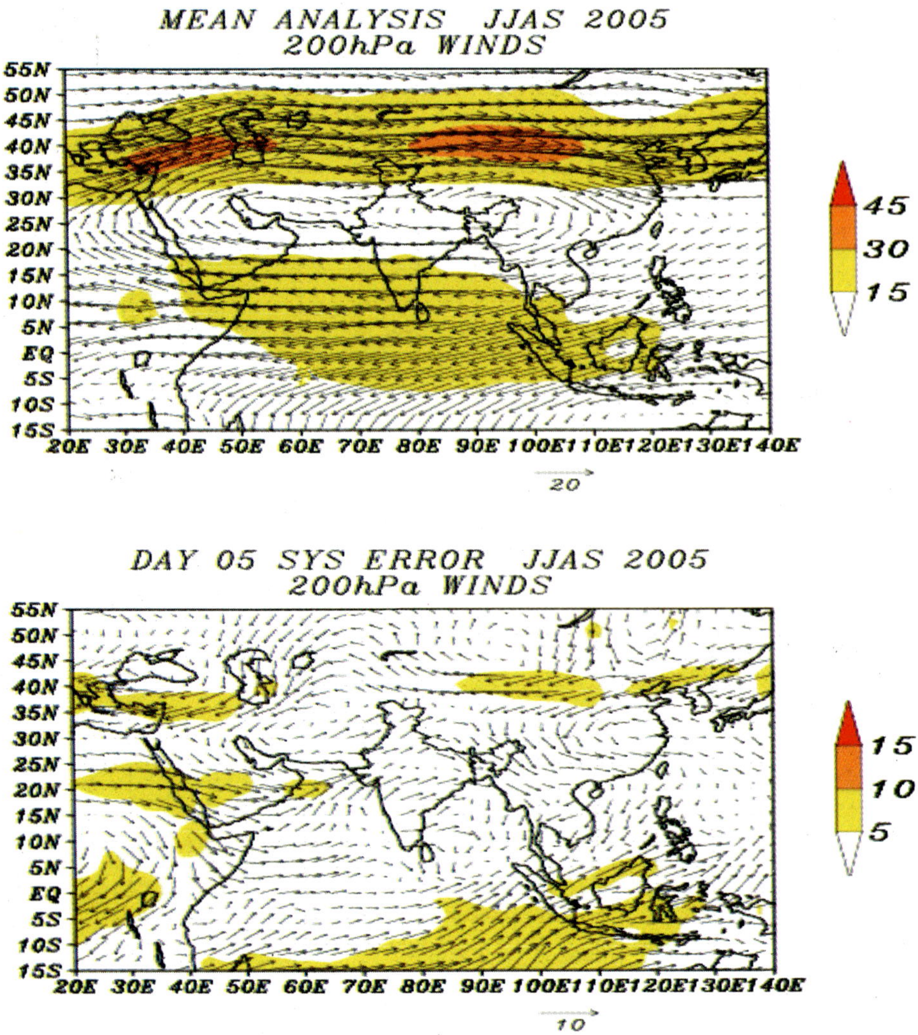

Figure 2: Mean and Systematic Error for the Monsoon Period of 2005 from NCMRWF Global Operational Analysis/Forecast System at 200 hPa

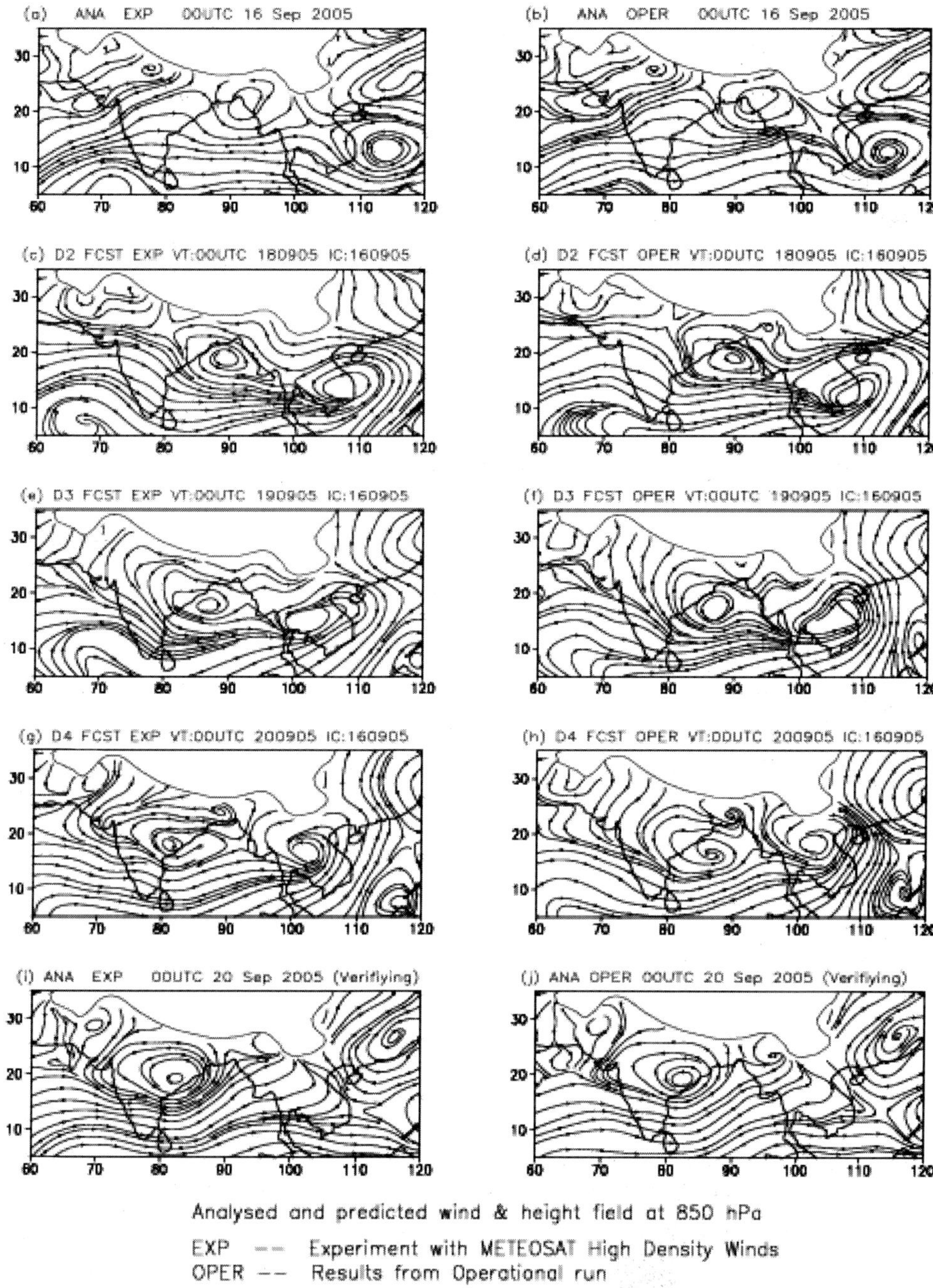

Figure 3: Improvements in Analysis and Forecasts of a Monsoon Rain Bearing System During September 2005 as Seen at 850 hPa Level

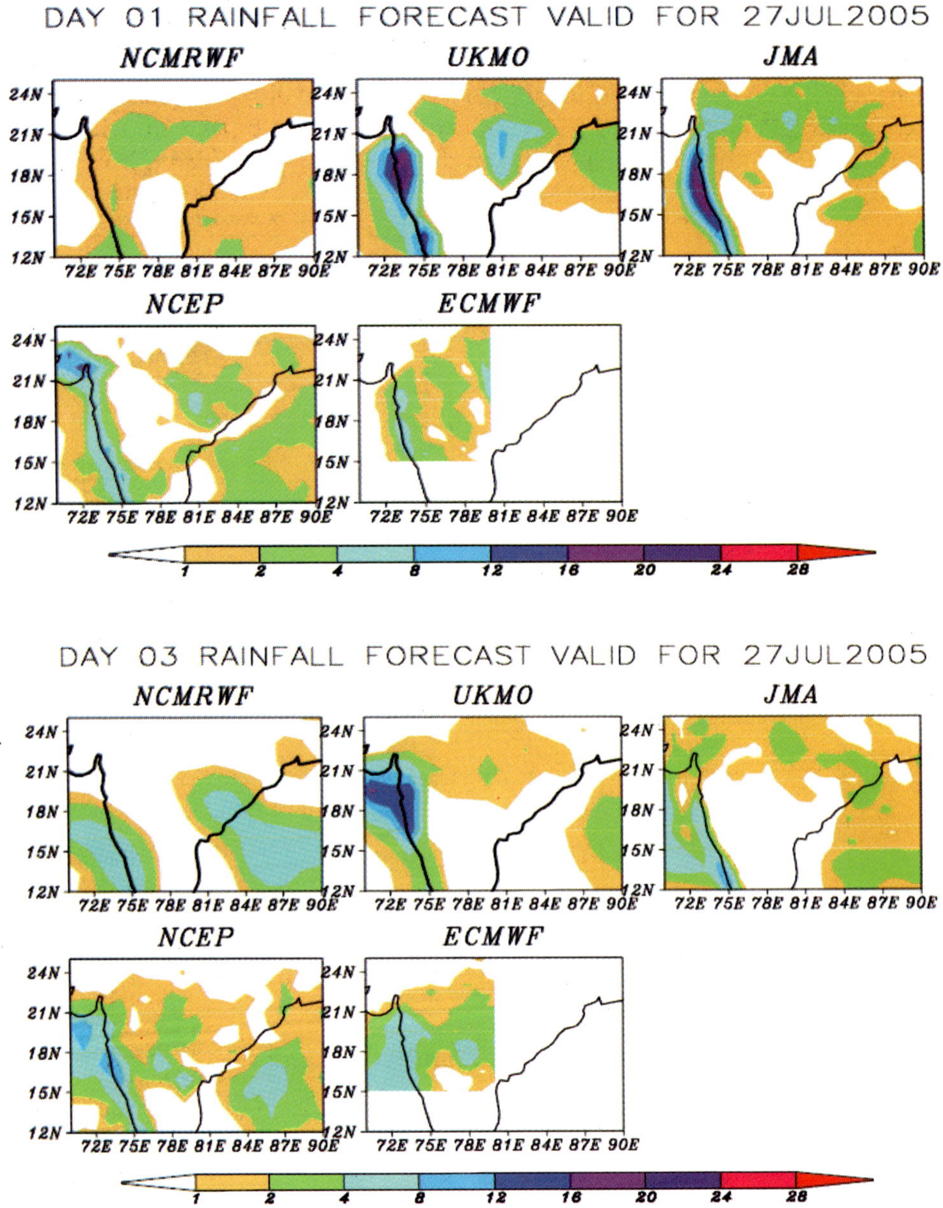

Figure 4: Forecast of a Very Heavy Rainfall Event During Monsoon 2005 by Different Global Models from Operational Centres

Ocean Forecasting

For improving the performance of the extended range prediction, at NCMRWF efforts are being made to implement the ocean models and the assimilation systems. Recently the NCEP ocean surface wave model WAVEWATCH III (Version 1.18) has been implemented at NCMRWF for the global domain at 1 degree lat/lon resolution, and the output is available on real time on the Centre web page on daily basis. Figure 10 shows the sample output from the model for the Indian Ocean region during the pre-monsoon period. Model Inputs are 6 hourly Winds at 10 m level from

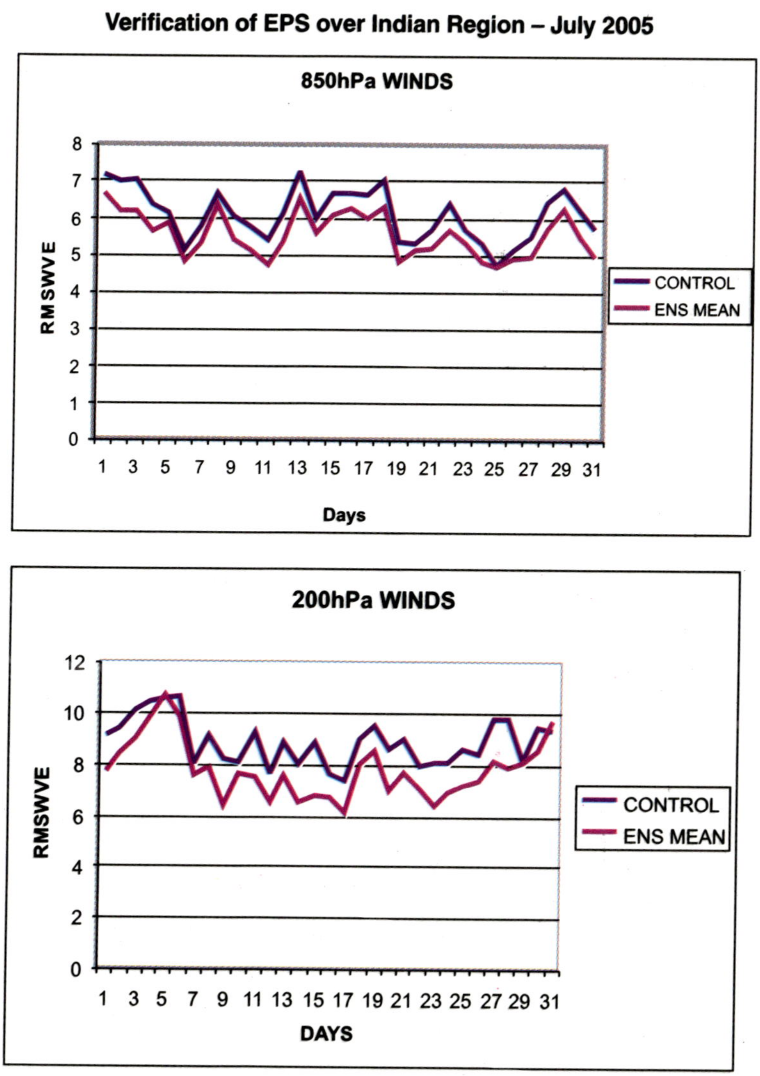

Figure 5: Improvements in Monsoon Prediction by Use of Ensemble Technique

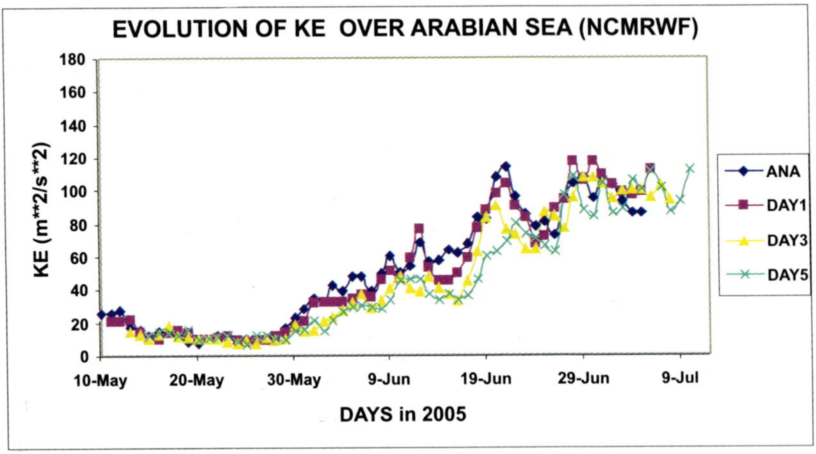
EVOLUTION OF KE OVER ARABIAN SEA (NCMRWF)
KE (m**2/s**2)
180
160
140
120
100
80
60
40
20
0
10-May
20-May
30-May
9-Jun
19-Jun
29-Jun
9-Jul
DAYS in 2005
ANA
DAY1
DAY3
DAY5

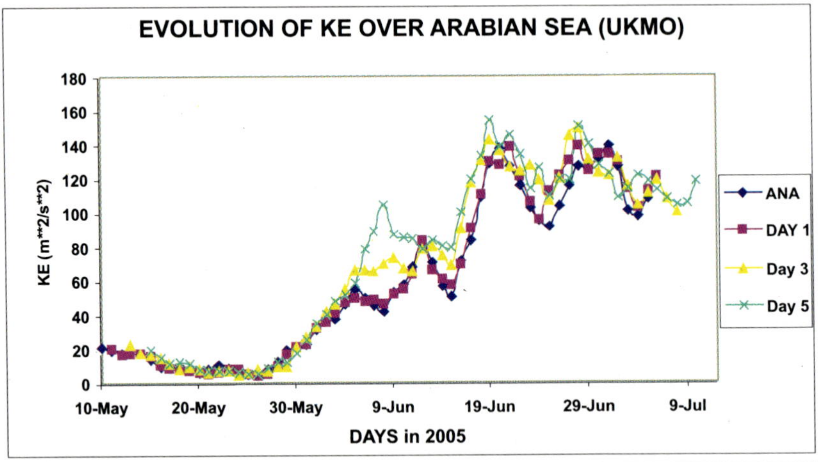
EVOLUTION OF KE OVER ARABIAN SEA (UKMO)
KE (m**2/s**2)
180
160
140
120
100
80
60
40
20
0
10-May
20-May
30-May
9-Jun
19-Jun
29-Jun
9-Jul
DAYS in 2005
ANA
DAY 1
Day 3
Day 5

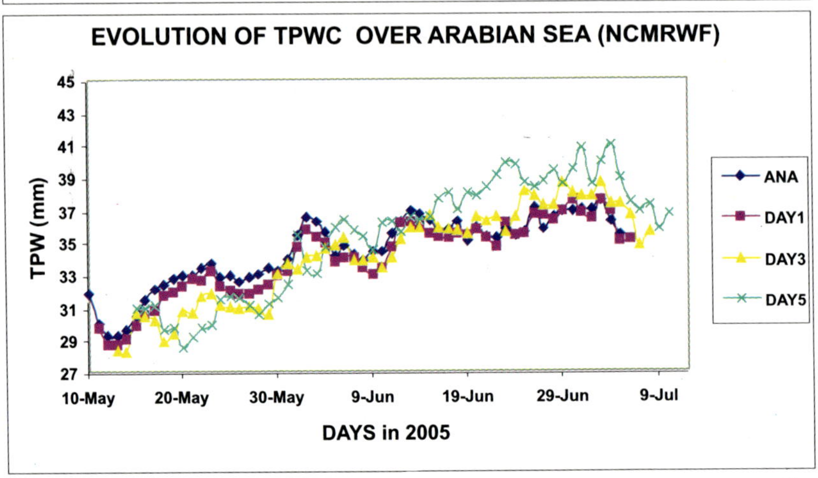
EVOLUTION OF TPWC OVER ARABIAN SEA (NCMRWF)
TPW (mm)
45
43
41
39
37
35
33
31
29
27
10-May
20-May
30-May
9-Jun
19-Jun
29-Jun
9-Jul
DAYS in 2005
ANA
DAY1
DAY3
DAY5

Contd...

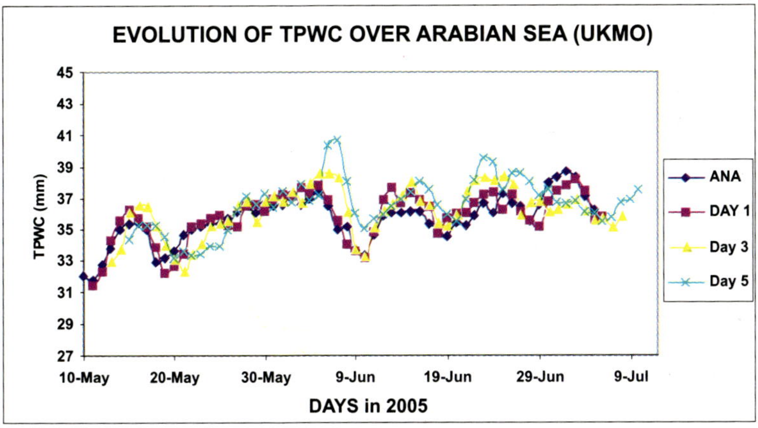

Figure 6: Evolution and Onset of Monsoon as Seen in Global Models

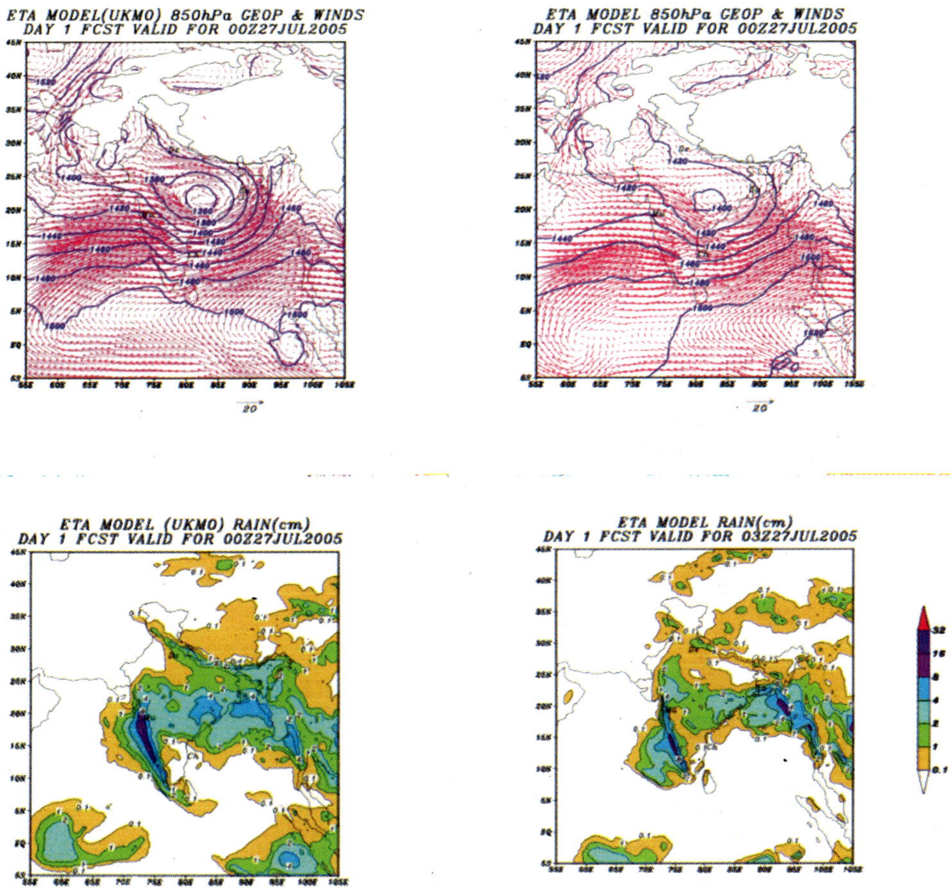

Figure 7: Improvements in Rainfall Prediction from Mesoscale Model Eta for a Heavy Rainfall Event by Including a Better Initial Analysis from UKMO

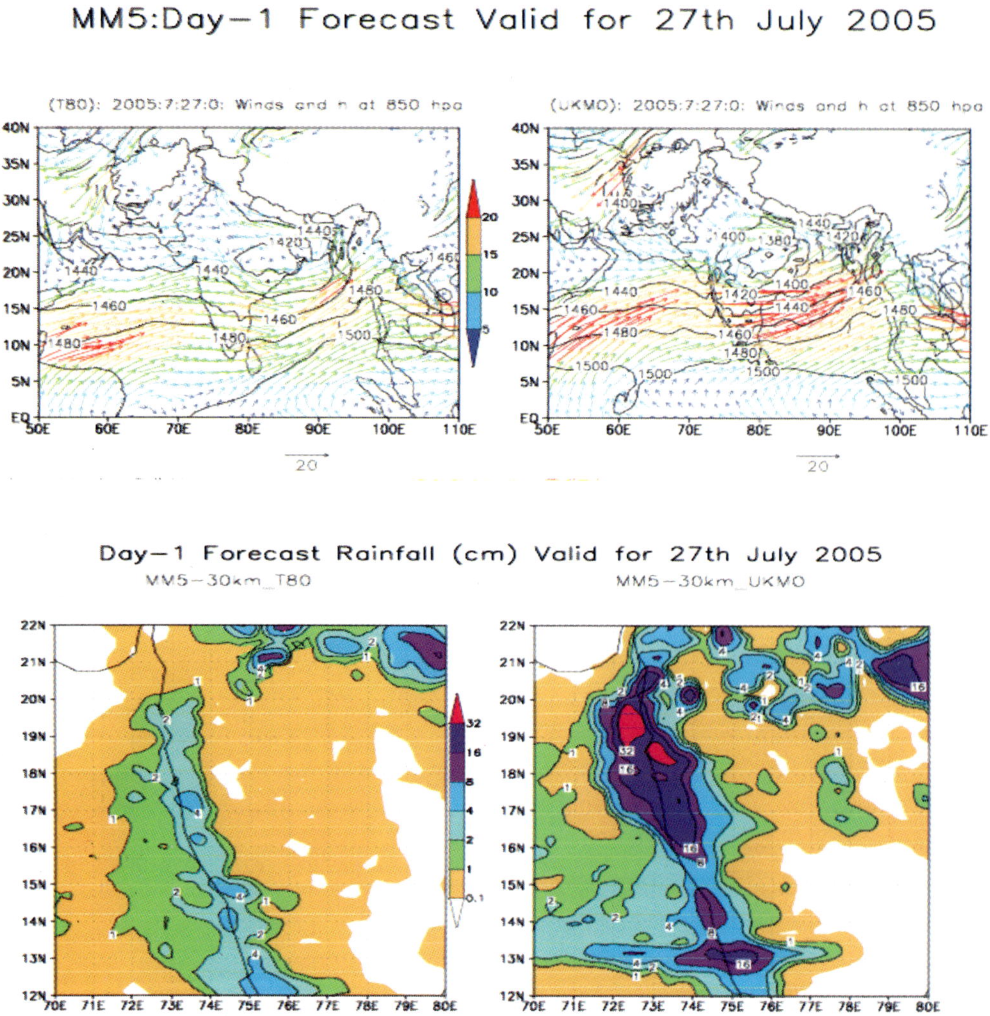

Figure 8: Improvements in Circulation and Rainfall Prediction from Mesoscale Model MM5 for a Heavy Rainfall Event by Including a Better Initial Analysis from UKMO

operational NCMRWF global analysis-forecast system. The 6 hourly Air-Sea temperature differences from operational NCMRWF global analysis-forecast system are also taken as input to the wave model.

Summary and Future Plan

In this presentation operational systems used for medium and extended range forecasts of monsoon in India have been presented. The mesoscale regional models are also discussed for high impact weather and dynamical downscaling of the details. Though the systems have shown satisfactory performance but there is a lot of scope

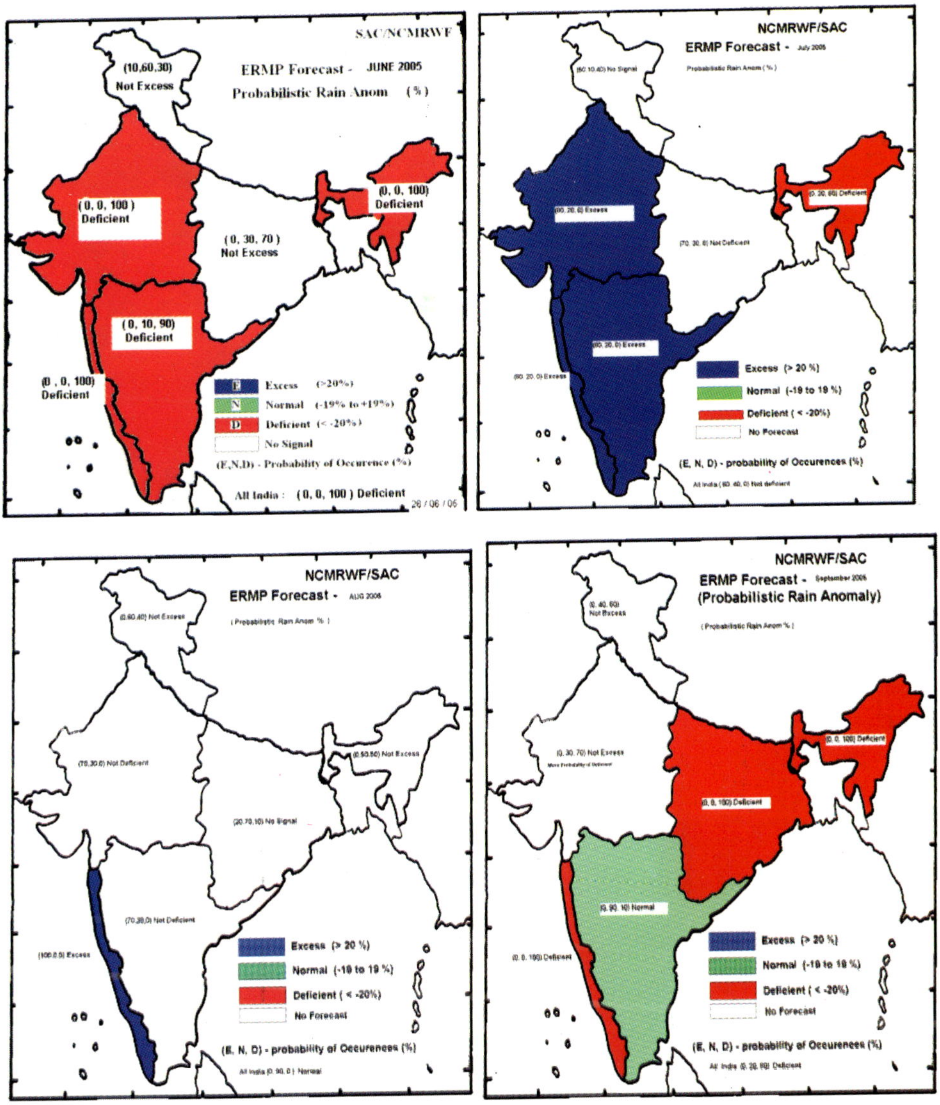

Figure 9: Experimental Extended Range Monsoon Prediction from a 10 Ensemble System Using NCMRWF Global Model

for improvement. Considerable developments have taken place in the recent times in the availability of high power computers, communication facilities and observational techniques. Forecasting daily weather in the monsoon region is a tough task and much remains to be done to improve accuracy of forecasts on different temporal/ spatial scales. Recent studies on the role of internal dynamics versus the boundary forcing are going to provide clues to the monsoon predictability and capturing the intra-seasonal predictability (Goswami 1998, Fu and Wang, 2004; Goswami and Xavier, 2003). At NCMRWF concerted efforts are put in to improve physical processes.

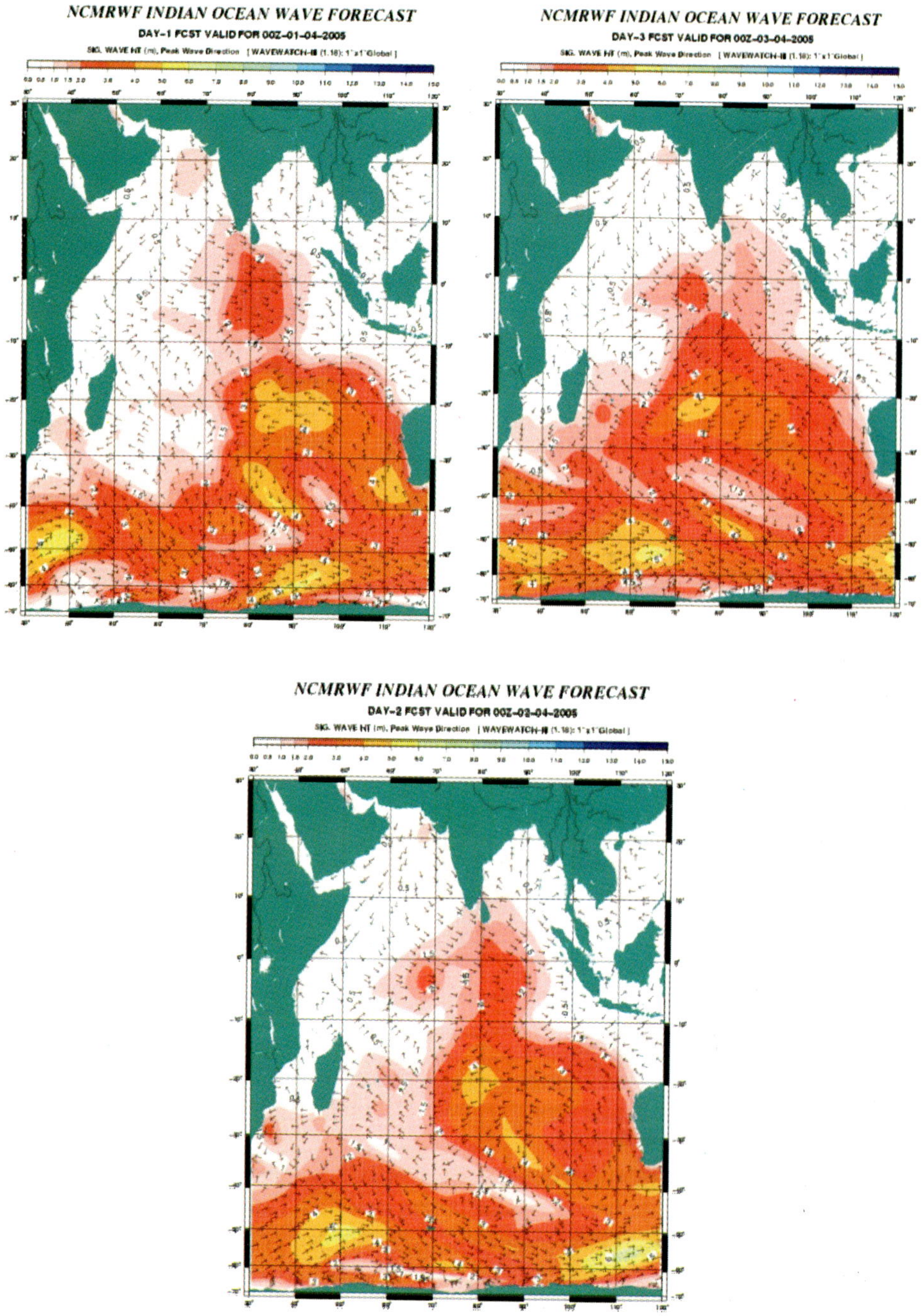

Figure 10: Sample Output from Wavewatch III Model Implemented at NCMRWF for the Global Domain

Also NCMRWF has been participating in comparison of performances of NWP systems (COMPARE Project), and in coordinated national and international Field Observation Programs (ARMEX, BOBMAEX, INDOEX etc.) It is time that more concerted efforts by all the countries affected by the monsoon are made to improve the observation and prediction system so that benefits of these developments become available to the populace of these countries.

In India, the plan is to increase the horizontal and vertical resolution of the operational models, develop schemes/procedures to ingest large volumes of satellite and other non-conventional data, carry out in-depth impact and sensitivity/diagnostic studies to improve physical processes included in the model, and seek international collaborations for intensive field observational and modelling experiments. Proper assimilation of direct radiances from the satellite might provide key improvements for the tropical region. Augmentation of observational platform and development of integrated disaster management system in which weather and climate prediction play important role is going to add value to these modelling activities.

References

1. Basu, B.K., 2005: Some Characteristics of Model-Predicted Precipitation during the Summer Monsoon over India, J. of Appl. Meteor., 44(3), 324-339.
2. Basu, S., G.R. Iyengar and A. K. Mitra, 2002: Impact of non-local closure scheme in simulation of Monsoon system over India, Mon. Wea. Rev., 130 (1), 161-170.
3. Bohra, A.K., S. Basu, E.N. Rajagopal, G.R. Iyengar, M. Dasgupta, R. Ashrit and B. Athiyaman, 2005: Heavy rainfall episode over Mumbai on 26 July 2005: Assessment of NWP guidance, Current Science (Communicated).
4. Das, Someswar, A.K. Mitra, G. Iyengar and S. Mohandas, 2001: Comprehensive Test of Different Cumulus Parameterisation Schemes for the Simulation of the Indian Summer Monsoon, Meteorology & Atmospheric Physics, vol. 78, No.3-4, 227-244.
5. Das, S., A.K.Mitra, G.Iyengar and J.V.Singh, 2002: Skill of medium range forecasts over the Indian monsoon region using different parameterisations of deep convection, Weather & Forecasting, 17 (6), 1194-1210.
6. Das Gupta M., A. K. Mitra, V. S. Prasad and D. Rajan, 2003: Utilisation of ATOVS temperature and moisture at NCMRWF - Results from recent experiments, Mausam, 54(1), 215-224.
7. Derber, J.C., and W. S. Wu, 1998: 'The use of TOVS cloud cleared radiances in the NCEP's SSI analysis system ', Mon. Wea. Rev., 126, 2287-2299.
8. Fu X. and Bin Wang, 2004: Differences of Boreal Summer Intraseasonal Oscillations Simulated in an Atmosphere–Ocean Coupled Model and an Atmosphere-Only Model, J Clim., 17(6), 1263–1271.
9. Gadgil S, P. N. Vinayachandran and P. A. Francis, 2003: Droughts of the Indian summer monsoon: Role of clouds over the Indian Ocean, Current Science, 85(12), 1713-1719.

10. George J P and Z.N.Begum, 1997: Impact of different radiation transfer parameterisation schemes in a GCM on the simulation of the onset phase of Indian summer monsoon, Atmosfera, 10,1-22

11. Goswami, B. N., 1998: ' Interannual variation of Indian summer monsoon in a GCM : external conditions versus internal feedback ', J Climate,11, 501-522

12. Goswami, B. N., and P. K. Xavier, 2003: Potential predictability and extended range prediction of Indian summer monsoon breaks, *Geophys. Res. Lett.*, 30(18), 1966.

13. Kar, S.C., 2002: 'Description of a high resolution global model (T170 / L28) developed at NCMRWF', *NCMRWF Technical Report* No. 1 / 2002, 28 pages.

14. Parrish, D.F., J.Derber, J.Purser, W.Wu and Z.Pu, 1997: 'The NCEP global analysis system: Recent improvements and future plans', *J. Met. Soc. Japan*, 75, 18 359 - 18 365.

3

Prediction of Local Rainfall from GCM Output Using Projection Pursuit Technique

A.H. Wigena*, Aunuddin* and Rizaldi Boer**

***Dept of Statistics, Faculty of Mathematics and Natural Sciences,**

****Dept of Geophysics and Meteorology,**

Faculty of Mathematics and Natural Sciences, IPB, Bogor, Indonesia

ABSTRACT

Statistical downscaling techniques have been used to predict local rainfall from GCM output. Since the characteristics of GCM output are nonlinear and do not follow any standard statistical distribution, the use of parametric technique will not be appropriate. Projection pursuit is one of the non parametric techniques which can be used to model the data that have such characteristics. The results of our analysis show that projection pursuit regression (PPR) performs better than the common parametric technique, i.e. principal component regression (PCR). Correlations of the predicted values of the PPR model with the observed data were much higher (between 0.71 and 0.84) than those of the PCR model (between 0.60 and 0.66) irrespective of the length of the data used in the analysis.

***Keywords**: Statistical downscaling, Projection pursuit, GCM.*

Introduction

Statistical downscaling is a functional relation (called as statistical downscaling model) between global scale (predictors) and local scale data (predicted) (Zorita and von Storch 1999). The model is used to predict a local climate variable based on GCM outputs (Fuentes and Heimann 2000). The goal of statistical analysis is to extract maximum information from the data.

GCM outputs can be strongly non-normal, non-linear, asymmetric and may have multiple modes. Extraction of information can become a tedious task as the dimensionality of the data increases and when data consist of several variables and observations. One solution to the problem is to apply a method that is able to take advantage of structures in the data, such as the dependence of the predicted only on few of the predictors. In the case of many predictors, *preprocessing* can be used to reduce large dimensional data, without the loss of much information. Both Principal Component Analysis (PCA) based on a linear combination and Projection Pursuit (PP) based on nonparametric technique can overcome some of these issues. Another method which has been commonly used for statistical downscaling of GCM outputs is Principal Component Regression (PCR). Projection Pursuit (PP) is an alternative technique which can be potentially used in statistical downscaling (Zorita and von Storch 1999).

Projection Pursuit Technique

In general statistical downscaling model is as follows:

$$\underline{Y} = f(\underline{X}) \tag{1}$$

where,

$\underline{Y}_{(t)}$: Local climate variable (such as monthly rainfall),

$\underline{X}_{(t \times g)}$: Global circulation variables (GCM output),

t: Number of time steps (*i.e.* daily or monthly),

g: Number of *grids* in the GCM.

The model needs calibration based on real data. The results of the statistical downscaling model depend on the length of the historical data used to calibrate the model. In spite of the length of records, good estimates depend on the following conditions: (1) a strong relation between predicted and predictors; (2) realism of the simulated predictor variables by GCM; and (3) stability of the relation between predicted and predictors with time (Busuioc *et al.* 2001).

Projection Pursuit is an exploration technique to extract interesting information in the small dimension projection from multivariate large dimension data (Nason 1992). PP maximizes a function, called *Projection Index*, to reduce large dimensions to one or two dimensions. The value of the function is high for the projection of interesting information, and low otherwise. The technique is usually used to estimate nonparametric regression, especially if data structure is nonlinear. This method can be used to overcome the problem of nonlinear structure in large dimensional data (Sun 1998).

Let X be a matrix of t×g dimension, and Z be matrix of t × k (k<g) as the projection of X, that is:

$$Z^T = A\,X^T \qquad X \in \Re^g, Z \in \Re^k \tag{2}$$

where, A is the projection coefficient matrix. Friedman and Stuettzle (1981) used PP to estimate regression model (1) where f(X) is the sum of smoothing function, $S_{\alpha(m)}$, of Z,

$$\mathbf{Y} = \sum_{m=1}^{M} \mathbf{S}_{\alpha(m)}(\mathbf{Z})$$

where,

$Z=(\alpha_{(m)} \times X)$ and $\alpha_{(m)}$ is the projection coefficients of A which maximize the projection index (3).

PPR model is developed iteratively using the following algorithm (Friedman & Stuetzle 1981):

1. Setting initial values of residual (r_i) and M (number of functions).

$$r_i \leftarrow y_i, \qquad i=1,2,\ldots,n$$
$$M \leftarrow 0$$

where,

$\Sigma y_i = 0$ (standardized).

2. Finding α and function S_α.
   For any $Z = \alpha_m \bullet X$, find a smoothing function $S\alpha(Z)$, using projection index, $I(\alpha)$.

$$I(\alpha) = 1 - \frac{\sum_{i=1}^{t}(r_i - S_\alpha(\alpha \bullet x_i))^2}{\sum_{i=1}^{t} r_i^2} \tag{3}$$

   Find the coefficients α_{M+1} which maximize $I(\alpha)$ or $\alpha_{M+1} = argmax_\alpha(I(\alpha))$ and smoothing function, $S_{\alpha_{M+1}}(Z)$.

3. End of the algorithm.
   If $I(\alpha)$ is less than a *threshold*, then stop; otherwise, change the values of residual and MND, A continue to step 2.

$$r_i \leftarrow r_i - S\alpha(Z), \qquad i=1,2,\ldots,n$$
$$M \leftarrow M+1$$

Methodology

Data

Data used in this study are precipitation of years 1966 to 2001 simulated by GCM from ECHAM and rainfall data during those years at station Sukadana in Indramayu. The location of Indramayu is at 6.30 to 6.59 S and 107.87 to 108.48 E. Domain size for downscaling is 8x8 grids of GCM (Bergant *et al.* 2002) at 1.94 N to 18.14 S and 98.74 to 118.10 E (Figure 1).

Methods

PCR and PPR models are used to develop statistical models for predicting rainfall based on GCM outputs. The models are developed for different length of records (35, 30, 25, 20 years). Both models are compared based on the values of RMSEP (Root Mean Square Error of Prediction) and correlation (r) between the predicted and observed data

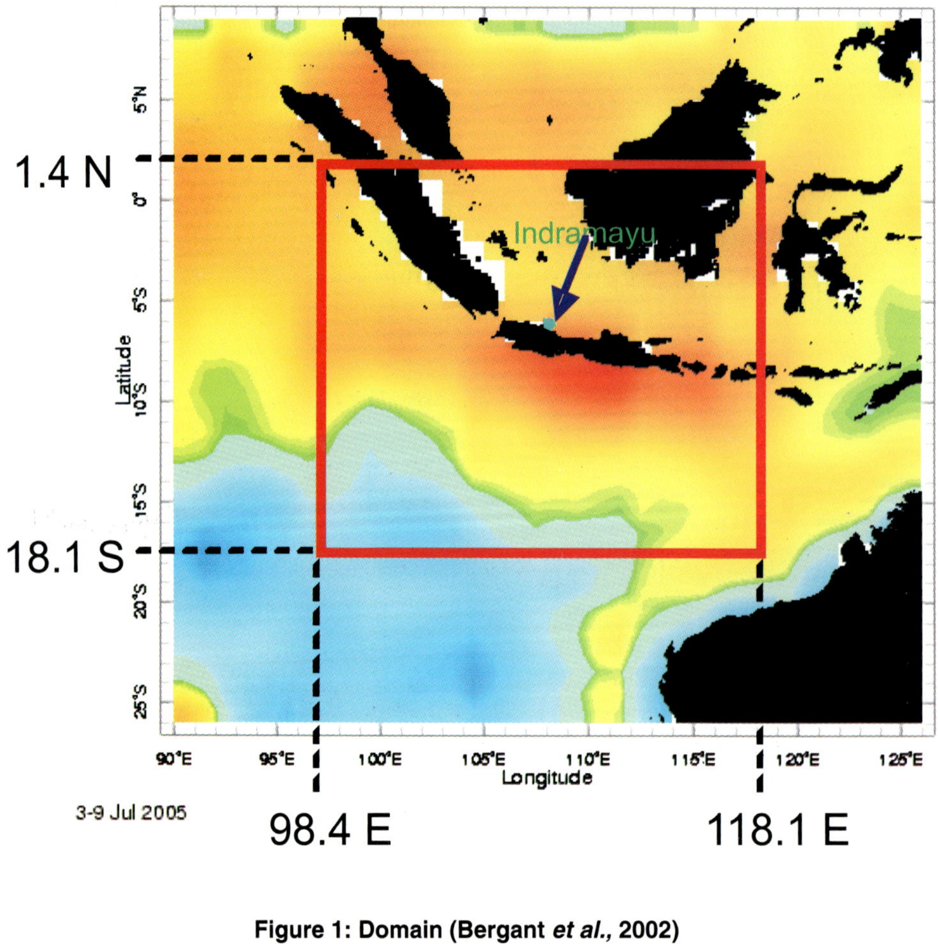

Figure 1: Domain (Bergant *et al.*, 2002)

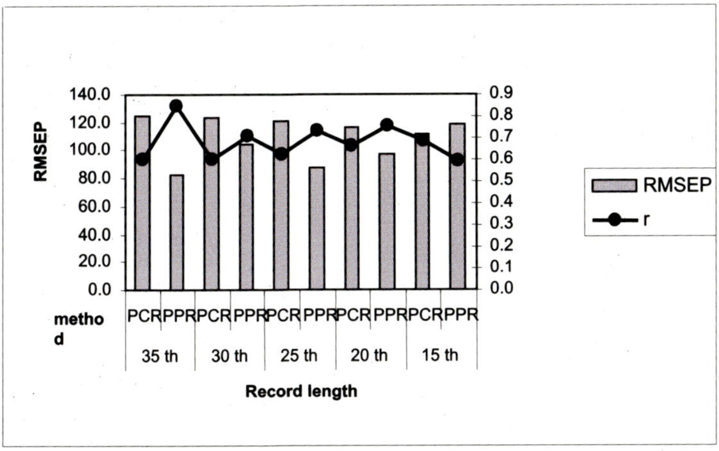

Figure 2: RMSEP and r of PPR and PCR

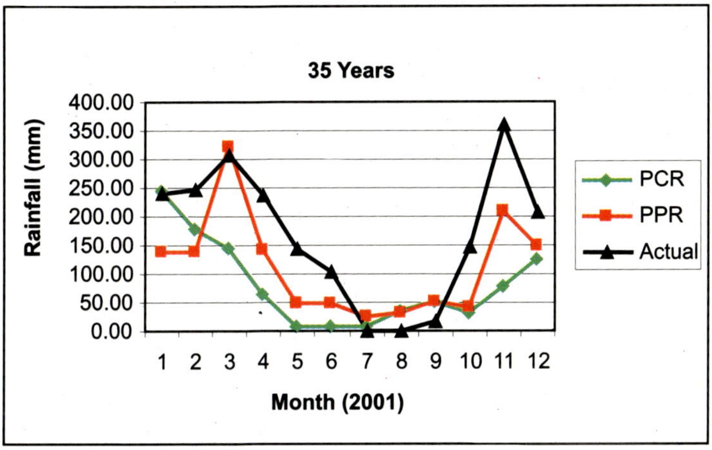

Figure 3: Predicted and Observed Rainfall (35 yr Record Length)

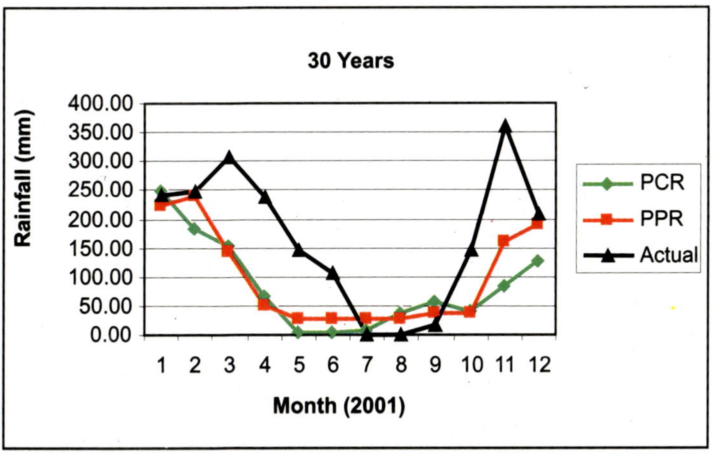

Figure 4: Predicted and Observed Rainfall (30 yr Record Length)

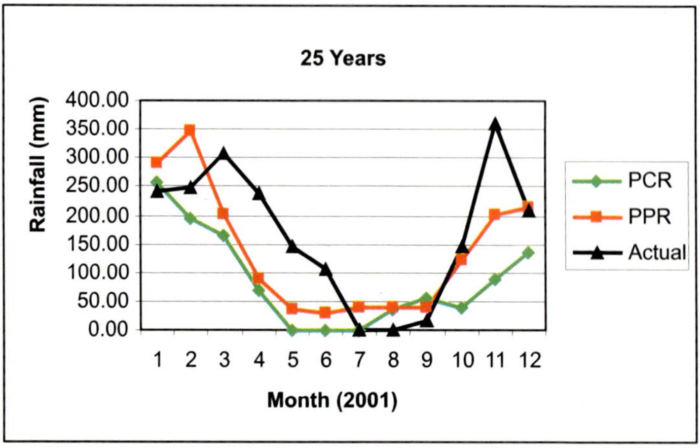

Figure 5: Predicted and Observed Rainfall (25 yr Record Length)

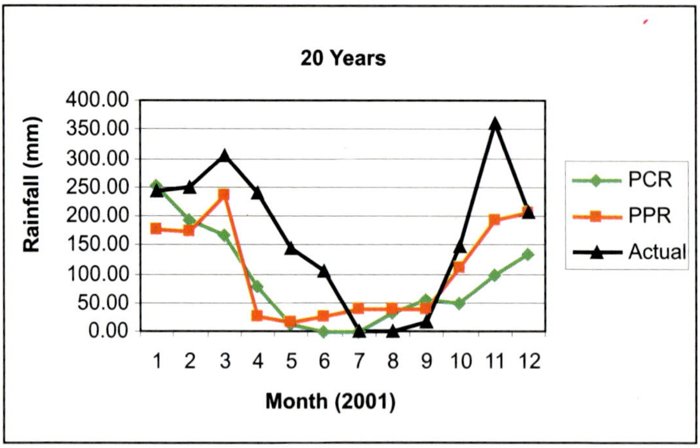

Figure 6: Predicted and Observed Rainfall (20 yr Record Length)

Results

The results are presented in Table 1 and Figures 2 to 6. It shows the values of RMSEP and r resulted by PPR and PCR models based on the four record lengths. Figures 3 to 6 show the comparison of observed rainfall and predicted rainfall of PPR and PCR. PPR model performed better than PCR model for each of the record lengths, that is 35, 30, 25, and 20 years. It indicates that PCR model give results almost the same for each the record length, *i.e.* the values of r are between 0.60 and 0.66; while the values of r of PPR model are between 0.71 and 0.84.

Conclusions

We conclude that PPR model is better than PCR model and can be an alternative technique for statistical downscaling. The estimate of rainfall based on 20 year historical data is not much different from that based on 30 year historical data.

Table 1: Predicted and Observed Rainfall

Month (2001)	Observed (mm)	Predicted (mm)							
		35 yrs		30 yrs		25 yrs		20 yrs	
		PCR	PPR	PCR	PPR	PCR	PPR	PCR	PPR
January	241	245.15	141.50	251.14	225.71	258.03	289.30	251.99	176.35
February	248	180.25	141.35	184.60	242.11	194.72	346.88	191.83	175.03
March	306	147.94	323.00	154.34	146.32	163.92	203.17	166.12	237.09
April	238	67.20	143.15	68.41	51.86	70.71	88.13	80.05	27.25
May	144	11.30	49.84	5.43	30.21	0.17	36.89	11.52	17.53
June	105	11.48	50.29	7.44	29.94	0.00	28.88	0.00	27.75
July	0	9.42	28.00	9.62	28.67	1.25	40.29	0.00	38.20
August	0	37.76	32.06	41.30	30.53	37.48	38.21	34.04	38.06
September	17	53.02	52.44	58.27	39.45	57.10	38.96	55.15	38.92
October	147	31.97	43.46	41.62	40.68	41.24	121.09	50.57	111.75
November	360	79.24	208.71	85.42	163.16	89.33	203.07	98.90	191.97
December	207	127.97	148.72	130.05	191.94	136.00	216.48	135.26	206.22
RMSEP		124.58	82.91	122.65	104.69	120.94	87.26	116.05	97.25
R		0.60	0.84	0.60	0.71	0.62	0.73	0.66	0.75

Note: PCR: Principal component regression

PPR: Projection pursuit regression.

References

1. Bergant, K, L. Kajfez-Bogataj, and Z. Crepinsek. 2002. Downscaling of general-circulation-model-simulated average monthly air temperature to the beginning of flowering of dandelion (*Taraxacum officinale*) in Slovenia. *Int. J. Biometeorol*, 46: 22-32.

2. Busuioc, A, D. Chen, and C. Hellstrom. 2001. Performance of statistical downscaling models in GCM validation and regional climate change estimates: Application for Swedish precipitation. *Int. J. of Climatol*, 21: 557-578.

3. Friedman, J.H. and W. Stuetzle. 1981. Projection pursuit regression. *JASA*, 76: 817-823.

4. Fuentes, U. and D. Heimann. 2000. An improved statistical-dynamical downscaling scheme and its application to the Alpine precipitation climatology. *Theoretical and Applied Climatology*, 65: 119-135.

5. Nason, G.P. 1992. Design and Choice of Projection Indices. Dissertation. University of Bath. *http://www.stats.bris.ac.uk/~guy/Research/PP/PP.html* (April 2004).

6. Sun, J. 1998. Projection Pursuit. *http://sun.cwru.edu/~jiayang/pp.ps* (January 2004).

7. Von Storch, H and F.W. Zwiers. 1999. *Statistical Analysis in Climate Research.* Cambridge University Press. Cambridge.

8. Wilby, R.L and T.M.L. Wigley. 2000. Precipitation predictors for downscaling: Observed and general circulation model relationships. *Int. J. of Climatol*, 20: 641-661.

9. Zorita, E. and H. von Storch. 1999. The analog method as a simple statistical downscaling technique: Comparison with more complicated methods. *J. of Climate*, 12: 2474-2489.

4

Long-range, High-resolution Forecast of Monsoon Rainfall

P. Goswami[#], G.K. Patra*, K.C. Gouda* and V.S. Prakash**

**Centre for Mathematical Modelling and Computer Simulation*
Wind tunnel Road, Bangalore-37
[#]E-mail: goswami@cmmacs.ernet.in
***Drought Monitoring Cell, Bangalore, Karnataka, India*

ABSTRACT

Accurate forecast of monsoon rainfall can be valuable input for many sectors and in particular, for agricultural planning. However, for these to be truly effective, they must have long range and high spatial resolution. The long range is critical for a large country like India with complex logistics to allow sufficient lead time. Similarly, given the tremendous spatial variability of monsoon rainfall as well as agricultural practices, only forecasts with sufficient spatial resolutions are meaningful. Long range, high-resolution forecasting of monsoon rainfall, however, continues to be a major scientific challenge worldwide. We propose and evaluate a methodology using multi-grid ensemble as an efficient strategy for long-range forecasting of monsoon. Unlike in a conventional multi-lead ensemble using initial conditions from a number of observations (days); the multi-grid ensemble uses the variations in the forecasts due to small changes in the grid structure. The methodology is based on a variable resolution general circulation model, which can provide higher resolution over a selected area (zoom) and allows small changes in the grid structure without changing the global grid. Comparison of 5-member multi-grid ensembles for the years 2002, 2003 and 2004 with the corresponding forecasts from 9-member multi-lead ensemble forecasts shows that the former is superior in a number of ways. In particular, for anomalies in area-averaged weekly rainfall for 2002, 2003 and 2004, the multi-grid ensemble average shows significant correlation with the corresponding anomalies from NCEP in 9 out of 12 cases. We have then generated experimental long-range, high-resolution forecast of monsoon 2005 and 2006 based on the multi-grid configuration with a combination of multi-grid and multi-lead for the latter. The forecasts are based on a 15-year model climatology which provides a reliability estimation of the forecasts as well as a quantitative procedure for calculating anomalies. In addition, we also evaluate forecasts at district level for the state of Karnataka for two years to explore possibilities of forecasts at such scales.

Introduction

Given the scientific challenges of monsoon forecast with scientific groups world-wide reporting of limited skill [Kang *et al.*, 2002; Sperber and Palmer, 1996; Webster *et al.*, 1998], there is an urgent need to develop and assess methodology for enhanced range, resolution and reliability of monsoon forecasts. There are important questions related to predictability restricting forecast skill at a given scale and range [Goswami, 1998; Goddard *et al.*, 2001]. However, improved forecast methodology and better resolution can be expected to lead to higher forecast skill [Bovile, 1993; Boyle, 1993; Kentarchos *et al.*, 2000; Krishnamurti *et al.*, 1999]. There are three major aspects which can contribute towards significant improvement in range and quality of monsoon forecasting, the relative importance of which still awaits careful assessment. The first one involves model physics including parameterisation of convection. The second one involves numerics and model configuration involving finite difference algorithms, resolution and related issues. The third aspect involves forecast methodology including data assimilation schemes and ensemble forecasting. The purpose of the present work is to explore and evaluate a forecast methodology that significantly enhances range and skill of long-range monsoon forecasting.

Multi-Grid Forecasting

The methodology involves creating an ensemble average of forecasts that result from slightly different grid structures. In a complex system like a GCM numerics is intimately connected to physics and dynamics; thus a change in the grid structure leads to a change in the resolved scale interaction which results in a change in the forecast. In a conventional GCM with uniform horizontal resolution, a change of (horizontal) grid, of course, would require a change of resolution globally. However, a new class of GCM, the so called variable resolution GCM (hereafter VR GCM) that allows selectively high resolution around a location (zoom) provides a better alternative. In a VR GCM, an alteration in the centre of the zoom results in a change in the model dynamics, which leads to a change in the forecast. As the overall resolution remains unchanged, the changes due to a change in the zoom centre can be thought of as small perturbations. The principle of multi-grid (MG) ensemble forecasting is to average forecasts from a number of essentially comparable (variable-resolution) grids.

The forecast model is adopted from the variable resolution GCM developed at LMD, France. The basic formulation and validation of the model, including formulation of variable resolution, have been discussed in a number of studies [Sadourny and Laval, 1984; Sharma and Sadourny, 1986; Laval *et al.*, 1996]. The version used in the present studies uses a diurnal cycle, a land surface module and convective parameterisation scheme of Tiedtke [Tiedtke, 1989]. The model grid has 192x145 points in the horizontal direction with a zoom over the monsoon domain, which provides a horizontal resolution of about 60 km x 50 km around the zoom which merges smoothly to about 2° × 2° away from the zoom. The number of vertical levels is 19. The initial conditions are extracted from daily fields from NCEP [Kalnay, 1996] available on a 2.5° × 2.5°.

As the simulations are carried out in a forecast setting, the SST field must be either dynamically generated or prescribed, for example from climatology. While the important role played by SST in monsoon dynamics has been emphasised in many studies [Ramusson *et al.*, 1983; Latif *et al.*, 1994] it must be also remembered that the response of organized convection to SST is a threshold process. Thus small errors in SST field (say from a coupled ocean-atmospheric model) can lead to the wrong convective regime and thus completely off-set the gain. Our strategy here is to avoid such error in expense of the inter-annual variations of SST by adopting a (monthly) climatology of SST field from AMIP (Atmospheric Model Inter-comparison) data set. Instead, we expect that the inter-annual variability of (convective) dynamics in the model in response to different initial conditions can also generate a significant part of the inter-annual variability of monsoon.

We have generated model climatology from 15 hind cast for 15 past monsoons chosen to represent relative occurrence of excess, normal and deficit monsoons. The years considered are 1979, 1982, 1987, 1988, 1990, 1991, 1992, 1994, 1995, 1996, 1997, 1998, 1999, 2000, 2001. The simulations for the model climatology were carried out with a single (variable-resolution) grid with zoom centre over 75°E, 15°N as shown in Figure 1.

The corresponding observed climatology was created by taking the corresponding fifteen years from NCEP Analysis. Figure 2 compares the 15-year model climatology with the corresponding NCEP climatology in terms of area-averaged weekly rainfall; the four areas considered are as indicated in the figure.

Although the model has certain bias, the correlation coefficients between the two climatologies represented by the numbers within brackets in each panel, are significant over each location. The bias is particularly strong over south India; however, there is a significant correspondence in trend which is reflected in the correlation coefficient. Over the other three areas, and especially over all-India and north-India, the correspondence between the two climatologies is particularly good for the June-July period. Figure 3 shows the comparison of 15 year climatology between CMMACS, NCEP and CMAP for June, July and August.

Next, forecasts for 2002, 2003 and 2004 (not included in the fifteen-year climatology) were generated through MG ensemble average. We have used five different grids with five different zoom centres given in Table 1. The total number of (horizontal) grid points (192x145), however, is same in all the simulations, including

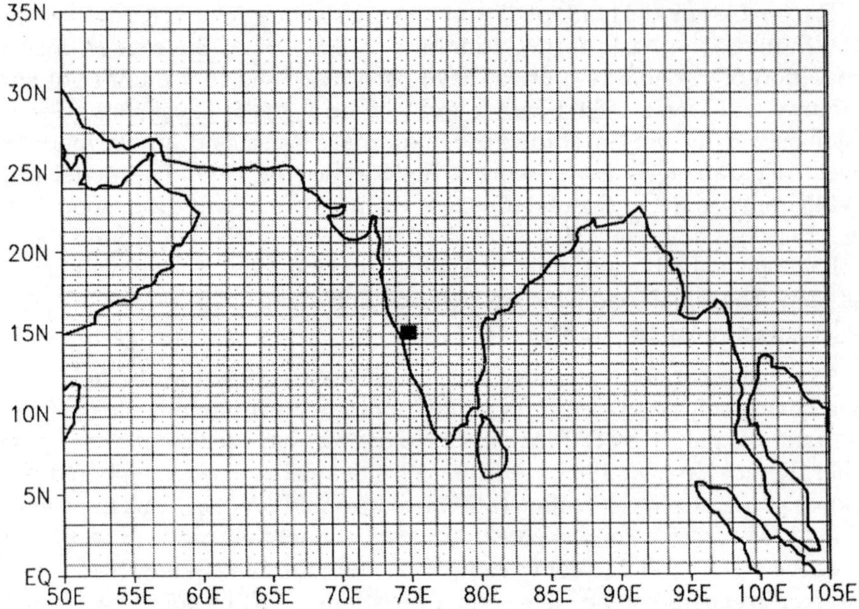

Figure 1: Grid Zoom Centred at 75°E, 15°N Used for Generating the 15 Years Climatology

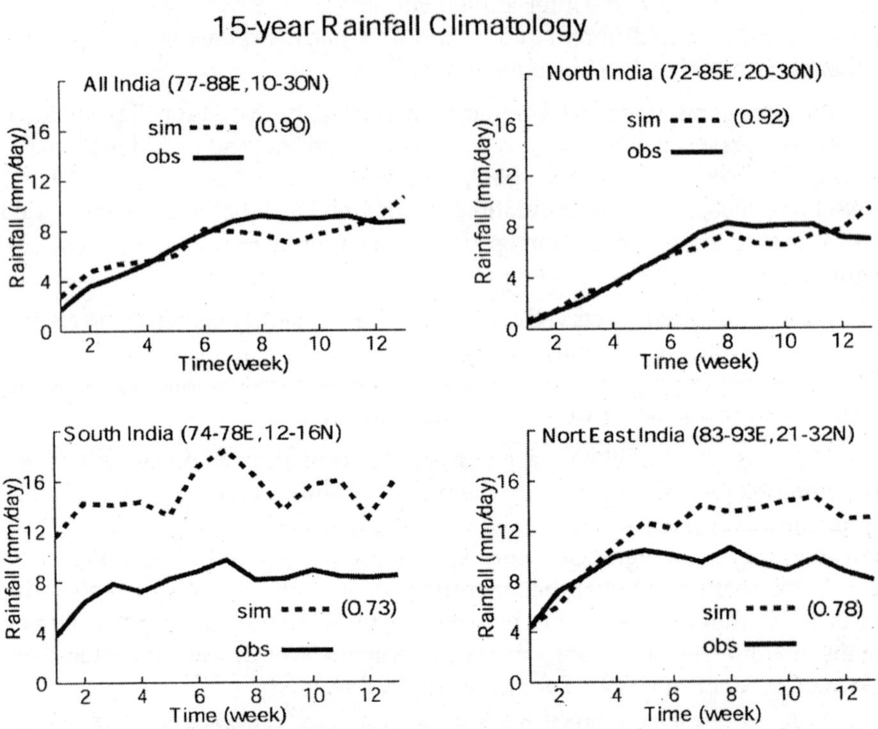

Figure 2: Climatology of Area-averaged Weekly Rainfall from NCEP (Solid Line) and Model Simulation (Dash Line) Over Four Areas as Indicated. The number in bracket in each panel represents the correlation coefficient between the two climatologies. Week 1 on x-axis corresponds to the first week of June.

the simulations for creating the climatology. The MG ensemble average forecasts discussed below thus represent a 5-member average, with equal weight (1). For comparison, we also consider a 9-member multi-lead (ML) forecast with multiple leads; the predictable part is taken as the average of the ensemble. The initial conditions for the MG ensemble forecast was taken from May 1 of the respective year, while for ML forecasting, the initial conditions were taken for days between April 1 and May 30; the average range of the forecast is thus about one month for June and about 3 months for August.

Table 1: Longitude and Latitude of Different Zoom Centres

Sl. No.	*Longitude*	*Latitude*
1.	75	15
2.	70	20
3.	75	10
4.	75	20
5.	80	20

Figure 4 compares the anomalies in all-India weekly rainfall for the three years 2002, 2003 and 2004 from NCEP (thick solid line), MG ensemble (upper panels) and ML ensemble (lower panels). The thin lines in each panel show forecasts with representative members of the corresponding ensemble. The number in bracket in each panel represents correlation coefficient between the weekly anomalies from NCEP and the ensemble average forecast. A scrutiny of Figure 4 clearly shows the sensitivity of the model forecasts to changes either in the initial condition or in the grid structure. In general, however, MG forecasts perform better than ML forecasts.

Table 2 summarises the performances of MG and ML ensemble forecasting in terms of correlation coefficients between weekly rainfall anomalies from NCEP and the respective ensemble forecasting for different years and different regions.

Table 2: Correlation Coefficients Between Weekly Rainfall Anomalies for NCEP and Forecasts

Year	*Area*	*Correlation*	
		Multi-Lead	*Multi-Grid*
2002	AI	0.28	0.22
	NI	-0.40	0.32
	SI	0.00	-0.29
	NE	0.17	0.40
2003	AI	0.34	0.55
	NI	0.69	0.58
	SI	0.00	0.58
	NE	0.37	0.55
2004	AI	-0.31	-0.16
	NI	-0.62	0.00
	SI	-0.42	0.58
	NE	-0.52	0.28

Out of 12 (four regions, three years) cases, the MG ensemble shows very small or negative correlation in three cases, while the ML ensemble shows in 7 cases. This roughly translates to a skill of about 75% for MG forecasts and 30% for ML forecasting.

Table 3 shows the normalised (with respect to corresponding climatology) anomalies in area-averaged seasonal (JJA) rainfall for the three years and the four areas, as indicated. Once again, out of the twelve cases, the MG forecasts have anomalies in the same direction as that of NCEP for nine cases (the cases for which ML forecast has opposite sign to NCEP anomaly are highlighted), implying a success rate of 75%; the corresponding number for ML forecasting is 6, which represents a corresponding skill of 50%. However, the magnitudes of anomalies, in most cases, are smaller than those in NCEP for both MG and ML forecasting. Two main results emerge from the present study: the first is that the forecast platform, based on the VR GCM, provides a viable option for long-range forecasting of monsoon rainfall.

Table 3: Normalised Rainfall Anomalies for Different Areas for ML and MG Forecasting

Year	*Area*	*Rainfall (JJA)*		
		Obs	*MG*	*ML*
2002	AI	-0.21	-0.06	0.15
	NI	-0.21	-0.16	0.22
	SI	-0.25	-0.07	-0.03
	NE	-0.14	-0.07	0.05
2003	AI	-0.04	-0.06	0.16
	NI	0.15	-0.11	0.23
	SI	-0.14	-0.02	0.06
	NE	-0.19	0.06	0.07
2004	AI	0.08	0.06	0.06
	NI	0.11	-0.04	0.08
	SI	0.09	0.06	0.02
	NE	0.02	0.04	0.07

The second important result is that the MG ensemble averaging provides higher forecast skill than that with ML forecasting. This is particularly true at smaller scales, as a scrutiny of Figure 4 and Table 2 reveals. The correlation coefficients between NCEP and MG forecasting and NCEP, and that between ML forecasting and NCEP are somewhat comparable at All-India scale; however, the latter is much more significant than the former at smaller (regional) scales, in general.

A very strong point of MG forecasts is its detail spatial distribution. This aspect is particularly important given the tremendous spatial variability of monsoon rainfall. Figure 5 to Figure 7 compares the distribution of rainfall anomalies in forecasts with those from observations for June, the year 2003 to 2005. It should be noted that the forecast grid is not restricted to fit state (zone) boundaries and areas of excess/deficit can cut across boundaries.

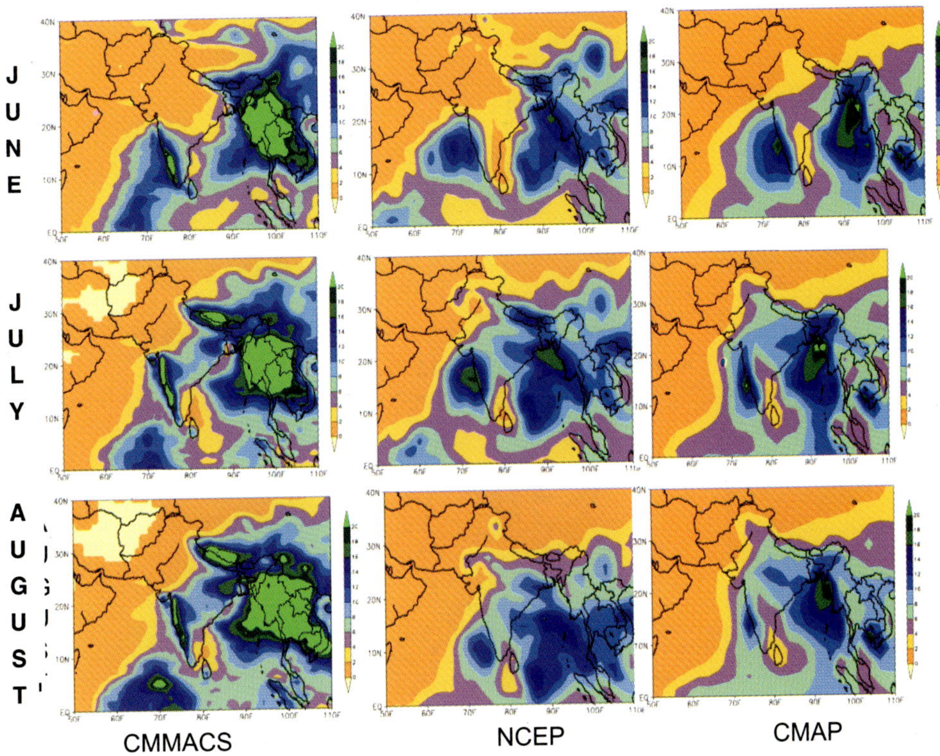

Figure 3: Comparison of Climatology Between C-MMACS, NCEP and CMAP

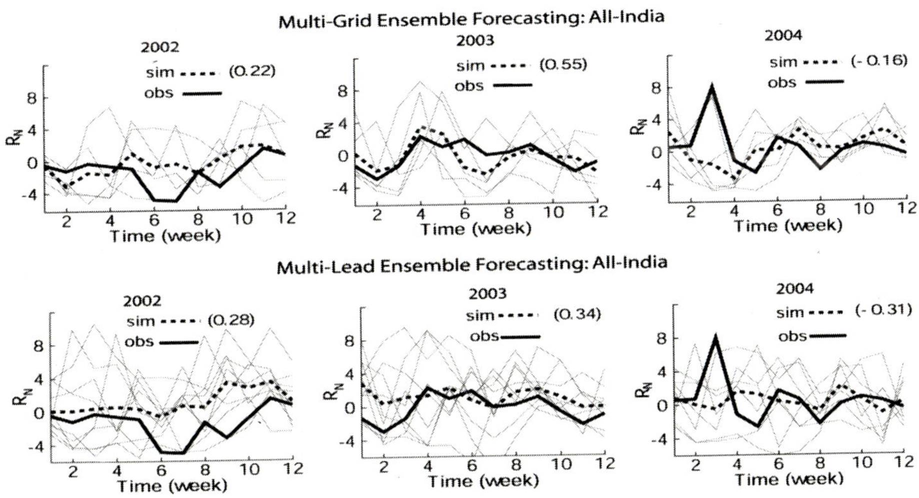

Figure 4: Normalised Anomalies in All-India Weekly Rainfall (R_N) for Three Years from NCEP (Thick Line), MG (Top Panels) and ML (Bottom Panel) Ensemble Forecasting. The thin lines in each panel represent forecasts from the members of the ensemble in each group.

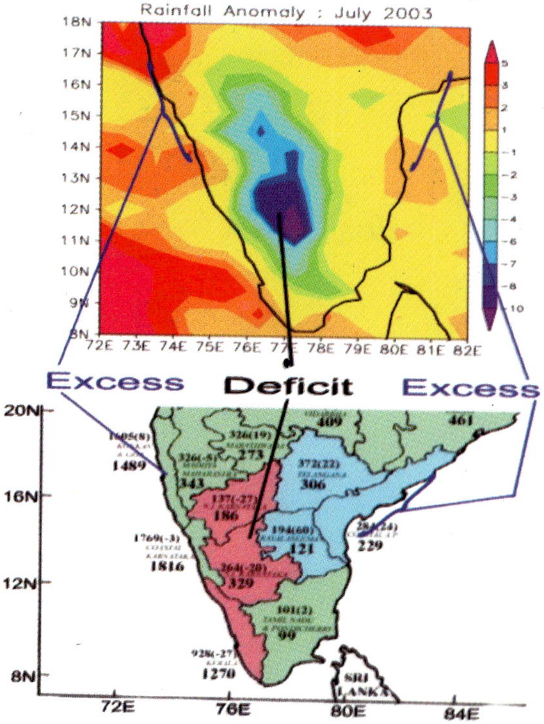

Figure 5: Comparison of C-MMACS Rainfall Anomaly Forecast with IMD Observation for June-July 2003 for the South Indian Region. The forecast was issued in May 2003. The forecast anomalies are with respect to 15 year model climatology.

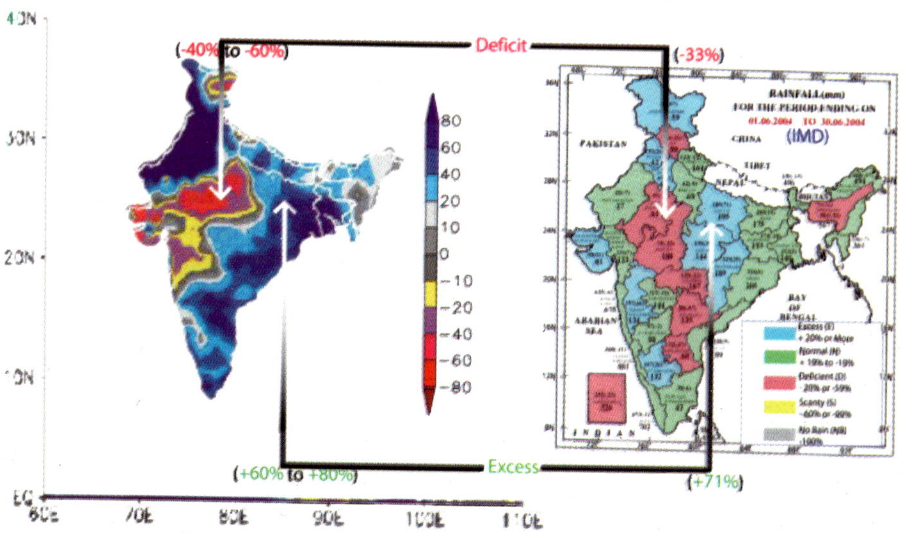

Figure 6: Comparison of C-MMACS Rainfall Anomaly Forecast with IMD Observation for June 2004 for the All Indian Region. The forecast was issued in May 2004. The forecast anomalies are with respect to 15 year model climatology.

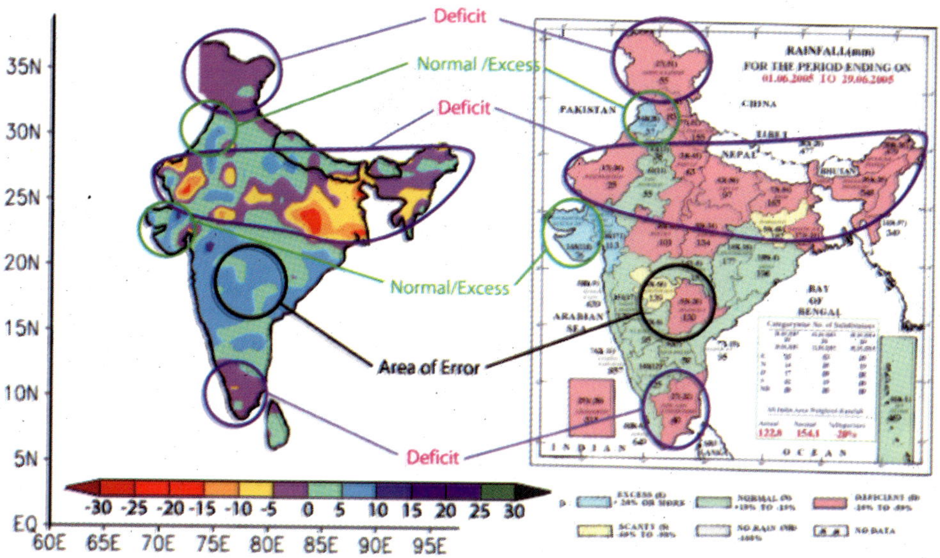

Figure 7: Comparison of Anomalies in Monthly Rainfall for June, 2005 from C-MMACS Experimental Forecasts and Observations (www.imd.ernet.in). The forecast anomalies are with respect to 15 year model climatology.

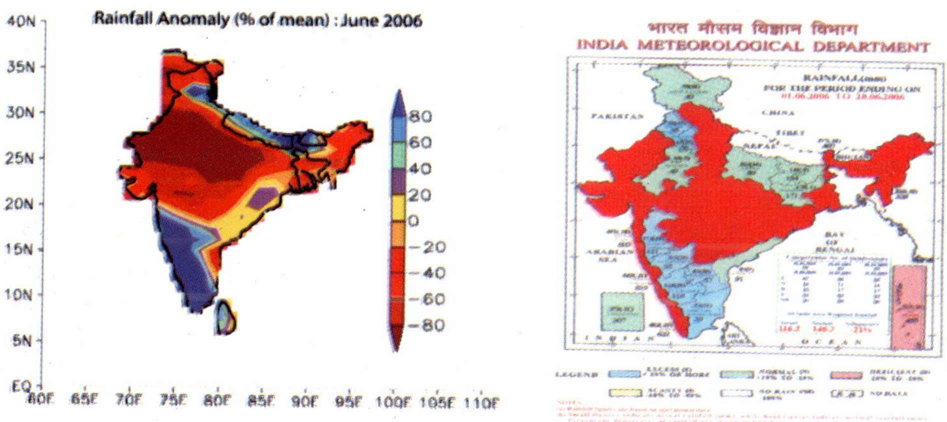

Figure 8: Multi-Grid Forecast for June, 2006 with Initial Conditions from April–May, 2006

A quick comparison of anomalies in monthly rainfall from observations and forecasts for June 2005 reveal the following features:

Successes

1. The north-west part of India was characterised by a strong spatial variation: while Gujrat recorded an excess, the neighbouring west Rajasthan experienced a strong deficit, Punjab, neighbouring WR on the other hand,

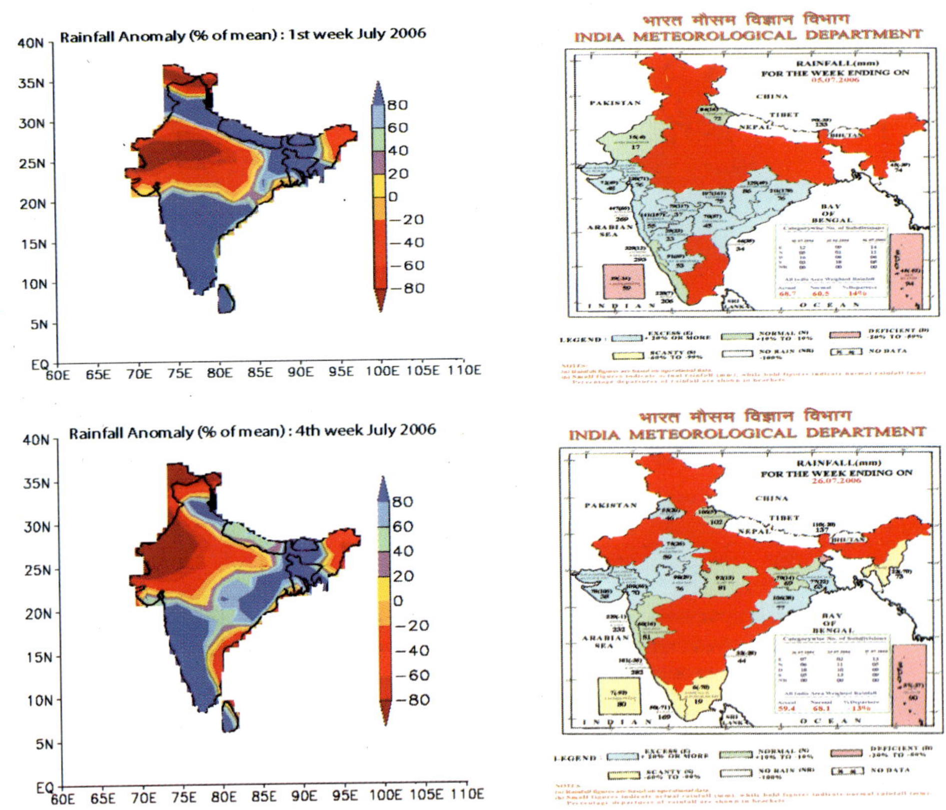

Figure 9: Mixed-ensemble Forecast for 1st and 4th Week of July, 2006 with Initial Conditions from April–May, 2006

experienced an excess rainfall in June. These features are well captured in forecast.

2. The forecasts captured well the belt of severe deficit extending from east to wet, including the severe deficit over.
3. The forecasts also captured well the normal to excess rainfall over the south-central India.
4. The forecasts indicated deficit rainfall over the north-eastern states as observed.
5. The forecasts correctly indicated deficit rainfall over the peninsular India.

Failures

1. The amplitudes of the anomalies in the forecasts are smaller than those observed in some cases.
2. The forecasts could not capture the severe deficits over Marathawada and Telengana, although they indicated relatively weaker rainfall.

3. The forecasts failed to capture the severe deficits over eastern and western Uttar Pradesh.

Mixed Ensemble Method

While ML forecasting addresses the issue of forecast uncertainly arising from uncertainties in the initial conditions, the MG forecasting allows us to handle uncertainties due to numerics. It is conceivable, therefore, that a combination of ML and MG forecasting will result in better forecast skill. Figure 8 presents a post-forecast evaluation of C-MMACS forecasts for June, 2006 from such a mixed ensemble through a comparison with the corresponding observed spatial distribution (right panel). The observed spatial distribution has been adopted from IMD, in which anomalies less than or equal to -10% have been shaded in red for easy comparison with the forecast. It is clear that the forecasts capture the pattern of distribution quite well; however, there are significant differences in the amplitude of the anomalies in observation and forecasts. An accurate knowledge even the category of the anomaly with a long range, however, can be very useful, especially in the areas of crop planning, which requires a long preparation time. The mixed ensemble forecasts, were found to be better than the corresponding forecasts from only ML (not shown) or MG ensemble.

Weekly and District-level Forecasts

Finally, we had explored the model performance in two of the grand challenges of monsoon forecasting: higher (weekly) temporal and spatial resolution.

Figure 9 compares the forecast (left panels) and observed (right panels) distribution of anomalies for the first (top panels) and the fourth (bottom panels) week of July, 2006 from mixed ensemble. Once again, the observed anomalies of less than or equal to -10% have been shaded red for ease of comparison. It is clear that the model skill at such temporal scales is yet to reach acceptable level, although it does show certain promise. For example, the severe and persistent droughts over the north-eastern India as well as over Jammu and Kashmir were well captured by the forecasts. However, more case studies are needed to quantify such skill statistically.

The district-level forecasts were generated for the state of Karnataka since 2003 in response to a request from the Government of Karnataka; the forecasts were subsequently verified from observations collected by the Department of Economics and Statistics (DES), Govt. of Karnataka. These forecasts for 2004 and 2005 were supplied to the Government of Karnataka on request, who then carried out a post forecast evaluation with data from their rain gauge network. We briefly present these results in Tables 4 (2004) and 5 (2005). In each of these tables, compares the observed and predicted anomalies for each of the twenty seven districts for June, July and August. At present, however, we focus on phase synchronisation.

The phase synchronisation in terms of percentage of cases for which the observed and the forecast anomalies are in phase (for 27 districts) is given at the bottom of each table for each month. While there are cases for which the phase synchronisation is as high as 70%, there are two cases (out of six), June 2004 and July 2005, where it is less than 50%. Obviously, a primary requirement is to evaluate skill for such high-resolution forecasts with more cases.

Table 4: Comparison of District Wise Rainfall Forecast with Actual for June, July and August 2004

Sl. No.	District	June(% dep)			July(% dep)			August(% dep)		
		Pre-dicted	Ac-tual	Phase	Pre-dicted	Ac-tual	Phase	Pre-dicted	Act-tual	Phase
1.	BANGALORE -URBAN	-24	25	-1	25	138	1	-25	-27	1
2.	BANGALORE -RURAL	-21	-24	1	20	146	1	-22	-65	1
3.	KOLAR	-14	-51	1	36	94	1	-18	-69	1
4.	TUMKUR	-19	2	-1	17	112	1	-13	-46	1
5.	CHITRADURGA	-18	16	-1	20	43	1	-16	-22	1
6.	DAVANAGERE	-23	17	-1	15	-6	-1	-24	38	-1
7.	CHAMARAJANAGARA	-15	11	-1	23	68	1	-17	-62	1
8.	MYSORE	-22	-9	1	2	4	1	-16	-33	1
9.	MANDYA	-25	25	-1	3	109	1	-25	-56	1
10.	BELLARY	-18	39	-1	17	16	1	-26	-57	1
11.	KOPPALA	-17	78	-1	15	14	1	-22	-80	1
12.	RAICHUR	-27	-24	1	33	-4	-1	-26	-81	1
13.	GULBARGA	-42	-44	1	36	-14	-1	-26	-76	1
14.	BIDAR	-52	-53	1	35	33	1	-33	-36	1
15.	BELGAUM	-14	74	-1	25	-71	-1	-29	38	-1
16.	BAGALKOTE	-23	74	-1	20	7	1	-29	-57	1
17.	BIJAPUR	-26	-27	1	22	53	1	-26	-68	1
18.	GADAG	-21	51	-1	15	71	1	-25	-34	1
19.	HAVERI	-26	8	-1	15	-58	-1	-25	51	-1
20.	DHARWAD	-19	40	-1	17	-74	-1	-25	62	-1
21.	SHIMOGA	-32	40	-1	17	-58	-1	-24	41	-1
22.	HASSAN	-23	70	-1	6	-38	-1	-17	26	-1
23.	CHIKKAMANGALUR	-32	51	-1	23	-49	-1	-18	41	-1
24.	KODAGU	-19	40	-1	12	-52	-1	-4	41	-1
25.	DAKSHINA KANNADA	-15	-10	1	33	-41	-1	-12	-4	1
26.	UDUPI	-2	4	-1	33	-24	-1	-25	11	-1
27.	UTTARA KANNADA	-16	2	0	22	-47	-1	-25	32	-1
	Phase Sync.(%)			*29*			*52*			*70*

A major advantage of MG forecasting over ML forecasting is the scope for enhanced lead in the former. In the present case, the MG forecasts have been generated with initial condition of May 1 of the respective year, which gives a forecast lead of 1-3 (June-August) months. The corresponding lead in ML forecasting is reduced by almost a month, if the initial conditions from the later part of May are used, as in the present case.

Table 5: Comparison of District Wise Rainfall Forecast with Actual for June, July and August 2005

Sl. No.	District	June(% dep)			July(% dep)			August(% dep)		
		Predicted	Actual	Phase	Predicted	Actual	Phase	Predicted	Actual	Phase
1.	BANGALORE -URBAN	-5	42	-1	-25	38	-1	-20	14	-1
2.	BANGALORE -RURAL	0	-25	-1	-15	55	-1	-15	29	-1
3.	KOLAR	-10	33	-1	-20	48	-1	-30	38	-1
4.	TUMKUR	10	-36	-1	-15	145	-1	-15	92	-1
5.	CHITRADURGA	10	20	1	-5	205	-1	-10	88	-1
6.	DAVANAGERE	10	35	1	-5	205	-1	15	58	1
7.	CHAMARAJANAGARA	10	104	1	-20	64	-1	-10	60	-1
8.	MYSORE	10	69	1	0	46	-1	25	59	1
9.	MANDYA	10	43	1	-15	139	-1	20	136	-1
10.	BELLARY	15	1	1	-10	102	-1	-15	23	-1
11.	KOPPALA	15	22	1	-5	82	-1	-10	-16	1
12.	RAICHUR	0	-53	-1	-25	54	-1	-20	14	-1
13.	GULBARGA	-10	-45	1	-30	27	-1	-20	4	-1
14.	BIDAR	-15	-50	1	-25	63	-1	-25	-37	1
15.	BELGAUM	10	72	1	10	34	1	15	26	1
16.	BAGALKOTE	10	-2	-1	0	62	0	5	-6	-1
17.	BIJAPUR	10	-22	-1	-10	73	-1	-10	30	-1
18.	GADAG	10	19	1	10	132	1	5	17	1
19.	HAVERI	10	21	1	10	70	1	20	29	1
20.	DHARWAD	10	25	1	10	83	1	25	20	1
21.	SHIMOGA	10	14	1	10	1	1	20	10	1
22.	HASSAN	10	9	1	10	64	1	15	55	1
23.	CHIKKAMANGALUR	15	-5	-1	10	17	1	20	32	1
24.	KODAGU	10	-10	-1	10	19	1	25	25	1
25.	DAKSHINA KANNADA	5	3	1	25	-17	-1	25	-19	-1
26.	UDUPI	5	-12	-1	5	-18	-1	15	-20	-1
27.	UTTARA KANNADA	10	7	1	5	11	-1	10	-11	-1
	Phase Sync. (%)			*63*			*33*			*48*

It is clear that model forecasts still have large errors in forecasting actual amplitudes of the anomalies, while it has useful skill in capturing the complex spatial distribution of the anomalies.

It is however, important to adopt an evaluation strategy that is based on user needs. The value of a forecast is a complex function of range, precision, spatial and temporal distribution and, of course, accuracy. For example, even an accurate category forecast (that is, forecast of only excess or normal) with long range and high spatial resolution may be more useful than a short-range but more accurate forecast. The useful range of the forecast itself, in case of the monsoon rainfall, must be defined based on the activity and the associate logistics. For example, the preparation time for planning crop type is much longer than that for irrigation. Accordingly the useful range of the forecast for the former is much larger than the latter. A very simple minded evaluation of a monsoon forecast based on some area-averaged and time-averaged quantity thus may not have much meaning.

There are reasons to believe that the skill of the MG ensemble forecasting can be further improved. One obvious, but computationally expensive, improvement is to adopt a climatology derived form MG averaging. Similarly, a mixing of ML and MG ensemble averaging, say MG ensemble with initial conditions from nearby days, has potential for further improving the forecasts. Further, the weights for different members of the ensemble can be determined using techniques like statistical regression or neural networks instead of equal weights adopted in the present study. As mentioned in the beginning, a multi-pronged approach is required to improve monsoon forecasts. We next present a diagnostic study that brings out the importance of organisation of dynamics in monsoon variability.

References

1. Bovile, B.A. 1991. Sensitivity of simulated climate to model resolution, *Jou. Climate*, 4, 469-485.
2. Boyle, J.S. 1993. Sensitivity of dynamical quantities to horizontal resolution for a climate simulation using ECMWF (cycle 33) model. *Jou. Climate*, 6, 796-815.
3. Goddard, L. *et al.* 2001. Current Approach to seasonal and interannual climate predictions. *Int. Jou. Climatology*, 21, 1111-1152.
4. Goswami, B.N. 1998. Inter-annual Variations of Indian Monsoon in a GCM: External Conditions versus Internal Feedbacks. *Jou. Climate*, 11, 501-522.
5. Kalnay, E., *et al.* 1996. The NCEP/NCAR 40 Years Reanalysis Project. *Bull. American Meteorl. Soc.*, 77, 437-471.
6. Kang, I. S. *et al.* 2002. Intercomparison of the climatological variation of Asian summer monsoon precipitation simulated by 10 GCMs. *Climate Dynamics* 19, 383-395.
7. Kentarchos, A. S. *et al.* 2000.Simulation of Extratropical Synoptic-scale Stratosphere-Troposphere Ex change Using a Coupled Chemistry GCM: sensitivity to Horizontal Resolution *J. Atmos. Sci.*, 57, 2824-2838.
8. Krishnamurti T. N. *et al.* 1999. Improved Weather and Seasonal Climate Forecasts from Multimodel Superensemble, *Science* 285, 1548-1550.
9. Latif, M. *et al.* 1994. Climate Variability in a coupled GCM, Part II: The Indian ocean and monsoon. *J. Climate*, 7, 1449-1462.
10. Laval, K. *et al.* 1996. Simulation of 1987 and 1988 Indian monsoon using LMD GCM. *Jou. Climate*, 9, 3357-3371.

Introduction

IMD is the weather service provider to the nation and also part of global hub for generating and disseminating weather data for the general public as well as specialised department for operations such as those related to aviation, agriculture, hydrology, water resource management and disaster management. Since the Indian sub-continent and its environment are battered by damaging cyclones, heavy precipitation leading to floods during monsoon with regularity; cyclone warning and heavy precipitation warning are among the important tasks performed by IMD. Along with periods of severe drought, hard winter cold waves, heat waves and fog are common in the different respective seasons in India, which are mostly region specific. The nature of specialised weather services vary widely from accurate long period area estimates of rainfall for use in hydrology, through long range forecast of monsoon activity for agriculture to fast update of high resolution observation and short period forecast (of the order of tens of minutes) of local winds, rain for aviation application. The spatial and temporal scale of this wide spectrum of weather phenomena across the country needs strong observation system for quick monitoring, understanding and prognostication. To achieve this mandate as envisaged to IMD by Govt. of India, IMD deploys a vast array of instruments for sensing meteorological parameters and surveillance of weather phenomena. The important components of these networks are surface observation, upper air observation and Radar, covering most of the coastal belt and significant area of its interior. Also, IMD has privilege of having satellite imagery through Indian Geo-Stationary satellite – Kalpana for weather monitoring. The network of these various observation tools/instruments has been built up gradually over the past decades. There is thus a mixed individual instrument of diverse characteristics, origin, vintage and genre. As an ongoing process for further improvement of the objective and to meet demands of various users for meteorological products, IMD has continuously endeavoured to keep pace with the modern development-taking place around the world with available resource.

Network Terminology

In recent time and in modern usage, 'Network' has a range of connotation. It may simply refer to a chain of elements operating under common entity but without significant interconnection, intercommunication in one way. On the other hand, 'network' may mean a close knit and fully integrated system of elements, strongly interconnected and functionally coupled to one another, which work in a coordinated manner at every level. 'Network' is also often used to denote simply the interconnection between the elements of a connected system, without considering the elements, which is a case with Internet (11). When referring to present status of various existing networks of IMD, the term 'network' is meant as loosely coupled and separate functioning set of upper air, ground equipment and radars of diverse origin and vintage.

Status of Upper Air Network

In IMD upper air observations are taken from 38 Radiosonde / Radiowind (RS/RW) stations twice a day at 00 UTC and 12 UTC. These stations include three stations in the Himalayan mountain range. One RS station has been added in the network. These observations provide meteorological data *i.e.* pressure (P), temperature (T), humidity (U) and wind at various levels in the atmosphere up to an altitude of 25-30 kms. There are 62 Pilot Balloon Observatories spread across the country for conducting upper air wind measurement 2-4 times a day. They provide wind speed and direction up to a maximum altitude of 15-18 kms depending upon the sky condition, employing optical theodolites.

Types of Ground Equipment Used

RS/RW observatories are equipped with three types of equipment, *viz.*

- Radiosonde Ground Equipment (RSGE) along with X-Band wind finding Radars (EEC/BEL) (Auto tracking in RW mode)
- IMS-1500 Radio theodolite (Auto tracking)
- SAMEER Radio theodolite (Manual tracking)

All the stations are provided with standby RSGE so that if the primary unit becomes defective then the ascent can be taken with standby equipment.

Except IMS-1500 Radio theodolite (b) above, all other ground equipment are indigenously developed and manufactured.

Brief Description of Ground Equipment

RSGE

It receives RS data from in-house manufactured Radiosonde. Wind data is obtained from radar by auto tracking the balloon borne passive target. RSGE operates at frequency of 401 MHz, X-Band wind finding radars are installed at 16 numbers of RSGE stations. Out of 16 number wind finding radars, 7 are imported (EEC, USA) and 9 are of indigenous make, design based on IMD's requirement.

SAMEER Radio theodolite

These radiotheodolites operate at frequency of 401 MHz. The limiting angle of these equipments is 15 degree and balloon borne target can be tracked up to an altitude of 30 kms.

SAMEER R/T is basically a replica of German make Metox R/T having dipole phase array antenna. Manual tracking through "equalisation of four pips" is not effective in the wind reversal zone and is a limiting factor for wind accuracy.

Inter Met Services (IMS) 1500 Radio Theodolite

This is the state-of-the-art IMS-1500 radio theodolite. It operates at 1680 MHz. Recently IMD has installed 10 such systems replacing the old Weather Bureau Radio theodolite (WBRT) at 7 locations and 3 have been installed in the Himalayan mountain range.

Present Status of Radar Network

IMD operates a chain of 40 radars. These can be classified on the basis of their use *viz.*

1. Cyclone Detection Radar (CDR)
2. Storm Detection Radar (SDR)
3. Multi Met Radar (MMR)
4. S-Band Doppler Weather Radar (DWR)

Cyclone Detection Radar

Ten S-Band high power radars are located along the east and west coasts of India, primarily for detecting approaching cyclones. In periods outside the cyclone season, some of these radars are also used for detection of local severe storms and local weather phenomena for purposes of local weather forecasting. These radars have an effective detection range of 400 kms.

Storm Detection Radar

Eleven medium power X-Band radars and two high power S-Band radars, located mostly at or near airports, serve the primary purpose of detection of localised weather phenomena for aviation use and local severe local storm at range up to 300 kms around radar site.

Multi Met Radar

Seventeen radars in the present network are Multipurpose Meteorological Radar, which are X-Band wind-finding-cum-weather radars. IMD had conceptualised the idea of integrated upper air sounding system built around such radars with associated equipment for radiosonde observation at 401 MHz. The first of these radars was installed in 1979. Wind finding operations as earlier indicated under upper air network, are usually performed at 00 UTC and 12 UTC each day. At times, these radars are operated in the weather mode for local forecast and aviation use.

Doppler Weather Radar

A decision was taken in 1992 to replace three S-Band radars, located at Kolkata, Chennai and Machilipatnam with S-Band Doppler Weather Radars (DWRs). This was based on the worldwide trend to install such radars. One DWR developed indigenously by Indian Space Research Organisation (ISRO) has been installed at Sriharikota is functioning operationally since April, 2004. In pursuance of earlier decision and demand from various agencies, three imported DWRs have been installed at Chennai, Kolkata and Machilipatnam and are functioning with effect from 22nd February 2002, 29th January 2003 and 8th December 2004 respectively. Equipment for other imported DWR designated for Visakhapatnam has arrived in India and is due to be installed by end of 2005 and is likely to be functional from early 2006.

Council for Meteorology and Atmospheric Sciences (CMAS), Govt. of India, has further approved induction of two more imported DWRs at Paradip and Mumbai and two indigenously developed DWR through M/s Bharat Electronics Ltd., in future.

Present Status of Surface Observation Network

The present surface observational network of IMD consists of 188 observatories manned by IMD personnel and 358 numbers are non-departmental observatories manned by part-time staff. Surface observatories, as far as possible, are located one in each revenue district, so as to meet the requirements of agricultural, transport and other operations. Out of 546 observatories, about 66.7% are manned by staff of State Governments/Schools etc. on payment of an allowance by the Department. The Department provides the instruments and stores. These observatories mainly measure the following meteorological parameters: surface pressure, wet bulb and dry bulb temperature, wind speed and direction, rainfall, sunshine hour, radiation, cloud coverage and visibility. From these observatories, instrumental observations as well as some visual subjective observations are taken. All these observations are taken at every synoptic hour and hourly/half hourly (as required for forecasting, which depends on the prevailing weather) and are transmitted by conventional telecommunication channels, some of which are rather slow. Relatively few stations have continuous recording instruments.

Also there are hundred Automated Data Collection Platforms (DCP) transmitting basic meteorological surface parameters through satellite.

Further, under hydrometeorological observatories, there are 633 departmental observatories, which record only precipitation data, mainly set up in connection with flood forecasting, river studies (like Damodar Valley, Ganga, Brahmaputra), compilation of rainfall statistics for use in management of dams etc. These observations are mostly operative during monsoon season and part time in nature.

Besides raingauges maintained by IMD, State Governments are maintaining over 7610 raingauge stations, whose data are made available to IMD in manuscript form.

In addition to upper air, radar, surface network of observatories, IMD is maintaining the following observatories *viz.*

	Type	*No.*
1.	Agrometeorological observatories	228
2.	Evaporation observatories	238
3.	Evapotranspiration observatories	39
4.	Soil Moisture Recording stations	55
5.	Dew-fall recording stations	75
6.	Radiation observatories	
	a) Surface	45
	b) Upper air	8
7.	Aviation surface weather observatories	73
8.	Ozone observatories	
	a) Ozone-sonde observatories	3
	b) Surface ozone observatories	6
	c) Total ozone observatories	5

Also one each of above ozone observatories is functional at Maitri (Antarctica)

Modernisation and Augmentation of Various Observational Network of IMD

The scientific understanding of the atmosphere and ability to forecast large and small-scale hydrometeorological phenomena has increased rapidly during the last thirty years. This is largely because of advancement and assimilation of various types of meteorological data in computing system for weather forecasting. As a result, many National Weather Services have either modernised / upgraded the observation system or initiated action to do the same through deployment of proven observational information processing and communications technologies (Friday, 1994). IMD has also initiated this process of upgrading their observation system, which is basically now in the preliminary stage. The thrust is acquiring more on accurate, near real time observations such that same can be ingested in the computing system directly.

While formulating the schemes it is ensured that basic stations of surface and upper air generating TEMP and CLIMATE should not be changed to all automated system to avoid any erroneous effect on climate observation or reference. Thus modernisation will consist of phased conversion to a balanced mix of manual and automated observation. One of the major differences between the observational requirements of climate and weather concerns the treatment of observation beyond few hours of their recording and collection. While the operational value of observations to weather forecasters usually rapidly depreciates, it does not for climatologists. Climate data management systems generally sit between the observation systems and delivery, production of climate products and services(17). Thus data received at a central computer may be directly scrutinized and processed to create climatological records.

Rationale of Proper Size of Various Weather Observations Network in India

According to standards of World Meteorological Organisation (WMO), meteorological stations be distanced not far than 500 kms when on land and 1000 kms when at sea. For upper air stations, this distance is respectively 1000 kms and 1500 kms. Though IMD's observatories are well within these limits in some regions but it is not same for all regions. Hence, augmentation of data sparse area is essential for capturing both synoptic and mesoscale weather. As the vast distance between observatories would result in a poor data coverage thus affecting forecasting skill making weather forecast unreliable, an increase in the number of observatories would improve the initial data representation but cost of construction, supply and management of the observatories has impact on the economy of the service that is being provided.

It is always a major problem to define an optimal weather observatories network in tropic because of spectrum of scale of weather events occurring in this region. The problem is compounded by a need to take into account methods to be applied for arriving at a goal for which the network is oriented (Tarakanov).

Optimal Density of Surface Network

A nominal grid size of 75 kms is considered adequate for proper monitoring of mesoscale weather events in the plains and for mountainous regions of the country, even better monitoring with a grid size of 40 kms may be adequate. Of all the meteorological parameters, rainfall is the most important from the point of view of real-time monitoring, particularly during monsoon season. Since the spatial variability of rainfall is very high in the tropics, a very dense network of raingauges is essential for accurate assessment of rainfall in a given area. Hence, a nominal grid size of 25 kms may be adequate for monitoring rainfall over large parts of the country.

Based on the above, IMD intends to augment the surface observatories network with inducting 1000 Automatic Weather Stations (AWS), 4000 Automatic raingauges (telemetry type).

Optimal Density of Upper Air Network

Though present density of RS/RW network seems to be adequate in the peninsular India, it is unbalanced in spatial density in other parts of the country. Raghavan and Vaidyanathan (1969) found that the standard deviation of Indian data were comparable with the western hemisphere tropical data and they recommended that since the horizontal gradients of geopotential heights are small in the tropics, which become comparable to radiosonde errors, hence a high spatial density of RS/RW stations than warranted by small gradient is not useful. But it is felt that for detection of mesoscale phenomena and local forecasts, present density of RS/RW stations is not adequate, particularly in eastern and northeastern parts of the country. Further calculation based on an observational accuracy requirement of the order of 2.5 m/sec for wind velocity at 500 hPa and the interpolation accuracy requirement of the same order in the tropics (Tarakanov), it is found that optimal spacing between two upper air stations should be 180 kms. On this basis, the optimal number of wind observations stations in the country may be 100 in numbers. Hence, addition of 47 numbers of upper air wind observatories would suffice for the country.

There is a feeling among the numerical weather modeller that Indian radiosonde data quality requires improvement and is not at par with accuracy requirement laid down by WMO (WMO No.8, 1996). While no radiosonde in the world appears to meet completely the accuracy requirement as prescribed in WMO guidelines, the last international comparison held in 1985 (Schmidlin, 1988) showed that Indian Radiosonde's data quality was quite comparable with that of others, but the quality of IMD's radiosonde network data was not found consistent (Hollingsworth et al 1986, Schmidlin 1988, Kitchen 1989, Kuo et al 2005). The problem lies in other parts of the world too (Schwartz and Doswell, 1991). To meet these high standards, major upgradation in current IMD's radiosondes is essential, in terms of design, manufacturing processes, repeatability and quality assurance. It is observed that main source of Indian radiosonde error is in the pressure measurement, which is mechanical aneroid capsule. IMD has already initiated steps to improve quality in collaborative manner to develop MEMS based sensor indigenously, which is a state-of-the-art technology. This will take another about 18 months for field trial. As the development of the sensors is an R&D project, full implementation will take time after thorough test and evaluation; hence another parallel approach has also been made to replace the existing mechanical pressure sensor with a readily available solid-state pressure from international market. The trials of this system are expected to start from February 2006. With this change, it is likely that standard deviation of Indian radiosonde will reduce substantially. In near future, initially 5 numbers of wind profilers will be inducted at specific locations of the country for validation of the system. Many countries already have a network of wind profilers in their system (NOAA 1994 and 2004). Once wind profilers data are validated, there is a plan to induct total 45 nos. of wind profilers in IMD's network.

The wind profiler is a Doppler radar used to measure vertical profiles of atmospheric winds directly above the profiler site. Typical operation of a wind profiler results in a vertical stack of winds every hour from near the earth surface to 10-12 km above. The Radiowind is a point measurement of wind over a slant path whereas wind profiler measures a time averaged vertical profile of wind over the site. There are various Automation of Field operation and Services (AFOS) products that can be generated with wind profiler (Battel et al 1993). However, wind at particular height is dependent on atmospheric condition over WP site. This is a limitation of this system and hence cannot be taken as a replacement of RS/RW. It can only supplement for wind observation.

Optimal Network of Radar Network

Clouds in the tropics have wide range of size *i.e.* it ranges from isolated cumuli to meso-scale convective system (MCS) in term of Zipser (1982) definition of MCSs. These MCSs are often modulated by synoptic scale wave disturbance, which implies that MCSs are intricately tied to other scale of motion in the tropics and some MCS evolve into tropical cyclones (Reed and Rocker 1971). The spatial and temporal scales of tropical MCSs are ideal for Radar observation. The characteristics spiral each pattern of tropical cyclones was one of the first meteorological features described by (Maynard 1945).

In recent years the global trend in weather radar technology is to incorporate Doppler capability. The availability of more parameters (reflectivity, radial velocity, turbulence and host of derived products based on algorithm) higher resolution and accuracy of data relative to conventional and the versatility of digital processing permit the use of automatic detection, recognition and tracking algorithms for weather features such as thunderstorms, mesocyclone, cyclone etc. with quick update has made induction of Doppler Weather Radars (DWR) essential particularly for short range forecasting purpose.

Based on recommendation of the National Committee for IMD's weather radar network, IMD intends to adopt the following:

- To ensure nearly complete Doppler coverage of the Indian land mass and adjoining islands and focused coverage of operationally important areas, a network of 55 S-Band Doppler weather radars is considered adequate. A few of these may be replaced with C-Band weather radars, if necessary (may be 10% of total recommended numbers).

- The current Multimet radars used for deriving upper air winds by tracking of balloon borne target will not form part of the modern network. Such radars will be phased out and radiotheodolite will replace the same.

Ultimate Objective of Modernised Network

These modernised observational networks of IMD will provide quick update of data for ingesting to fast computing system for issuing weather forecasts and various weather related warnings in better way by all IMD offices which are involved in weather forecasting.

References

1. Battel, G.F. M.A, Leaphart J.T, Moeller M.A, Petrie. 1993. AFOS Profiler Software System, NWS, NOAA, 18 pp.
2. 1996. Guide to Meteorological Instruments and Method of Observation, Sixth edition, WMO NO. 8.
3. Friday, E.W.Jr. 1994. The Modernisation and Associated Restructuring of the National Weather Service; An overview, Bull. Amer. Meteo. Soc., 75. 43-52.
4. Hollingsworth, A, D.B.Shaw, P. Lonnberg, L. Illari, K. Arpe and A.J.Simmons. 1986. Monitoring of observation and Analysis Quality by a data Assimilation System, Mon. Wea. Rev., 114, 861-879.
5. Kitchen, M., 1989. Compatibility of Radiosonde Geopotential measurements, WMO instruments and observing methods, Report No. 26, WMO/T.D. No. 344, 79 pp.
6. Kuo Y.H., W.S. Schreiner, J.Wang, D.L.Rossiter and Y.Zhang. 2005. Comparison of GPS radiooccultation sounding with radiosondes, Geophy. Res. Letter, 32.
7. Maynard, R.H. 1945. Radar and Weather, J.Meteor. 2, 214-216
8. Read and Recker. 1971. The structure and properties of synoptic scale wave disturbances in equatorial western pacific, J.Atmos.Science, 28, 1117-1133.
9. Raghavan, S. and Vaidynathan. 1969. Performance of the Audiomodulated Radiosondes of the India Meteorological Department, Prepublished Scientific Report No. 89.
10. Raghavan and Viswanathan G. 1999. A modern surface and upper air observational network for India, Proceeding of TROPMET-95, Chapter 6.
11. 2005. Report of National Committee for IMD's Weather Radar Network (April).
12. Schmidlin, F.J. 1988. WMO International Radiosonde Comparison Phase II, 1985, WMO Instrument and Observing Method Report No. 29, WMO /TD No. 312, 113 pp.
13. Schwartz, B.E., and Doswell, C.A., III. 1991. North American Radiosonde Observations: Problems, concerns and a call to Action, Bull. Of Amer. Meteor. Soc., 72, 1885-1896.
14. Standard Brief, India Meteorological Department (2004).

15. Tarakanov, G.G., Tropical Meteorology, Mir Pubhishers Moscow, Chapter I
16. Upper Air Manual, India Meteorological Department
17. Weather Climate Water in the Information Age, WMO-No.970 (2004).
18. Weather Radar Mannual (Revised), India Meteorological Department, 1994.
19. Wind Profiler Assessment Report and Recommendation, 1987-1994, NOAA (1994).
20. Wind Profiler Observation Report and Storms Report, NOAA (2004).
21. Zipser, E.J. 1982. Use of Conceptual model of the Life Cycle of Mesoscale Convective System to improve very short range forecasts, Nowcasting, K.Browing ed. 199-204 pp.

6

Data Assimilation at NCMRWF: Case Study of Recent Monsoon System

M. Das Gupta*, John P. George, R. Ashrit
National Centre for Medium Range Weather Forecasting (NCMRWF)
Ministry of Earth Science, Govt. of India,
A-50, Sector-62, Noida – 201 307, U.P., India
Phone: +91-120-2403900; Fax: +91-120-2400062
**Email: munmun@ncmrwf.gov.in*

ABSTRACT

Global and mesoscale data assimilation scheme implemented at National Centre for Medium Range Weather Forecasting (NCMRWF) utilises various conventional and satellite observations received through global telecommunication system (GTS) at India Meteorological Department (IMD). Though the large-scale monsoon flow is well captured in the analyses the predicted rainfall is underestimated compared to observations and predictions by other Numerical Weather Prediction (NWP) centres. Numerical experiments have been carried out assimilating QSCAT sea surface winds and high-density atmospheric motion vectors (AMV) from METEOSAT in global as well as mesoscale data assimilation systems during active monsoon phase. Assimilation of the satellite winds in global data assimilation system resulted in strengthening lower level westerlies over Arabian Sea and weakening of cross-equatorial flow over Bay-of-Bengal in the analyses. This inturn generates realistic prediction of maximum rainfall zone along west coast of India. As expected, the monsoon systems are analysed better organised in mesoscale analyses and subsequent track prediction by mesoscale model is also improved.

Keywords: *Global data assimilation, MM5-3DVAR, Satellite observations, QSCAT.*

Introduction

The data scarcity over the Indian Ocean and adjoining region poses a major problem in defining the large-scale flows associated with south-west monsoon. The simulation of large scale monsoon flow and associated rainfall prediction by NCMRWF assimilation-forecast system were compared to that of other major operational NWP centres (Basu *et al.*, 1999). The study revealed that although most of the large-scale monsoon features are captured well, yet the predicted rainfall is underestimated compared to observations and predictions by other NWP centres.

Various studies have already shown that quality of initial analysis over data sparse Indian Ocean region and adjoining Indian Seas has an important role in rainfall prediction. Low-Nam (1982) carried out such experiments over the monsoon region with multi-level primitive equation model, using satellite derived cloud motion vectors over Indian ocean and also various in-situ observations from research ships, buoys, constant level balloons, dropsonde etc. deployed during 1979 Global weather and Monsoon Experiments. He found that the additional data, especially satellite derived winds were quite beneficial to simulate a devastating tropical storm of May, 1979 over southeastern India 96- hr. in advance. An experiment had been carried out at NCMRWF to see the impact of high-density CMVs of METEOSAT-5 (63°E) on the simulation of monsoon flow and its subsequent impact (Das Gupta *et al.* 2002). Study showed that inclusion of high-resolution satellite winds from various geostationary satellites in the NCMRWF operational assimilation-forecast system produced a more realistic monsoon flow pattern. The cross equatorial flow and low-level westerly jet were better represented. The depth of monsoon circulation was also enhanced. The unrealistic equatorial-ward penetration of mid-latitude westerly in the middle troposphere was also corrected by inclusion of satellite winds. This improved monsoon flow pattern resulted in better medium range rainfall prediction over Indian sub continent.

The present study is motivated by the need to fill the data gaps with satellite-derived winds, specially sea surface scatterometer winds and atmospheric motion vectors of METEOSAT-5, for better analysis and prediction of a monsoon system associated with heavy rainfall over west coast of India. Numerical experiments have been carried out by assimilating high-density satellite winds, in global as well as mesoscale assimilation systems for a period of 21st–31st July 2005. The analyses and subsequent predictions of the monsoon system by global as well as mesoscale models after ingesting satellite winds are presented in this paper.

Global Data Assimilation-Forecast System

The Global Data Assimilation system (GDAS) operational at NCMRWF is a six-hourly intermittent three-dimensional scheme, where analysis is performed four times a day *i.e.* at 0000, 0600, 1200, 1800 UTC. It mainly consists of three components, namely (i) Data reception and quality control (ii) Data Analysis and (iii) the NWP model. A six-hour prediction from NWP model (T80L18), with a previous initial condition, valid for the current analysis time is used as the background field, or the first guess for the subsequent analysis. The analysis scheme used in GDAS is based on the concept of Spectral Statistical Interpolation (SSI) technique developed at NCEP,

USA (Parrish and Derber, 1992), which is basically a 3-Dimensional variational analysis scheme. In SSI, the observation residuals are analysed in spectral space on sigma surfaces. The forecast model at NCMRWF is a T80/L18 spectral global model, the initial version of which is developed at NCEP (Kanamitsu, 1989).

MM5-3DVAR Data Assimilation System

A non-hydrostatic version of the Pen State/NCAR mesoscale model MM5 (v3.6) (Grell *et al.*, 1995), with a triple-nested domain at 90, 30 and 10 km resolutions and 23 vertical levels is operationally running at NCMRWF, since 2002 (Das, 2002). The initial and lateral boundary conditions (every 12 hrs.) required for this model are provided by NCMRWF's operational global data assimilation and forecast system run at T80/L18 resolution. A mesoscale data assimilation system (MM5-3DVAR) compatible to MM5 has been recently implemented at NCMRWF to provide the initial condition for the mesoscale MM5 model over Indian region. MM5-3DVAR (Barker *et al.* 2004) assimilation system is also designed as a cyclic 6-hrly intermittent assimilation scheme. In cyclic mode, the boundary conditions for MM5 run are taken from global models analysis and 6 hrly forecasts. However the lateral boundary conditions are updated after each analysis. Subsequently after each analysis, six-hour forecasts are made using MM5 model. 6-hour forecast of each run (valid for next analysis time) is used as the first guess for the next analysis. Background error (BE) co-variances are vital input to any variational analysis scheme as they influence the analysis fit to observations and also completely define the analysis response away from the observations. In the current implementation of 3DVAR, climatological background errors have been used which has been derived using NMC-method (Parrish and Derber, 1992). Cyclic mode application requires errors representative of a short-range forecast run from a previous 3DVAR analysis. BE has been computed over Indian region (Domain-1), using 12 hr. and 24 hr. predictions (sample size of 1-month) from MM5-3DVAR assimilation system and the same is used in the current study. In this study mesoscale assimilation is done over Domain-1 (90 km) only and other domain use the interpolated analysis from Domain-1 analysis.

Data Used

The meteorological data from various observing platforms from all over the globe is received at IMD through GTS and the same is made available to NCMRWF. At NCMRWF, meteorological observations from all over the globe is assimilated four times a day *viz.* 0000, 0600, 1200 and 1800 UTC of everyday. Data used in the operational assimilation system of NCMRWF during the period of study are SYNOP/SHIP, BUOY, TEMP, PILOT, AMDAR/AIREP, satellite winds (SATOB) from INSAT, METEOSAT, GMS and GOES and SSM/I sea-surface wind speed. The observations falling within ±3 hours of the respective hour of assimilation are being used in the corresponding hour assimilation.

Apart from these operationally archived conventional data sets, the satellite winds used in this study are sea surface wind direction and speed from polar orbiting satellite Quick-Scat(QSCAT) of USA, high density visible and water vapour channel winds form European geo-stationary satellite METEOSAT. Global and Mesoscale

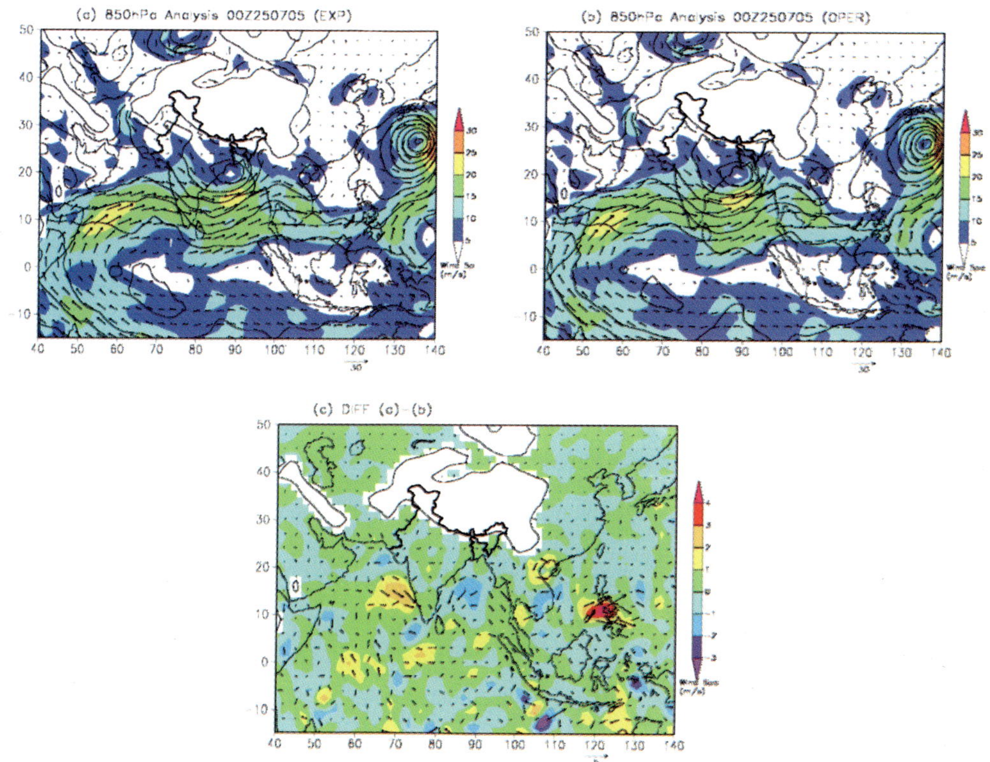

Figure 1: Analysed Wind and Height Fields at 850hPa on 0000UTC 25th July 2005
(a) EXP; (b) OPER; (c) Diff (EXP-OPER)

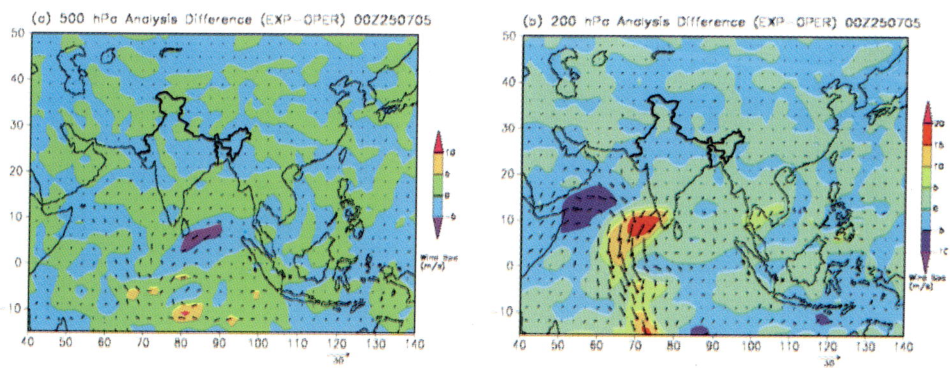

Figure 2: Analyses Difference (EXP-OPER) for Wind and Height Fields on 0000UTC 25th July 2005
(a) 500 hPa; (b) 200 hPa

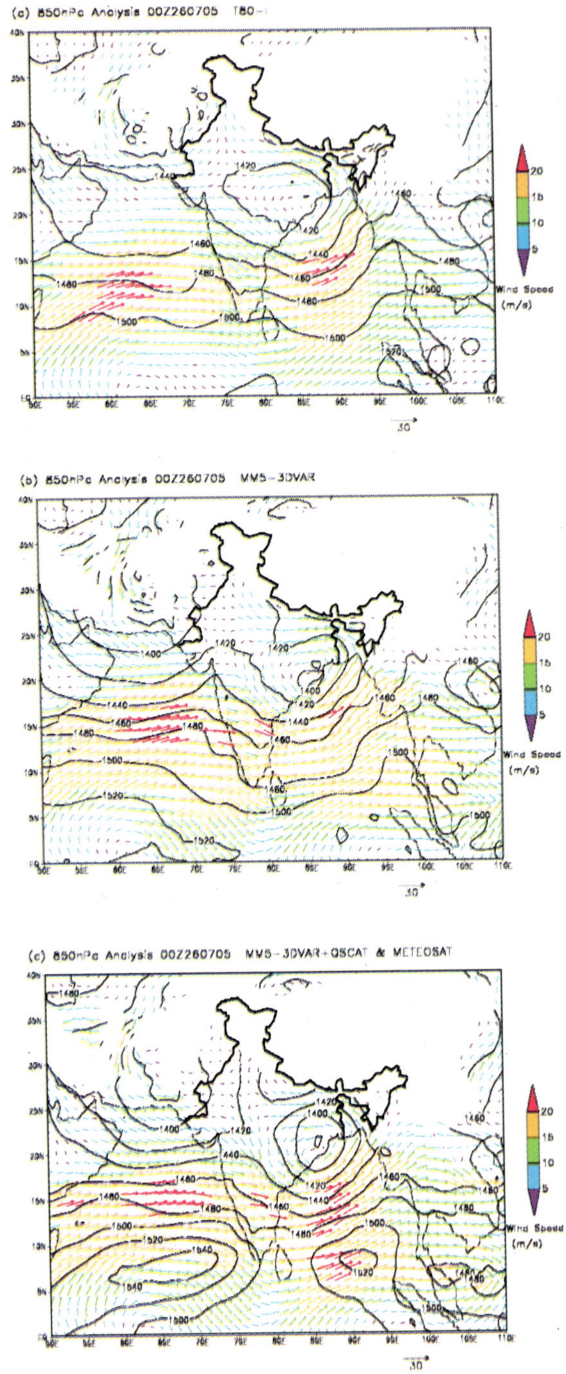

Figure 3: Analysed Wind and Height Fields at 850hPa on 0000UTC 26th July 2005 (a) T80 Interpolated (T80-I); (b) MM5-3DVAR; (c) MM5-3DVAR +QSCAT+METEOSAT

assimilation system rerun with these satellite winds and impact of these data in simulating active monsoon phase over Indian subcontinent will be presented in next few sections.

Case Study

Monsoon was fairly active over Indian subcontinent during last 10 days of July 2005. A low-pressure system formed over North Bay of Bengal off Gangetic West Bengal – Orissa coast on 23rd. The system persisted on 24th & 25th and became well marked. It moved inland and lay over Orissa & neighbourhood on 26th. During this period the Arabian Sea Branch of cross equatorial flow was also very strong. Confluences of lower level westerly jet winds and easterlies associated with low-pressure system resulted in very heavy rainfall along the west coast of India.

Impact on Global Data Assimilation-Forecast System

Assimilation of the satellite winds in general resulted in strengthening (~3m/s) lower level westerlies over Arabian Sea along the west coast of India. At the same time slight weakening of cross-equatorial flow over Bay-of-Bengal along east coast of India is also noticed. Figure 1 depicts analysed wind and height fields at 850hPa on 0000UTC 25th July 2005 for experimental (EXP) and operational run (OPER) along with their difference.

In the lower level the impact of data is seen mainly over the oceanic region. However, it has almost negligible impact in defining the analysed position of low-pressure system over Orissa and adjoining Bay of Bengal. Not much improvement is seen in subsequent track prediction of the system. Maximum impact of data is seen in the analysis of middle and upper level winds, which is due to assimilation of water vapour channel winds. Figure 2 depicts the analyses differences of both the runs *i.e.* EXP and OPER for the same day at 500 and 200 hPa levels.

Strong upper level divergence is seen over peninsular India and adjoining Arabian Sea in EXP. These lower level convergence and upper level divergence over Arabian Sea and adjoining peninsular India results in realistic prediction of maximum rainfall zone along west coast of India, although there is not much change in rainfall amount.

Impact on Mesoscale Assimilation-Forecast System

MM5 model was run up to 72 hours during this period with initial condition from (i) interpolated from T80/L18(T80-I), (ii) MM5-3DVAR with conventional and satellite data from operational archive and (iii) MM5-3DVAR with QSCAT and METEOSAT winds along with operationally archived data sets. Figure 3 depicts the initial height and wind analyses at 850 hPa level on 0000UTC26th July 2005 for (a) T80-interpolated field and (b) MM5-3DVAR and (c) MM5-3DVAR + QSCAT + METEOSAT. The low-pressure system over Orissa and adjoining Bay of Bengal is analysed stronger and better organised in MM5-3DVAR analysis compared to T80-I. However MM5-3DVAR along with QSCAT and METEOSAT winds make it further stronger with two closed isoheights. Winds over Indian peninsula in MM5-3DVAR are also stronger than T80-I and closer to observations. Lower level jet and the winds over Bay of Bengal have also strengthened after utilisation of QSCAT and METEOSAT winds. Track of this low pressure system and associated rainfall is also predicted better in subsequent predictions with satellite winds.

Acknowledgement

Authors sincerely acknowledge the help and cooperation received from NCAR scientists specially, Dr. D. M. Barker, S. R. H. Rizvi, Y. R. Guo and W. Huang to carry out the study. Encouragement shown by Head, NCMRWF is also acknowledged.

References

1. Barker D. M., W. Huang, Y.-R. Guo and Q. N. Xio, 2004: A three dimensional Variational (3DVAR) Data Assimilation System with MM5: Implementation and Initial results. *Mon. Wea. Rev.*, 132, 897-914.
2. Basu, B.K., K.J. Ramesh, and P.A. Harathi, 1999: Intercomparison of the characteristic features of the Southwest monsoon over India as reproduced in the mean monthly analyses and forecasts of some operational NWP centres during 1995, *Meteor. and Atmos. Phys.* 69, 157-178.
3. Das, S., 2002: Real time mesoscale weather forecasting over Indian region using MM5 modelling system, NCMRWF report no. NMRF/RR/3/2002.
4. Das Gupta M, A.K. Mitra, S.C. Kar, V.S. Prasad, G.R. Iyengar, D. Rajan, R.K. Paliwal and S.V. Singh, 2002a: Impact of High Density Atmospheric Motion Vectors in NCMRWF Global Data Assimilation-Forecast System, *Proceeding of Sixth International Wind Workshop*, EUMETSAT, EUM P 35,ISSN 1023-0416, pp. 155-162.
5. Grell, G. A., J. Dudhia and D. R. Staufferr, 1995: A description of the 5th generation Peen State/NCAR Mesoscale model(MM5), *NACR Technical Note, NCAR/TN-398+STR, pp 122*
6. Kanamitsu, M., 1989: Description of the NMC global data assimilation and forecast system. Wea. Forecasting, 4, pp 335-342.
7. Low-Nam S., 1982: On the Impact of Data Sets in the Prediction of a Tropical Storm during MONEX, *Report No. 89-9, Department of Meteorology, Florida State University Tallahassee, Florida*, 122pp.
8. Parish, D. F. and J.C. Derber, 1992: The National Meteorological Centre's Spectral Statistical Interpolation analysis system. *Mon. Wea. Rev., 120, 1747*-1763.

7

Development of Statistical-Dynamical Models at NCMRWF for Predicting Location Specific Weather During Monsoon

P. Maini* and Ashok Kumar

National Centre for Medium Range Weather Forecasting (NCMRWF), Ministry of Earth Science, Govt. of India, New Delhi, India

Phone: +91-120-2403900; Fax: +91-120-2400062

**E-mail: pmaini@ncmrwf.gov.in*

ABSTRACT

Small scale features, those only a few tens of kilometers in extent, and surface (or near-surface) weather variables are many a times not predicted directly by the General Circulation Models (GCM), and when they are, the accuracy may be fairly low. This is because the GCM's are known to have errors because of coarse representation of model topography and deficiencies in model physics. Skill further reduces when the forecast is made at a location. This necessitates the development of statistical-dynamical models. Thus an operational system for forecasting rainfall (quantitative, probability of precipitation) by statistical interpretation (SI) of Numerical Weather Prediction (NWP) model output using the Perfect Prog Method (PPM) approach, has been developed at the centre and implemented since 1992. Daily forecasts for rainfall are then obtained from these equations by using T80L18 model output, running operationally at NCMRWF. Initially, PPM model equations are developed by using European Centre for Medium Range Weather Forecasts

(ECMWF) analysis data (1985-90). Subsequently PPM models are also developed based on T80L18 model analysis using data from 1994-99. Comparative verification of rainfall forecast obtained from the two types of SI models and the Direct Model Output (DMO) of the T80L18 model is presented for monsoons 2002 and 2003. The two objective forecasting systems (DMO and SI) are then used to prepare the final forecast, by man-machine mix approach, to be disseminated to different units in the 127-agro climatic zones of the country. A comparative study of the verification between the SI, DMO and the final forecast has indicated that SI forecast improves over the DMO considerably and hence can be developed as a fully automatic operational weather forecasting system.

Keywords: Statistical-dynamical models, Quantitative and Probability of Precipitation (PoP), PPM

Introduction

The monsoon is the most spectacular weather phenomena that affect the Indian sub-continent during June-September and its prediction in different time scales is the most challenging task facing the scientists today. It is more so when the prediction has to be made in the medium range. The geographical character of the Indian region and adjoining tropical region, due to typical dominance of the physical forcing over the dynamics in determining the atmospheric circulation, and data sparse regions around the Indian subcontinent, makes the task of prediction in the medium range even more difficult to accomplish. The limitation of the NWP models in predicting surface weather over a location further adds to the problem.

Surface weather parameters like rainfall, maximum and minimum temperatures play an important role not in agriculture but also in other sectors such as power, water, shipping, fisheries etc. that decide the economy of a country. Hence, their accurate prediction is necessary for the farmer to plan his day-to-day agricultural operations so that adverse impact due to these can be minimized. Local topographic and environmental conditions play an important role in the distribution of precipitation. For these reasons, the direct prediction of precipitation amounts (or even precipitation occurrence) with a numerical model becomes difficult, particularly for the tropical regions. With the limitations of NWP models and complexity of the Indian subcontinent, location specific forecast of temperature, precipitation occurrence and its amount becomes a challenging task. In order to overcome this difficulty, statistical-dynamical models are developed to downscale the NWP models by developing empirical relationships between the concurrent circulation, certain thermodynamic quantities, and the resulting precipitation. The uncertainties involved in the relationships between the circulation and weather can also be formally expressed through such SI. At NCMRWF an attempt has been made to develop an objective system for giving location specific forecast by developing statistical-dynamical models. Models have been developed for rainfall and surface temperatures.

Section 2 describes the method employed, data used, and equation development including the bias correction method of the statistical dynamical models. Section 3 discusses the method of obtaining location specific forecast by DMO. In section 4 the preparation of final forecast that is disseminated to the Agromet Field Units (AMFU) is explained. Section 5 deals with the verification of the forecasts. Finally, important conclusions are drawn in section 6. Two types of SI models one based on ECMWF analysis and the other based on T80 analysis has been discussed.

Statistical- Dynamical Models

Statistical Interpretation Scheme Used at NCMRWF

There are basically three methods of doing statistical weather forecasting (Murphy and Katz 1985; Wilks 1995). They are the classical approach, Perfect Prognostic Method (PPM) (Klien *et al.* 1959) and the Model Output Statistics (MOS) (Glahn and Lowry 1972). For medium range prediction both MOS and PPM methods are used. Both of these methods utilise a two-step procedure. At the first stage, equations are developed between the upper airfields and the surface parameter to be predicted. In PPM, the upper airfields are the past observations or analysis and in MOS it is the past forecast. In the second stage these equations are used to prepare the actual forecast.

The decision on whether to use the MOS or PPM approach depends primarily on the availability of an adequate developmental sample (Carter *et al.* 1989) and on whether the numerical model is expected to change significantly in the future. With sufficient data, MOS is generally the more accurate approach. It has been well established that MOS gives better forecast than PPM because of its ability to account for some of the systematic errors in the NWP model. It is being used operationally for the past couple of decades in the United States and elsewhere. However, today's rapidly changing model environment prevents the wide usage of the MOS technique. This is because every time a significant change in the numerical model is made, the MOS equations have to be redeveloped. On the other hand the PPM forecasts do not deteriorate when a model is changed, and the same equation holds good.

Studies by Carter (1986) have indicated that stability is achieved with a larger sample of archived data. However, it is required that during the archival period, the model configuration should be kept frozen. The T80L18 spectral model that has been operational at the centre since 1994 and is run every day to produce forecasts up to 7 days has undergone many changes in the model physics in recent years (planetary boundary layer, convection and radiation). Under such unstable model environment, the MOS technique is apparently not a suitable method for reinterpreting forecasts. Thus at NCMRWF, development of equations based on PPM technique was taken up. Multiple linear regression (MLR) technique was adopted for the prediction of precipitation and temperature using PPM method.

Predictors

Development of statistical-dynamical models commenced at NCMRWF in 1994. At that time the T80L18 model, which had just been made operational, could not provide the necessary output to the development of statistical dynamical model.

Owing to the limited amount of developmental data from the T-80 model, neither PPM nor MOS equations could be developed using these data.

In order to cover all type of variability in the monsoon season, at least five to six years of data is required. Southwest monsoon season for the Indian station has duration of three to four months. Carter in his paper (Carter 1986) accepts that three seasons of six months duration are sufficient for giving stable statistical relationships. Thus the PPM models are developed for rainfall and temperature during monsoon seasons using six years (1985-90) of data from ECMWF TOGA analysis. The data is available on a $2.5^0 \times 2.5^0$ latitude-longitude grid. These models have been developed for about 45 stations covering different regions of India and have been made operational in a phased manner since 1994. These models along with DMO and synoptic interpretation techniques are used to prepare the final forecast, which is disseminated on a bi-weekly basis to each of the agromet field units (AMFU's) located in the 127 agro-climatic zones of the country.

Recently efforts have also been made at NCMRWF to develop models based on T80 analysis using data from 1994-99. This data is available on a $1.5^0 \times 1.5^0$ latitude-longitude grid. PPM approach is adopted for developing these models. These models have been developed for over 30- stations. The period of the monsoon season is taken as June-August or June-September depending upon the location of the station.

Forty-seven meteorological parameters at 1000, 850, 700 and 500 hPa level are chosen as possible set of predictors (Table 1). This set includes a few basic variables (*e.g.* geopotential height, temperatures, winds, vertical velocity) and a few other derived variables (*e.g.* mean sea level pressure, divergence, vorticity, 1000–500 mb precipitable water, saturation deficit, thickness and the rate of change of moist static energy). The same set of predictors is also used while predicting rainfall and temperature using T80 analysis. In the present paper, results of precipitation forecasting are presented.

Predictands

Predictands chosen initially for the development of SI models are quantitative precipitation (*QP*) and probability of precipitation (*PoP*). Forecast for Yes/No rainfall is subsequently derived using the *PoP* forecast. Rainfall is highly variable in the tropics and follows a skewed distribution. The distribution is made nearly normal by taking the cube root of the data values. Hence rainfall equations are developed using cube root of *QP*. The observed value of *PoP* is taken as 1 if measurable precipitation is observed and 0 otherwise. The threshold value for measurable precipitation is 0.1 mm. While deriving equations based on T80 analysis, the same set of 47 predictors is chosen.

Reference Time

The valid time of the predictors is taken near the time of occurrence of rainfall. Depending upon the reporting time of occurrence of rainfall, three reference times, namely 0000 UTC and 1200 UTC of the previous day and 0000 UTC of the same day, are considered (Figure 1). A "day" in this case is the calendar date on which 24-hour rainfall is reported. Thus, for development of equations for *QP* and *PoP*, there are $141 (47 \times 3)$ potential predictors.

Table 1: Meteorological Parameters Chosen as Predictors

Parameter	*Level (hPa)*
Relative humidity	1000, 850, 700, 500
Temperature	1000, 850, 700, 500
Zonal wind component	1000, 850, 700, 500
Meridional wind component	1000, 850, 700, 500
Vertical velocity	1000, 850, 700, 500
Geopotential	1000, 850, 700, 500
Saturation deficit	1000-500
Precipitable water	1000-500
Mean sea level pressure	
Temperature gradient	850-700, 700-500
Advection of temperature gradient	850-700, 700-500
Advection of temperature	1000, 850, 700, 500
Vorticity	1000, 850, 700, 500
Advection of vorticity	1000, 850, 700, 500
Thickness	850-500
Horizontal water vapour flux div.	1000-500
Mean relative humidity	1000-500
Rate of change of moist static energy	1000-500

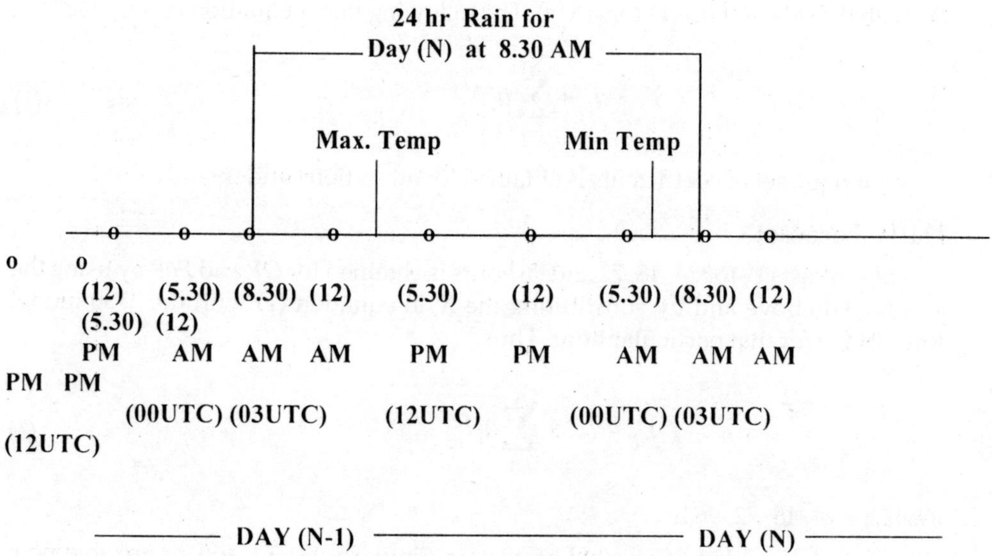

Figure 1: Reference Time for Rainfall Predictors

Predictors Selected

The value of a predictor at a station is best represented by its value at the nearest grid and the surrounding grid points. Hence using canonical correlations (Rousseau 1982), the best linear combination between the predictand (*QP* and *PoP*) and the predictors at the nine grid points surrounding the station of interest is obtained by using 6 years (1985-90) of monsoon season data. The best linear combination obtained has the maximum correlation with the predictand. This linear combination is obtained for each of the predictors to provide a new set of potential predictors. As the correlations are obtained between one predictand and several predictors, the canonical correlations in this case reduces to multiple linear regression.

To eliminate predictors that contain redundant information, the new set of potential predictors is screened with the stepwise selection procedure. The predictors that explain most of the variance are selected. The selection procedure is terminated when the addition of a further variable to the prediction equation contributes less than a critical value to the percentage of variance explained by the predictors already selected (Tapp *et al.* 1986). In order to have a significant percentage of variance explained by the predictors selected, this value is taken as 0.5% for *QP* and 1.0% for *PoP*. Four to eight predictors are selected for *PoP* and six to twelve predictors are selected for *QP*. Mean relative humidity (1000-500 hPa level), meridional wind component (850hPa) are frequently selected for both *QP* and *PoP*. For development of *QP* equations, vorticity at 850hPa is also important. A unique set of predictors is obtained for each station.

These selected predictors are then used to develop location specific PPM models. The regression coefficients (a_i's) are obtained by linearly regressing the predictands (Y) with the selected predictors (X_i's). The following linear equation is obtained.

$$Y = a_0 + \sum_{i=1}^{n} a_i X_i \qquad (1)$$

A unique set of coefficients is obtained for all stations under study.

Daily Forecast

SI forecast (*Y*) for 24, 48, 72 and 96 hours is obtained for *QP* and *PoP* by using the a_i obtained above and by substituting the X_i in equation (1) with the T-80 model forecast (F_i) for that particular hour. Thus:

$$Y_j = a_0 + \sum_{i=1}^{n} a_i F_{ij} \; ; \qquad (2)$$

where, j = 24, 48, 72, 96 h

where, *n* is the number of selected predictors. Similarly Y_{48}, Y_{72} and Y_{96} are obtained. During each monsoon, the SI forecast is obtained for 45 stations by using the daily output from T-80 model and the PPM equations developed for the monsoon season.

Bias-free Forecasts

The forecasts generated on any independent sample are known to have some bias. Owing to this, the predicted value of Y obtained from equation (2) may be either over- or under-predicted, and it is advisable to remove this bias.

The bias from the SI forecast obtained in monsoon season is removed by using the observations and SI forecast of the predictand during two to three previous seasons. A linear regression is carried out with the observed weather as the dependent variable, and the forecast weather as the independent variable. Using the coefficients (a_i) thus obtained, an equation of the form:

$$Y_{\text{new}} = a_0 + a_1 Y_{\text{old}} \tag{3}$$

is used for producing a bias-free SI forecast for *QP* during the current season, where Y_{new} is the bias-free forecast and Y_{old} is the original forecast (Glahn *et al.* 1991). Before fitting the regression line, the optimal threshold value for *QP* is obtained by maximising the skill scores. Optimal threshold value implies that if the rainfall amount is less than the threshold then *QP* is taken as zero, otherwise it is taken as the forecast value. Similarly for *PoP* a constant factor is added to the forecast probability by maximising the skill. Rainfall is obtained as a hybrid of both *QP* and *PoP* (Tapp *et al.* 1986). More weight is given to *PoP* forecasts as they show superiority in differentiating between a rainy and a non-rainy day (Kumar *et al.* 1999).

- If $PoP < 0.5$ and $QP = m$ then give $rain = 0.0$ mm
- If $PoP \geq 0.5$ and $QP = m$ then give $rain = m$ mm
- If $PoP \geq 0.5$ and $QP = 0.0$ then give $rain = 0.1$ mm

where, m is the forecast value of rainfall from *QP* equation and 0.1 mm is the minimum possible rainfall that can be measured. Thus a bias-free SI is obtained for rainfall in monsoons 2002, 2003 and 2004.

A similar approach is adopted for development of SI models based on T80 analysis. The only difference is in the developmental sample of the T80 analysis that is taken from 1994-99 at $1.5^0 \times 1.5^0$ latitude-longitude grid.

Yes/No Rainfall

The *Yes/No* rainfall forecast is obtained from *PoP* forecast by using a simple approach in which 0.5 is used as threshold for deciding rain or no rain case, because it is the best asymptotic threshold value which is not sample dependent (Mason 1979). That is

If $PoP < 0.5$ = no rain (Value=0.0)

If $PoP \geq 0.5$ = rain. (Value=1.0)

Direct Model Output (DMO)

The T80L18 model has been operational at NCMRWF since 1 June 1994 (upgraded to T170L28 in January 2002) for providing medium range weather forecasts upto 7 days in advance. The forecast values for different surface and upper air weather elements can be obtained at the 256X128 Gaussian grids of T-80 model. From 256X128 Gaussian grids of T-80 model, an Indian window of size (25X25) covering India is considered. The model output is then obtained at each time step at each of the 625 grid points for the six surface weather elements, namely, surface pressure (mb), rainfall rate (mm/sec), zonal wind component (at 10ft or 3.048 mts) (m/sec), meridional wind component (at 10ft or 3.048 mts) (m/sec), temperature (at 4.5ft or 1.3716 mt) (°c) and specific humidity (gm/gm). The forecast at a specific location is obtained by bi-linear interpolation of the values at the four grid points surrounding it.

Final Forecast (FNL)

NCMRWF issues bi-weekly forecasts to 107 AMFU's spread in different agroclimatic zones of the country. To issue this forecast, objective forecasts are obtained from DMO (nearest grid, interpolated) and SI models. Using these objective inputs, and the subjective judgment of the forecaster, final forecast (FNL) is issued by a man-machine approach (Kumar *et al.* 2000) for the subsequent 4 days for average cloud amount (okta), accumulated 24 hrs rainfall (mm), average wind speed (km/hr), and predominant wind direction (degree), maximum temperature trend (°C), minimum temperature trend (°C). These forecasts are regularly verified against observations.

Forecast Verification

Monsoon 2002 was a deficient year with most parts of the country suffering under drought conditions. Total seasonal monsoon rainfall over the country as a whole was 81% of its long period average, thus deficient by –19% (IMD, 2003). In contrast monsoon 2003 was a normal year. The rainfall was well distributed both in space and time. Total seasonal monsoon rainfall over the country as a whole was 102% of its long period average (IMD, 2004). As the two monsoons have contrasting characteristics, they form the best sample set to judge the quality and skill of a forecasting system. Here a comparative verification of all the three products namely, SI models based on ECMWF analysis (hereafter referred to as SI_ECMWF), SI models based on T80 analysis (hereafter referred to as SI_T80) and the Direct Model Output (DMO) from T80 model is presented. The verification is done for *QP*, *PoP* and *Yes/No* rainfall forecast.

Verification of the forecast is carried out at the end of the monsoon season (Maini 2002). Different measures of accuracy and skill scores (Wilks, 1995) are used for the assessment of the location specific forecast. For the *Yes/No* rainfall verification, Ratio Score (*RS*), Probability of Detection (*POD*), False Alarm Rate (*FAR*), Hanssen and Kuipers' Score (*HKS*) and Equitable Threat Score (*ETS*) are calculated. The 24-, 48-, 72- and 96-hour forecasts obtained by the DMO and SI_ECMWF, SI_T80 are verified against the actual (*i.e.* the observed data of the 2002 and 2003 monsoon) and are compared. Figures 2, 3 and 4 show the 24 and 72 hrs comparative verification of *HKS*, *ETS* and *RS* respectively obtained at 12 stations located in different regions of India. The upper panel in each figure shows the verification in monsoon 2002 and the lower panel shows the results obtained in monsoon 2003.

From Figure 2 it is seen that the *HKS* is higher in SI (ECMWF/T80) models than DMO in both 24 and 72 hrs forecast. *HKS* of SI_T80 and SI_ECMWF are comparable.

It is seen that SI_ECMWF performs best at locations in east India (Nadia, Ranchi, Sabour). This is because the T80 model has a systematic bias in the east and thus has a tendency to form a low pressure over the eastern states giving rise to more rainfall. As the SI_T80 models are developed using the PPM approach, the systematic error of the T-80 model creeps into the SI forecast obtained from SI_T80 models, hence leading to less skill. It is also seen that the *HKS* is in the range of 0.3 to 0.6 in both SI_ECMWF and SI_T80 which is nearly twice than the score of DMO forecast. In Kanpur, the DMO has a higher *HKS* than SI_ECMWF, though SI_T80 performs the best. This is because Kanpur is situated in the plains and has a good representation of observations from the Indian radio-sonde and these are assimilated in the T80 model. As SI_T80 models are developed based on T-80 model, hence they are able to predict the occurrence/non-occurrence of rainfall events correctly. On the other hand SI_ECMWF, which is developed, based on ECMWF analysis does not take into account the Indian radio-sonde data leading to a less skilful score. Thus both DMO and SI_T80 are performing better than SI_ECMWF at Kanpur.

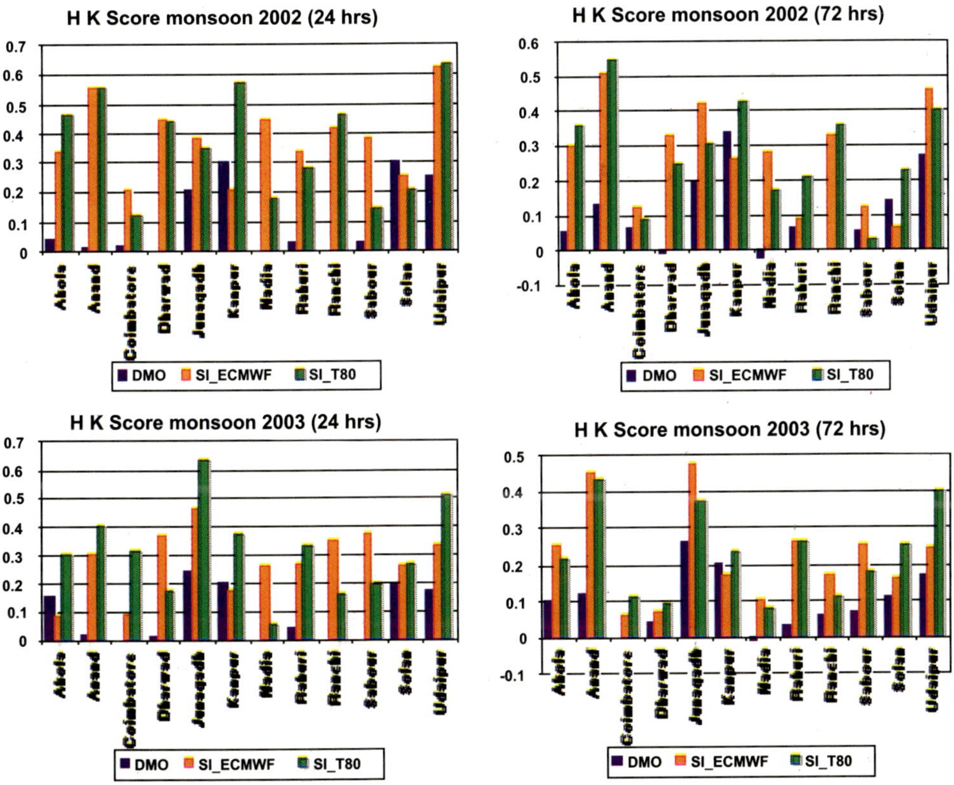

Figure 2: HKS Between SI_ECMWF, SI_T80, DMO during Monsoon 2002 and 2003

Figure 3 gives the *ETS* in 24 and 72 hrs forecast obtained using SI_ECMWF, SI_T80 and DMO forecast. The *ETS* (Schaefer 1990) is a modified version of the threat score. Thus a chance forecast will score 0, as will a constant forecast. A perfect forecast

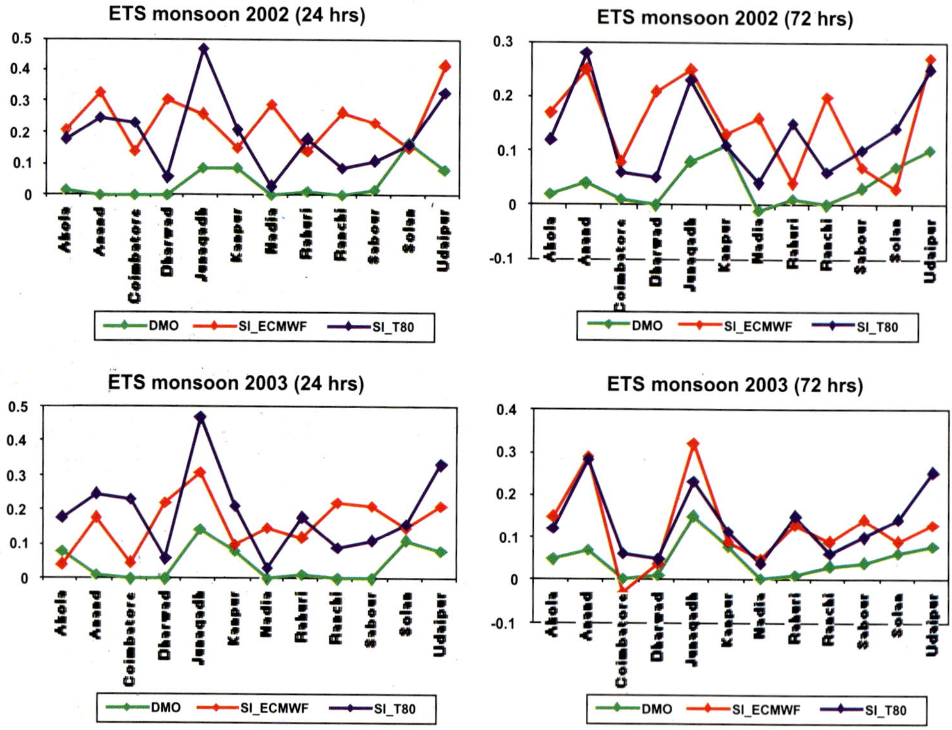

Figure 3: Equitable Threat Score (*ETS*) Between SI_ECMWF, SI_T80, DMO During Monsoon 2002 and 2003

will have an *ETS* equal to 1. Figure 3 shows that the *ETS* obtained from the SI models is higher than that obtained from DMO for most of the stations and the *ETS* is many a times 0 for DMO forecast. This shows that SI has the ability to forecast a rare event more accurately than DMO. Moreover a value of 0 for *ETS* in some of the stations shows that the DMO has the tendency to give a random and constant forecast.

The SI_T80 models are generally performing better than SI_ECMWF models except for stations located in the east. The values of *POD* and *FAR* are also obtained for the SI (ECMWF/T80) and DMO forecast. It is observed that for most of the stations, the value of both *POD* and *FAR* obtained from DMO is higher than SI for all the lead times. Here the higher value of *POD* for DMO can be attributed to over-forecasting. This fact is further strengthened by the higher values of *FAR* for DMO. This shows that the proportion of forecasts that fail to materialise is much higher in DMO than in the case of SI.

Figure 4 shows the *RS* obtained in monsoons 2002 and 2003. In general the *RS* obtained in DMO is of the order of 40-50% and in the case of SI (ECMWF/T80) it is around 60-70%. This again shows that the ratio of correct forecast in the case of SI is better than DMO. Moreover in stations like Coimbatore, Rahuri, and Dharwad the *RS* and *HKS* of SI (ECMWF/T80) is much higher when compared to the DMO. This is

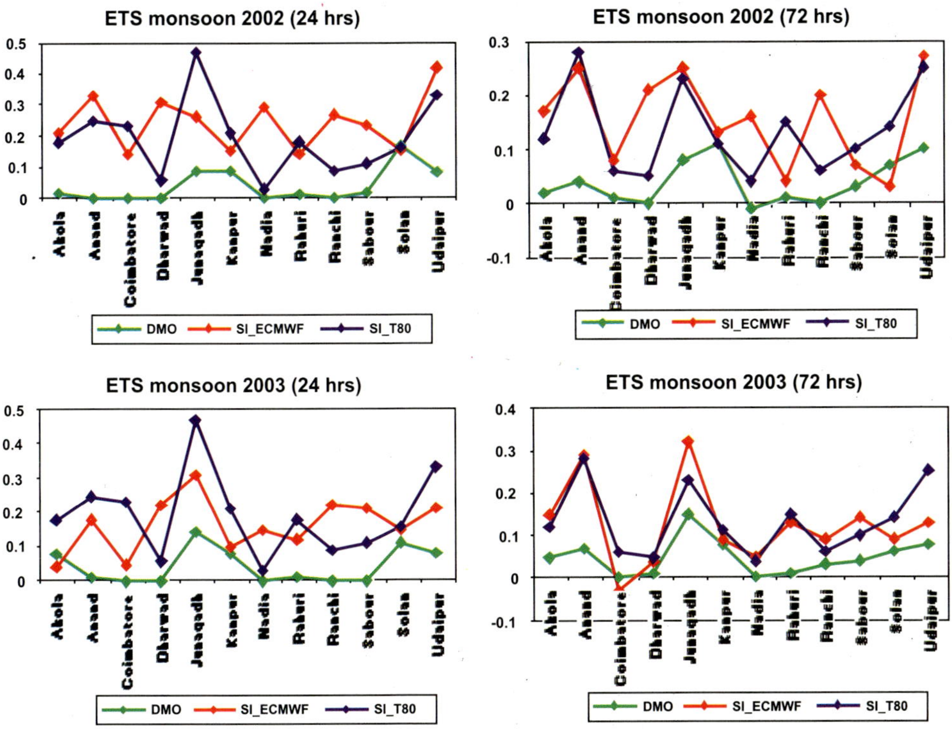

Figure 4: Ratio Score (*RS*) Between SI_ECMWF, SI_T80, DMO During Monsoon 2002 and 2003

because these stations are located near the Ghats in the southern peninsula and so most of the rain here is dominated by orography which is not very well captured by the DMO

Table 2 shows the comparative verification of *Yes/No* rainfall between SI_ECMWF, DMO and the final forecast (FNL) obtained at 12 stations in monsoon 2004. It is seen from both *HKS* and *RS* that SI is superior to DMO and comparable to the final forecast at most of the stations and hence can be developed as a fully automatic operational weather forecasting system.

It is also observed that DMO is performing better than SI at stations situated in the hills like Srinagar and Solan. The reason to this can be attributed to the type of rain that is generally occurring at these stations. Both Solan and Srinagar generally receive rainfall from the western disturbances (WD) rather than from the monsoonal flow. This is because WD is an extra tropical system that is mainly driven by atmospheric dynamics rather than physical forcing. Due to this, rainfall associated with this is captured quite well by the T80 model; hence DMO has a score at par with the SI models.

Table 2: Comparison of *Yes/No* Rainfall Forecast During Monsoon 2004

Station	*SI*		*DMO*		*FINAL*	
	Ratio	*HKS*	*Ratio*	*HKS*	*Ratio*	*HKS*
Anand	75	0.53	52	0.24	74	0.49
Bhubneshwar	63	0.23	56	-0.01	70	0.32
Coimbatore	84	0.47	27	0	57	0.07
Delhi	73	0.33	52	0.15	66	0.29
Dharwad	60	0.28	59	0	65	0.21
Junagadh	60	0.26	56	0.21	69	0.4
Nadia	58	0.18	73	0.02	71	0.11
Raichur	76	0.23	35	0.07	53	0.16
Ranichauri	71	0.44	68	0.38	70	0.41
Sindewahi	71	0.42	52	0.13	57	0.18
Solan	58	0.14	58	0.16	54	0.11
Srinagar	49	0.05	75	0.13	67	0.15

Conclusion

In this paper an operational forecasting system, developed at NCMRWF, for issuing rainfall forecasts has been described. It has been shown that in order to give a skilful forecast, it is necessary to statistically downscale the model products to the specific locations. The results of monsoon 2002 and monsoon 2003 suggest that SI (ECMWF/T80) has the capability of capturing rare rainfall events and performs much better at stations that are driven by orography. Although SI_T80 models are performing better than the SI_ECMWF models, yet they are not able to resolve the systematic bias of the model fully. The DMO due to its tendency to give constant and random forecast perform with equal skill at stations where the numbers of rainy days are more (Nadia, Ranchi, Sabour). The DMO also performs better at stations that are affected by the WD's. SI has an edge over the DMO in places where the variability in rainfall is more (Udaipur, Coimbatore).

Statistical interpretation of NWP model output has been performed and applied for the first time in India at NCMRWF. The results obtained are quite encouraging. Continuous efforts are being made at improving the forecast with different approaches and techniques. The development of MOS equations based on the operational T-80 model forecast will be taken up so that the systematic errors of the model are taken care of. Rainfall in India is basically categorised as light, moderate, heavy and very heavy depending upon the amount in centimeters. Therefore one of the future plans is to develop probability of precipitation type (*PoPT*) equations to forecast different categories of rainfall. For this, techniques such as discriminant analysis and logistic regression will be used. Work on predicting rainfall using neural network has already been initiated to study the non-linear behaviour of rainfall.

References

1. Carter, G. M., 1986: Moving towards a more responsive statistical guidance system. Preprints, *11th Conf. on Weather Forecasting and Analysis*, Kansas City, MO, Amer. Meteor. Soc., 39-45.
2. Carter, G. M., J.P. Dallavalle, H.R. Glahn, 1989: Statistical forecasts based on the National Meteorological Centres numerical weather prediction system. *Wea. Forecasting*, 4, 401-412.
3. Dallavalle, J. P. and H. R.Glahn 1989: Statistical forecasts based on the National Meteorological Centres numerical weather prediction system. *Wea.Forecasting.*, 4: 401-412.
4. Glahn, H. R., and D.A. Lowry, 1972: The use of Model Output Statistics (MOS) in objective weather forecasting, *J. Appl. Meteor.*, 11,1203-1211.
5. Glahn, H. R., A. H. Murphy, L. J. Wilson, and J. S. Jensenius, Jr., 1991: Interpretation and verification for non probabilistic forecasts. *Lectures, WMO Training Workshop on Interpretation of NWP products in terms of local weather phenomena and their verification*, Wageningen, The Netherlands, AREP/RDP/PTD, PSMP No.34, WMO/TD No. 421, xx, var. pags.
6. India Meteorological Department (IMD), 2003: Weather in India, Monsoon Season, (June to September 2002), *Mausam*, 54, No. 3, 775-810
7. India Meteorological Department(IMD), 2004: Weather in India, Monsoon Season, (June to September 2003), *Mausam*, 55, No. 3, 515-548
8. Klien, W.H., B. M. Lewis, and I. Enger, 1959: Objective prediction of 5-day mean temperature during winter, *J. Meteor.*, 16, 672-682.
9. Kumar, A., P. Maini, and S. V. Singh, 1999: An operational model for forecasting probability of precipitation and Yes/No forecast. *Wea. Forecasting*, 14(1), 38-48
10. Kumar, A., P. Maini, L. S. Rathore, and S. V. Singh, 2000: An operational medium range local weather forecasting system developed in India. *Int. J. Climatol.*, 20, 73-87.
11. Maini, P., A. Kumar, S. V. Singh, and L. S. Rathore, 2002: Statistical interpretation of NWP products in India. *Meteor. Appl.*, 9, 21-31.
12. Mason Ian, 1979: On reducing probability forecasts to Yes/No forecasts. *Mon. Wea. Rev.*, 107,207-211.
13. Murphy, A.H., and R.W.Katz, 1985: *Probability, Statistics, and Decision Making in the Atmospheric Sciences.* Westview Press, 545 pp.
14. Rousseau, D., 1982: Work on the statistical adaptation for local forecasts in France. In *Proceedings of Statistical Interpretation of Numerical Weather Prediction Products, Seminar/Workshop*, Reading, United Kingdom, ECMWF: 395-415.
15. Schaefer, J.T., 1990: The critical success index as an indicator of warning skill. *Wea Forecasting.*, 5, 570-575.
16. Tapp, R.G., Woodcock, F., Mills, G. A., 1986. Application of MOS to precipitation prediction in Australia, Mon. Wea. Rev., 114, 50-61.
17. Wilks, D. S., 1995: *Statistical Methods in the Atmospheric Sciences. An Introduction.* Academic Press, 467 pp.

8

A Tropical Mid-Range Forecast Model based on the Single Value Decomposition of the Madden-Julian Oscillation

Chien Wan Tham

National Environment Agency, Singapore

Phone: +65-6545-1492; Fax: +65-6545-7192

E-mail: en_wan@nea.gov.sg

ABSTRACT

The Madden-Julian Oscillation (MJO) which modulates the amount of precipitation received over South East Asia is modelled statistically. Using satellites derived outgoing longwave radiation (OLR) as a proxy for convective clouds, the MJO basic modes are obtained with the single value decomposition (SVD) of 20 years (1974-1994) of band-passed OLR data. The essential idea in using the SVD to predict MJO is to treat the predictors (past data) as the left fields and the predictands (forecast data) as the right fields. The current fields are then projected into the predictors fields and the forecast is obtained from reassembling the predictands fields based on the expansion coefficients. Experiments are performed with different lead times of the predictands and different lag times among the predictors. Based on the validation of the model on 4 years (1995-1998) of data, it is found that that the SVD forecasting methodology, when applied to MJO has predictive skills of up to 3 weeks.

Introduction

Numerical Weather Predictions models, which have been successfully used for weather prediction in the mid-latitudes, have not had much success in the equatorial region. Specifically, weather phenomena such as the El Niño-Southern Oscillation, the Tropospheric Biennial Oscillation (see Li *et al.*, 2001), the Madden Julian Oscillation (Madden and Julian, 1971; Madden and Julian, 1972), the Asian-Australia Monsoon, and the complex interactions among them have not been consistently modelled. On the other hand, empirical techniques, which are mainly statistical in nature, have had better prediction skills than these dynamical models (Webster *et al.*, 1998; Tham *et al.*, 2002). There are two reasons for this disparity. Firstly, the weather systems in the temperate region are more organised with a longer time scale, comprising the growth, movement, and decay of high and low pressure systems and fronts; whereas the weather systems in the tropics are more chaotic with a shorter time scale, consisting of mostly local convective systems that are due to heating. Secondly, the computational adage "garbage in garbage out" succulently describes the tropical modelling problem, where meteorological observational data available as dynamical model input in the tropical region is sparse and incomplete.

With these knowledge, a tropical mid-range statistical forecast model based on the phenomenon MJO is built. There are 3 advantages. Firstly, among the low-frequency variabilities of the tropics such as the ENSO, which has been exploited for climate forecast, MJO has one of the shortest time scale, of ~40 days that can be used for weather forecast. At this intraseasonal time scale, MJO is an excellent candidate for forecast as it is fairly well organised and influences the large-scale distribution of convective clouds over our region. Secondly, by using statistical methods, the difficulties of the lack of observational data have been avoided, as empirical models have a higher tolerance to data incompleteness and data error than dynamical ones. Thirdly, forecasts of dynamical model have a useful range of less than 5 days over the tropics, due to the growth of initial errors as chaos; with statistical methods, because of its statistical nature, longer range forecast of a few weeks is achievable.

In the rest of this article, more details of the weather phenomenon MJO, the statistical method SVD, and the mid-range tropical forecasting model that is based on MJO and SVD, will be described.

Madden-Julian Oscillation

In the following we describe some of the more fundamental characteristics of the MJO (Madden and Julian 1994). The MJO, alias 30–60 days oscillation or 40–50 days oscillation, is the main intraseasonal fluctuation that explains the weather variations in the tropics. It manifests itself as global-scale atmospheric disturbances within the tropics that are confined mostly to the equatorial belt. These oscillation signals have a period of 30–60 days and a wave number of 1–2 (implying that at any one time 1–2 places on the equatorial will be either in the wet or dry phase), with a eastwards propagation speed of ~5 ms–1. They impact our local precipitation variability significantly, and influence the onset and breaks of the Australian-Asian monsoons (Chen *et al.*, 1988; Hendon and Liebmann, 1990).

Observations of MJO

Globally, across the whole tropical strip, the MJO phenomenon can be observed in the wind fields especially the derived velocity potential, forming a full circle around the equator. However, with the outgoing longwave radiation (OLR), the MJO signals can only be seen in the Eastern Hemisphere, propagating at 5 ms^{-1}, from west to east between longitude 60E to 160E (see Figure 1). These are the two main signatures of the MJO, namely the westerly wind burst (WWB) and the super cloud cluster (SCC). These two meteorological variables are not always in exact phase with each other.

Observation studies have shown that the usual MJO development cycle is as follows. The MJO onset begins with convection building up and remaining stationary over the eastern Indian Ocean. The precipitating clouds then move eastward and weaken while over the maritime continent, Singapore, Malaysia, Indonesia, and northern Australia. After which the system continues in its eastward propagation

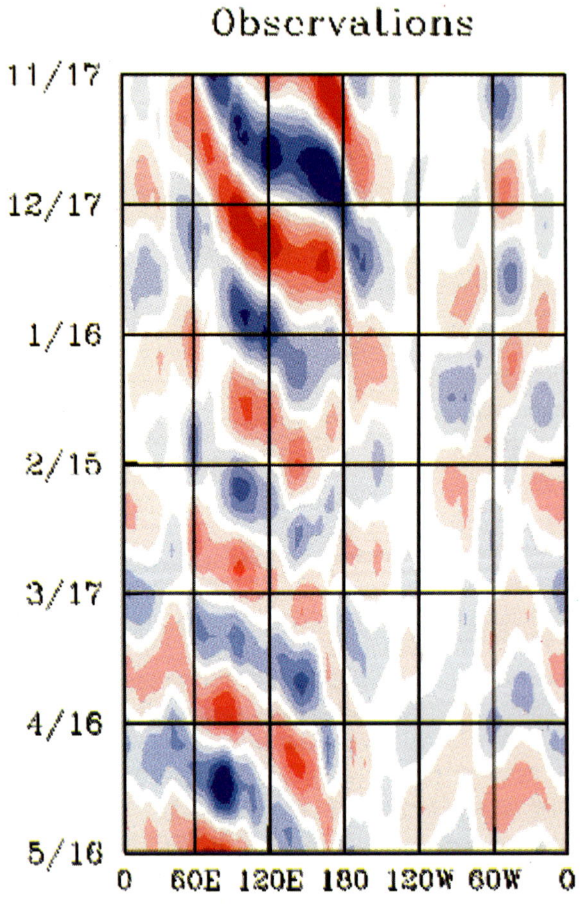

Figure1: A 30–70 Days Band-passed Time-longitude Diagram of the Observed OLR Averaged Over a Equatorial Band for the Winter of 1991

and intensifies above the warm pool over the western Pacific Ocean. This eastward migration slows as it reaches the dateline and weakens before moving toward the eastern Pacific Ocean.

Mechanisms of MJO

The equatorial trapped waves, Kelvin and Rossby waves, which have been deployed to explain the ENSO cycle in the delayed oscillator theory (see Tham 1996) can also be used in the description of the MJO mechanism. The origin of the MJO is still unsolved, although various works have refer to it as a atmospheric Kelvin wave, reconciling the difference in observed and theoretical phase speed with viscous damping (Chang 1977), and wave-CISK, conditional instability of the second kind (Chang and Lim 1988).

Statistical Methods

Multivariate statistical analyses are appropriate tools for geophysical datasets, where the number of variables is large with respect to the sampling time. However correlation and composition are, though computationally simple to implement, subjective in nature, depending on the choice of indexes and references. Thus objective matrix methods are considered, which are capable of determining the connected patterns among geophysical fields.

In this article, we review the following matrix methods: principal component analysis (PCA) and its variants, canonical correlation analysis (CCA) and its variants, and single value decomposition (SVD). In the following, the various methods and their trades off will be discussed. For comparative examples, see Bretherton *et al.*, [1992], where the methods are applied to a simple geophysically model.

Principal Component Analysis

Essentially, PCA is a technique used to reduce the dimensionality of a problem, by extracting uncorrelated components (linear combinations of the origin variables) that capture the largest variances of the fields. The mathematical operation of the PCA involves mainly the numerical computation of the eigenvalues and eigenvectors of the field covariance matrix.

PCA and its empirical orthogonal functions (EOFs) have been used successfully for decomposing meteorological fields into basic modes (*e.g.* Holmstrom 1963; Kutzbach 1967). There are two variants of PCA when applied to extracting coupled modes from the time series of two fields—combined field PCA (CPCA) and single field PCA (SPCA). In CPCA, the two variable fields are concatenated together as one and the EOFs are extracted as the coupled modes. On the other hand, in SPCA, the expansion coefficients of one the EOFs of the first fields are correlated with the variables of the second field (*e.g.* Wallace *et al.* 1990). The latter method is asymmetric while the former symmetric.

Canonical Correlation Analysis

The technique of CCA can be best explained in terms of multiple linear regression and correlation. In CCA, the first mode consists of linear combinations of the first and second fields that yield maximum correlation to each other. The other canonical correlations are found by considering linear combinations that have the next highest correlation on constrains that they are linearly independent to the more basic modes.

Various investigators for finding related patterns between meteorological fields have used CCA. For example, Barnett [1981; 1983] have employed CCA to find coupled modes between the Pacific seasonal sea surface temperature (SST) anomalies and the United States surface air temperature anomalies.

To deal with the sampling fluctuations in the CCA captured modes, it has been suggested that the data be prefiltered with SVD or PCA before the CCA procedure. For example, Barnett and Preisendorfer [1987] have proposed such an improvement for the CCA procedure, which will decrease the variability between the captured modes and the actual modes. In this procedure, the two meteorological fields are prefiltered by performing PCA to extract the basis, before applying CCA.

Single Value Decomposition

The SVD is a fundamental matrix operation that diagonalises a general rectangular matrix. For square matrices diagonalisation, the decomposed components are the eigenvalues and eigenvectors; with rectangular matrices, the end products are the left singular vectors, the singular values, and the right singular vectors.

Examples of the use of SVD in meteorology are given in the following. Prohaska [1976] has used it to capture the coupled patterns between the monthly mean surface air pressure of the United States and the sea level pressure of the northern hemisphere. Lanzante [1984] has employed it to document the patterns of the extratropical seasonal mean SST with the 700-mb height anomalies.

Comparison among PCA, CCA, and SVD

To facilitate the following discussions on the pros and cons of the various techniques of finding coupled patterns between two meteorological fields, we first define some nomenclature.

Arbitrarily, we assign one of the fields to be the left field, *s(t)* and the other, the right field *z(t)*. The variance and covariance matrices of the demean fields s(t) and z(t) shall be denoted by C_{SS}, C_{ZZ}, and C_{SZ}. Central to the idea of the techniques of PCA, CCA, and SVD, is the decomposing of original fields into modes, p_k for left modes and q_k for right. The left and right expansion coefficients, $a_k(t)$ and $b_k(t)$ respectively, are given by the left and right weights, u_k and v_k respectively. The subscript k refers to the mode number. Hence, we have:

$$s(t)=\sum_k a_k(t)\cdot p_k$$

$$z(t)=\sum_k b_k(t)\cdot q_k$$

where,

$$a_k(t)=u_{k^T}\cdot s(t)$$

$$b_k(t)=v_{k^T}\cdot z(t)\cdot$$

The PCA, CCA, and SVD techniques differ in the constraints placed upon the derivation of these patterns, weighting vectors, and expansion coefficients. In the following, we first compare CCA with SVD, and then PCA with SVD, showing the rational for choosing SVD.

In the SVD technique for isolating coupled modes, the optimising criterion is the maximising of the covariance between the expansion coefficients, with the condition that the next pattern p_k (q_k) is orthogonal to the previous patterns $p_1, p_2, \ldots, p_{k-1}$ ($q_1, q_2, \ldots, q_{k-1}$). As a consequence, the weight vectors are the same as the patterns themselves. Fulfilling these conditions is the numerical operation of SVD on the covariance matrix, C_{SZ}, in which the output left (right) singular vectors will be left (right) patterns, p_k (q_k). The output singular values will be the covariance of the left and right fields as explained by the patterns.

In the CCA technique, the criterion is to maximise the correlation between the expansion coefficients, with the condition that the next expansion coefficient a_k (b_k) is uncorrelated with the previous expansion coefficients $a_1, a_2, \ldots, a_{k-1}$ ($b_1, b_2, \ldots, b_{k-1}$). In doing so, the root mean square error between the rebuilt fields and that of the original fields are minimised. To attain the weights, patterns, the expansion coefficients, we perform SVD on the matrix $C_{SS}^{-½} \cdot C_{SZ} \cdot C_{ZZ}^{-½}$. The left (right) patterns and weights will be given by, $C_{SS}^{½} \cdot l_k$ and $C_{SS}^{1½} \cdot l_k$ ($C_{zz}^{½} \cdot r_k$ and $C_{zz}^{1½} \cdot r_k$) respectively, where l_k (r_k) is the left (right) singular vector of the SVD operation. The output singular values will be the canonical correlations, the correlation coefficients between the left and right expansion coefficients.

The problem associated with the CCA technique is that by minimising the differences between the rebuilt and original fields, it over-fits the patterns to the original fields. This problem is especially prominent in meteorological data sets where the time series of variables is small relative to the number of grid points. The variants in CCA address this problem by pre-filtering the data with SVD and PCA. However the numerical computation complexities increases many folds with no evidences of superiority over the SVD technique (Bretherton *et al.* 1992). Furthermore, there is a need for user subjectivity in the choice of the number of modes to retain in the prefiltered procedure of the modified CCA technique. Thus SVD is selected over CCA and its variants.

The PCA technique is considered a more elementary form of matrix operation when compared to SVD. Originally meant for separating single fields into modes using its own variance matrix, it has been extended to extract coupled modes from two fields by merging the left and right fields into one field (CPCA). In the second variant (SPCA), traditional PCA is performed on the left (right) field and the derived expansion coefficients are correlated with the right (left) field grids, thereby coupling the two fields together. The problem with these PCA methods is that there is a systematic bias in the derived coupled modes to the dominant modes of the individual fields. This is highly undesirable as it is possible that the true coupled modes are orthogonal to the individual EOFs. If this systematic error exists, the captured coupled modes would be orthogonal to the true couple modes. In addition, the problem is especially exacerbated in situation where the time series is short. Therefore, the PCA and its variants are not as suitable for deriving the coupled modes as SVD.

In summary, the SVD technique is both straightforward to implement and to interpret for extracting coupled modes. It avoids the difficulties of the classical CCA, the PCA, and the modified PCA techniques and yet is numerically more feasible that the pre-filtered CCA methods.

Single Value Decomposition of MJO

Being statistical in nature, the forecast model predicts the movements of the MJO large scale convective clouds, from the Indian Ocean into our maritime continents, by relying on twenty years of archived data. With the tracking of this MJO manifestation, we can predict the daily spatial distribution of wet and dry regions as attributed by the passing of these events over our regions.

The essential idea in using the SVD to predict MJO is to treat *the predictors (past data) as the left fields* and *the predictands (forecast data) as the right fields*. In doing so, the derived coupled modes will be the connection between the current and the future wet or dry conditions.

The model and its predictions are based on daily, 30-60 day bandpassed, 2.5 deg x 2.5 deg OLR data for the rectangular region, -10S to 10N and 80E to 120 E. The predictors (model inputs) comprise the two OLR anomalies daily maps separated by 10 days apart. As for the predictand (model forecasts), it consists of a relatively future daily OLR anomalies map which leads the most recent predictor by 1 to 21 days. For every lead day (ranges from 1 to 21 days), separately for winter and summer, the SVD technique is performed on the OLR dataset, for the years 1974-1994, to extract the modes and vectors. These left and right patterns, together with the singular values, form the essence of the model.

The summer and winter seasons are defined to be from 16 May-16 Nov and 17 Nov-15 May respectively because there is a discernable difference in the MJO migration between these periods (Salby and Hendon 1994). The first 3 modes of the model for a predictand lead of 10 days are given in Figures 2 and 3.

Discussion

Through SVD modelling, it is found that, from Figure 2, the first mode of the predictor-predictand pattern for each season is sufficient for accounting for about 36% of the covariance among the data. The second mode is orthogonal to the first mode, which is often the case with SVD decompositions. This accounts for 21% of the covariance. The third mode, unlike, the first two modes which depicts a symmetric eastward movement is asymmetrical with respect to the equator, account about 7%.

It was found that the foremost modes of the SVD model capture many of the features of the MJO. For example, as shown in the figures below, the first two coupled modes in both seasons show a general eastward progression of the anomalous dry and wet patterns from the Indian Ocean to our region. In addition, the bias of the MJO progression towards the north during summer (Figure 2) and the south during winter (Figure 3) can also be observed. Also, it was found that the total sum of covariance, captured by the three leading modes, is higher in the winter than in the summer. This

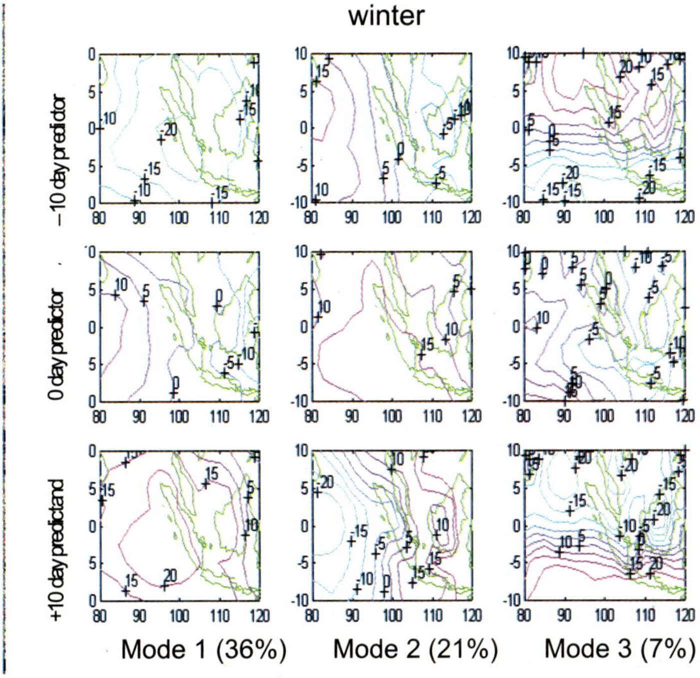

Figure 2: The Left (Predictors) and the Right (Predictand) Patterns for the First 3 Modes of the Model for the Northern Winter. The covariances as explained by the modes are given in brackets.

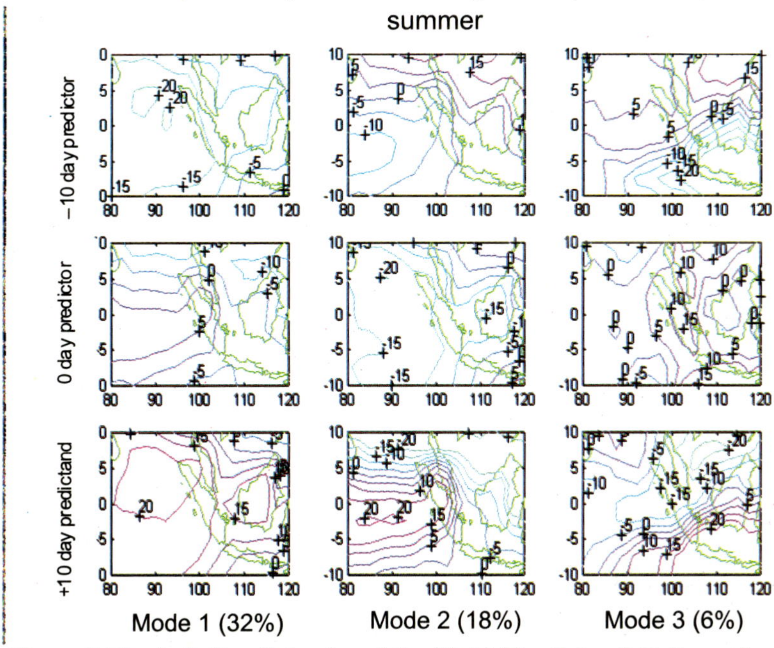

Figure 3: The Left (Predictors) and the Right (Predictand) Patterns for the First 3 Modes of the Model for the Northern Summer. The covariance as explained by the modes is given in brackets.

shows that the MJO phenomenon is more conspicuous in northern winter that in summer.

The research results comprise an extensive set of numerical experiments to determine the optimal lag between the predictors and the predictand lead day in which the model exhibit the best skills. In addition, the number of modes to retrain in the model filtering procedure is also varied to test its effect on the model skill. The model performance is gauged by comparing its forecast with the observations for the period 1995-1998. In this process, the Pearson correlation coefficients are calculated for a rectangular region (-5S to 5N and 100E to 110E) around Singapore.

The correlation coefficients score of the forecast with the actual observations for the winter season is given in the Figure 4. In general, the correlation drops as the number of forecast lead day increases. In fact, the correlation coefficients drop to below 0.4 for a 3-week or longer forecast, the upper limit on the model's forecast range. In addition, there is a low point in the forecast skills for lead-time of about 10 days. The reason for this is that a full MJO cycle is about 40 days and thus it has a maximum and minimum for every 20 days, thus the OLR anomalies on the 10th day (mid way between the maximal and the minima) would be least predictable.

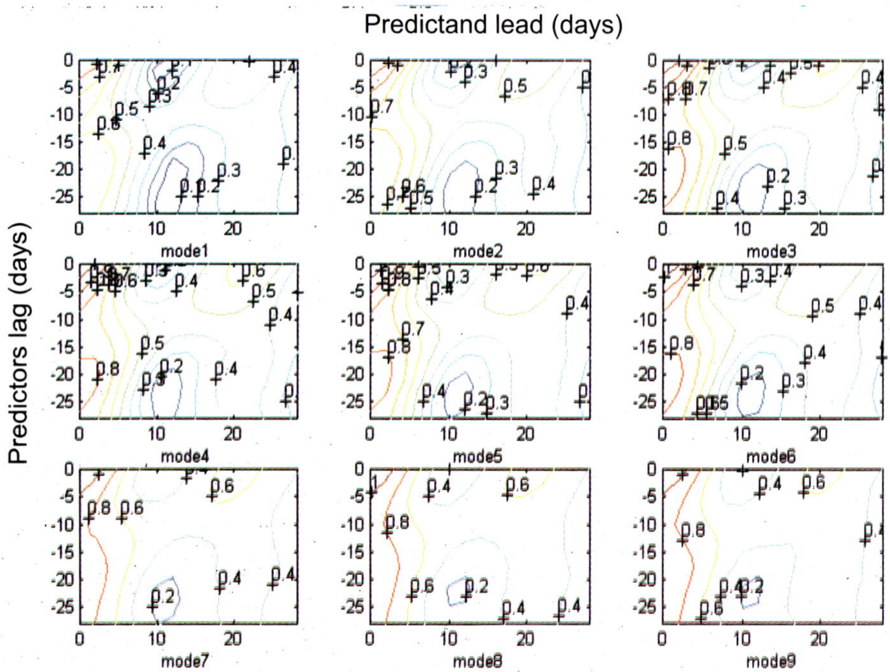

Figure 4: Correlation Contour Diagrams for Winter for the Different Model Parameters. Vertical axis: lag-days between the 2 predictors; horizontal axis: lead-days of the predictand; and diagram sequence: number of cumulative modes retained in the model.

In the verification studies (Figure 4), for the following configuration of the model: lag of 3 days between the predictors, retention of the first 4 modes, and forecast lead of 20 days, gives a *correlation of higher than 0.6,* between the observed and forecasted OLR values over Singapore.

The model constructed by applying the SVD technique shows a good correspondence to the actual MJO phenomenon; thereby verify the validity of this model to predict the MJO. The results of a numerical test performed to fine-tune the model's configurations based on correlation shows the useful forecast lead days of the model is taken to be up to 3 weeks.

Conclusion

In this project, we have described a matrix methodology for tracking and forecasting the MJO phenomenon as a means of providing 2-dimensional wet or dry weather guidance for the region for up to 3 weeks in advance. Tracking and forecasting of MJO, a component of the general circulation and because of its relative long time scale of ~40 days, aid in long-range forecast.

The SVD methodology could be applied to model and predict other phenomena such the diurnal cycle. Likewise, the MJO can also be forecasted with other techniques, such as the classical ideal of a linear interpolation of the time-longitudinal chart of the observed equatorial OLR anomalies.

References

1. Barnett, T. P., 1981: Statistical prediction of Northern American air temperatures from Pacific predictors. *Mon. Wea. Rev.*, 109, 1021–1041.
2. Barnett, T. P., 1983: Interaction of the monsoon and Pacific trade wind systems at interannual time scales. Part I: The equatorial zone. *Mon. Wea. Rev.*, 111, 756–773.
3. Barnett, T. P., and R.W. Preisendorfer, 1987: Origins and levels of monthly and seasonal forecast skill for United States surface air temperature determined by canonical correlation analysis. *Mon. Wea. Rev.*, 115, 1825–1850.
4. Bretherton, C. S., C. Smith, and J. M. Wallace, 1992: An intercomparison of methods for finding coupled patterns in climate data. *J. Climate*, 5, 541–560.
5. Chang, C. P., and H. Lim, 1988: Kelvin Wave-CISK: A possible mechanism for the 30-50 day oscillation, *J. Atmos. Sci.*, 45, 1709–1720.
6. Chang, C. P., 1977: Viscous internal gravity waves and low-frequency oscillations in the tropics, *J. Atmos. Sci.*, 34, 901–910.
7. Chen, T.-C. R. Y. Tzeng, M. C. Yen, 1988: Development and life-cycle of the Indian monsoon—Effect of the 30–50 day oscillation, *Mon. Wea. Rev.*, 116, 2183–2199.
8. Hendon, H. H., and B. Liebmann, 1990: A composite study of onset of the Australian summer monsoon. *J. Atmos. Sci.*, 47, 2227–2240.
9. Holmstrom, I., 1963: On a method for parametric representation of the atmosphere. *Tellus*, 15, 127–149.

10. Kutzbach, J., 1967: Empirical eigenvectors of sea-level pressure, surface temperature, and precipitation complexes over North America. *J. Appl. Meteor.*, 6, 791–802.

11. Lanzante, J., R., 1984: A rotated eigenanalysis of the correlation between 700-mb heights and sea surface temperatures in the Pacific and Atlantic. Mon. Wea. Rev., 112, 2270–2280.

12. Li, T., C.-W. Tham, and C.-P. Chang, 2001: A coupled air-sea-monsoon oscillator for the tropospheric biennial oscillation. *J. Climate*, 14, 752–764.

13. Madden, R. A., and P. R. Julian, 1971: Detection of a 40–50 day oscillation in the zonal wind in the tropical Pacific. *J. Atmos. Sci.*, 28, 702–708.

14. Madden, R. A., and P. R. Julian, 1972: Description of global-scale circulation cells in the tropics with a 40–50 day period. *J. Atmos. Sci.*, 29, 1109–1123.

15. Madden, R. A., and P. R. Julian, 1994: Observations of the 40–50 day tropical oscillation—a review. *Mon. Wea. Rev.*, 122, 814–837.

16. Prohaska, J., 1976: A technique for analysing the linear relationships between two meteorological fields. *Mon. Wea. Rev.*, 104, 1345–1353.

17. Salby, M L and H. H. Hendon, 1994: Intraseasonal Behaviour of clouds, temperature and motion in the tropics. *J. Atmos. Sci.*, 51, 2207-2224.

18. Tham, C.-W., 1996: *El Niño chaos in the delay oscillator.* M.Sc. Dissertation. University of Reading, 97 pp.

19. Tham, C.-W, S. H. Tian, and L. Ding, 2002: Weather Forecasting System Based on Satellite Imageries Using Neuro-fuzzy Techniques. *AFSS 2002*: 267-273.

20. Wallace, J. M., C. Smith, and C. S. Bretherton, 1990: Singular value decomposition of sea-surface temperature and 500-mb height anomalies. *J.Climate*, 5, 561–576.

21. Webster, P. J., V. O. Magana, T. N. Palmer, J. Shukla, R. A. Tomas, M. Yanai, and T. Yasunari, 1998: Monsoons: Processes, predictability and the prospects for prediction. *J. Geophys. Res.*, 103-C7, 14451–14510.

9

Association Between Indonesian Rainfall and the Indian Ocean Dipole

P. N. Vinayachandran* and Ravi S. Nanjundiah
Centre for Atmospheric and Oceanic Sciences,
Indian Institute of Science, Bangalore – 560 012, India
Phone: +91-80-2293 3065; Fax: +91-80-2360 0865
**E-mail: vinay@caos.iisc.ernet.in*

ABSTRACT

Interannual anomalies of Indonesian rainfall show large negative anomalies during the Indian Ocean Dipole mode years of 1994 and 1997. A coupled ocean general circulation model reproduces the seasonal cycle and interannual variability of the Indonesian rainfall. The model also simulates several dipole mode events and the model rainfall anomalies over Indonesia during these events are negative, similar to the observations.

Introduction

The seasonal cycle of the rainfall over Indonesia is characterised by high rainfall during November–February and low rainfall during July–September (Hendon, 2003). The former is generally known as the wet season and the later the dry season. The interannual variability of the Indonesian Rainfall is maximum during the dry season and minimum during the wet season (Haylock and McBride, 2001). The standard deviation of the monthly rainfall anomalies is the maximum and the interstation coherence is the highest during the dry season. The interannual variation of the Indonesian Rainfall is influenced by the El Nino Southern Oscillation (ENSO). The

Indonesian Rainfall is lower during El Nino years and higher during La Nino years. Hendon (2003) has suggested that the dry season rainfall anomalies are influenced by the sea surface temperature anomalies in the equatorial India Ocean. These SST anomalies are attributed to the influence of ENSO. Recent studies suggest that such anomalies develop due to the coupled ocean atmospheric process over the Indian independent of ENSO (Vinayachandran *et al.*, 1999, Saji *et al.*, 1999).

During the years of Indian Ocean Dipole (IOD) cold SST anomalies appear around Indonesia. The western equatorial Indian Ocean becomes warmer than usual. The winds along the equatorial Indian Ocean becomes anomalously easterlies and strong upwelling favourable winds appear along the coast of Sumatra. During IOD years convection is suppressed over the eastern Equatorial Indian Ocean and enhanced in the west. In the ocean, the thermocline rises in the east and deepens in the west (Vinayachandran *et al.*, 2001). Recent IOD events occurred during 1994 and 1997.

It has been shown by Gadgil *et al.* (2003) and Gadgil *et al.* (2004) that the Indian summer monsoon is influenced by the Equatorial Indian Ocean Oscillation which is the atmospheric component of the IOD. In fact, it has been shown that the unusual drought of 2002 summer monsoon and the excess during 1997 can be explained in terms of the unfavourable and favourable phases of this oscillation respectively. Not much is known about the relative importance of the IOD on Indonesian Rainfall in comparison to the influence of ENSO. Saji and Yamagata (2003) have suggested that significant variability of Indonesian Rainfall can occur associated with IOD. In this article we examine the relationship between Indonesian Rainfall and IOD using observations as well as a coupled ocean-general circulation model.

Methods

We have used the monthly CPC Merged Analysis of Precipitation (CMAP) data for the period of 1979 to 1998 which is available at a horizontal grid of 2.5° latitude by 2.5° longitude. In addition, we have used the monthly mean outputs of the Community Climate System Model Version 2 (CCSM2). This coupled model consists of four component models one each for ocean, atmosphere, land and ice. The model run has been carried out for 100 years. Details of the model configuration and experiment may be found in Janakiraman *et al.* (2005).

Results

Figure 1 shows monthly rainfall anomalies for Indonesia. Grid points nearest to Sumatra, Kalimanthan and Jakarta are selected. At Sumatra the rainfall anomalies show large negative values during the IOD years of 1994 and 1997. It is interesting to note that the negative rainfall anomalies were much smaller during the El Nino of 1982-83. Similar anomalies are also noted for Kalimanthan and Jakarta. However, it appears that the ENSO effects have larger influences on the southern and eastern parts of Indonesia. On the other hand, the influence of Indian Ocean Dipole appears to be dominant over Sumatra.

The performance of the model with regard to the monsoons as well as the climatology of the Indian Ocean has been evaluated by Janakiraman *et al.* (2005). In order to evaluate the performance of the coupled model in simulating the rainfall

The model also simulates several IOD events in its 100 year simulation. The dipole mode index defined as the difference in sea surface temperature anomalies between the eastern and western Indian Ocean (Saji *et al.* 1999) show that the year 32 had the strongest dipole in the model. Figure 4 (upper panel) shows the rainfall anomalies for the model years 10-40 for the Indonesian region. The variability in the model is similar to the observations. There are periods of low variability and extreme events in both model and data. Similar to the observations the model rainfall anomaly is negative during the dipole year and positive in the year following the IOD.

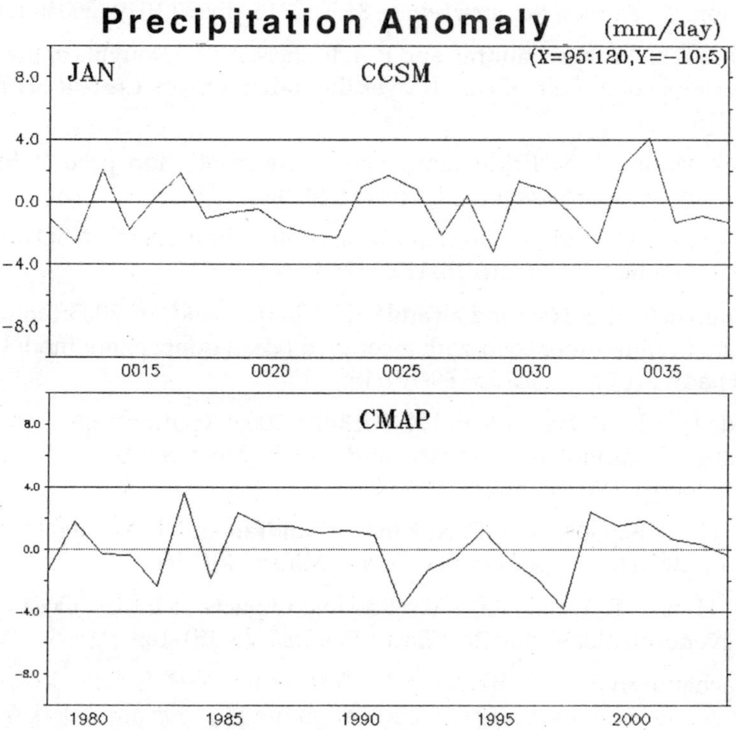

Figure 4: Monthly Rainfall Anomalies Averaged Over the Indonesian Region for the Years 10 to 30 from the Model (Upper Panel) and for 1997 to 2004 from CMAP (Lower Panel)

Summary

A preliminary analysis of the relationship between Indonesian rainfall and the Indian Ocean Dipole has been carried out. CMAP data shows that the rainfall over Sumatra had large negative anomalies during the IOD years of 1994 and 1997. A coupled ocean atmosphere model has a reasonable reproduction of the seasonal cycle of the Indonesian Rainfall. The coupled model also simulates several dipoles in the 100 year simulation and during the IOD years the model rainfall anomalies over Indonesia is negative similar to the observations. The mechanism that lead to such anomalies need to be investigated.

Acknowledgements

The couple model simulation was carried on the PARAM Padma computer at C-DAC, Bangalore. This study was partly funded by the INDOMOD program of the Department of Ocean Development.

References

1. Gadgil S., P. N. Vinayachandran, P. A. Francis and S. Gadgil, 2004: Extremes of the Indian summer monsoon rainfall, ENSO and equatorial Indian Ocean oscillation, *Geophysical Research Letters*, 31, L12213, doi:10.1029/2004GL019733.
2. Gadgil S., P. N. Vinayachandran and P. A. Francis, 2003: Droughts of the Indian summer monsoon: Role of clouds over the Indian Ocean, *Current Science*, 85, 1713-1719.
3. Haylock M. and J. McBride, 2001: Spatial coherence and predictability of Indonesian wet season rainfall, *J. Climate*, 14, 3882-3887.
4. Hendon, H., 2003: Indonesian rainfall variability: Impacts of ENSO and local air-sea interaction, J. Climate, 16, 1775-1790.
5. Janakiraman S., R. S. Nanjundiah and P. N. Vinayachandran, 2005: Simulations of Indian Summer monsoon with a coupled ocean-atmosphere model on the param padma, *Current Science*, 89(10), 1555-1562.
6. McBride J. L., M. R. Haylock and N. Nicholls, 2003: Relationships between the Maritime Continent heat source and the El Nino Southern Oscillation phenomenon, *J. Climate*, 16, 2905-2914.
7. Saji N. H., B. N. Goswami, P. N. Vinayachandran and T. Yamagata, 1999: A dipole mode in the tropical Indian Ocean, *Nature*, 401, 360-363.
8. Saji N. H. and T. Yamagata, 2003: Possible impacts of Indian Ocean Dipole mode events on global climate, *Climate Research*, 25, 151-169
9. Vinayachandran P. N., S. Iizuka and T. Yamagata, 2002: Indian Ocean dipole mode events in an ocean general circulation model, *Deep Sea Res. II*, 49, 1573-1596.
10. Vinayachandran P. N., N. H. Saji and T. Yamagata, 1999: Response of the equatorial Indian Ocean to and unusual wind event during 1994, *Geophys. Res. Lett.*, 26(11), 1613-1617.
11. Xie P., and P. A. Arkin, 1996: Global precipitation: a 17-year monthly analysis based on gauge observations, satellite estimates, and numerical model outputs. *Bull. Amer. Meteor. Soc.*, 78, 2539-2558.

10

Decadal to Interdecadal Time Scale Climate Variability: In Context of Asian/Indian Monsoon System

R.K. Tiwari* and S. Sri Lakshmi

National Geophysical Research Institute (NGRI),
Hyderabad - 500 007, India
Phone: +91-40-23434831; Fax: +91-40-27170491/ 27171564
**E-mail: rk_tiwari3@rediffmail.com*

ABSTRACT

South Asian monsoon is believed to be one of the possible drivers of global climate system. The relation between ENSO and Asian monsoon has been the subject of one of the largest standing debate in climatology. We have spectrally analysed here different sets of recently published climate indicator time series to search for statistically significant modes and teleconnection of ENSO in the context of Indian monsoon. In particular we examine: (1) Indian Rainfall (IRF) time series of the whole country covering the time span of 1826-1994, (2) coral growth rate time series for a period of 42 years spanning over 1948 –1990 from the Arabian sea, and (iii) NINO3 temperature record to investigate the signature of ENSO response in the Indian monsoon. Multiple spectral techniques (e.g. multi-taper method (MTM), and Wavelet analysis) are used to identify the coherent cyclic and non-stationary modes in these records. MTM analysis of IRF time series resolves statistically significant variability (>90% C.I) (i) at multi-decadal (66-70 year) scales related to the well-known global temperature variability of internal atmospheric-ocean origin; and (ii) the 2.5 to 7.5 year cycles associated with ENSO frequency band.

The MTM spectra of coral growth rate record also reveal statistically significant periodicities (>90% C.I.) within 1.8-4.2 ENSO frequency band, and a relatively weak signal at 12.8 years. Wavelet spectral analyses of the above time series reveal non-stationary "localised modes" of ENSO evolution corresponding to 2-7 years. Coherency analysis exhibits statistically significant spectral peaks (>80% CI) only at some selected periods suggesting possible role of ENSO dynamics in organising the subtle Indian monsoon at these frequencies. These results may provide significant implication for the modelling of Indian monsoon.

Introduction

The atmosphere, oceans and biosphere are globally coupled phenomena, which is often called the Earth system. In recent years, the study of climatic variability and its inter-relationships with the global climate system have been increasing tremendously on spatial as well as temporal scales. The climate system varies and changes quasi-periodically because of the complex interaction of the atmosphere with the other Earth system components. As a result there are recurrences of short-term extreme events such as floods and droughts; and long-term episodes such as dry and wet decades, cool or warm centuries, and glacial-interglacial cycles. There are different climatic oscillations that work on varying scales: (i) 2-2.5 years oscillation in the equatorial jet in the Lower stratosphere is known as the Quasi-Biennial Oscillation (QBO) (ii) El-Nino/Southern Oscillation (ENSO) has a periodicity of 4-5 years (iii) Decadal and inter-decadal variability is found in the North Atlantic Oscillation (NAO) (iv) Century to Millennial scales occur the Dansgaard-Oeschger Cycles. These climatic oscillations operating on interannual, decadal and multidecadal time scales impact the global oceanic and atmospheric circulations and can produce droughts and floods in certain regions.

The complexity in the precipitation record seems to be primarily associated with both external forcing as well as internal atmospheric-ocean processes. It is, therefore, somewhat difficult to assign a single causative mechanism for controlling the behaviour of monsoon over the Indian subcontinent. Recent wavelets analysis of (partially covered region of the Indian sub-continent) IRF monsoon time series has emphasised some role of solar/sunspot cycle (Kailash and Narsimha 2000). They have also noted that there is no evidence for ENSO signal in the Indian rainfall data.

The El Nino-Southern oscillation (ENSO) is widely known to be a quasi-periodic phenomena dominated by the coupled ocean-atmospheric interactions. This has far reaching hazardous impact including drought, floods and intense rainfall with severe human consequences as well as distinctive "telelinked" pattern of climatic anomalies. This phenomena has also impact on the Asian monsoon that drives the surface ocean seasonality in the Indian and western Pacific oceans and Atlantic inter-tropical convergence zone (Cole *et al.*, 1993). An event of this type affects the climate of a large portion of the globe. The strongest and most reliable effects occur in the tropical Pacific Ocean where El Nino and Southern Oscillation are strongly coupled. Other parts of the world, especially in the middle Latitudes, are affected through teleconnection. Many studies suggest the possibility of indirect link between ENSO and NAO and illustrate a direct impact of ENSO on tropical North Atlantic SSTs (Enfield and Mayer, 1997). Although the signatures of ENSO quasi-cycle have been recognised globally, the possible coupling between the IRF inter-annual variability and sea surface temperature (SST) anomaly in the Arabian Sea is yet to be quantitatively examined. Hence, the analysis of new proxy record of temperature variability (coral growth rate) record from sensitive location Arabian sea and West Pacific regions combined with IRF time series may shed some light on degree of coupling between the ENSO and Indian tropical monsoon. If there is a strong effect, this can be identified by the statistical and spectral analyses.

Hence in particular, we analyse here the sets of newly available data (*e.g.* Indian rainfall and coral growth record) and compare with similar El Nino record of ENSO activity. Our analysis revealed the signatures of ocean-atmospheric dynamics in IRF signal on multi-decadal and inter-annual (ENSO signal) scales.

Data

The annual coral growth record of forty two years long spanning (1948-1989 AD) (Chakraborty and Ramesh, 1998), analysed here, comes from a live coral head Favia Speciosa which has been collected in June 1990 off the coast of Pirotam island (22.6° N, 70° E) situated in the Gulf of Kutch (Northern Arabian sea) at a water depth of ~ 1 meter during low tide (Figure 1).

We use here the recently updated instrumental annual rainfall index of the whole country (Singh and Sontakke, 1996) to investigate the ENSO response in Indian monsoon spanning over a period from 1826 to 1994 (Figure 1). The present data (Singh and Sontakke, 1996) are area weighted and homogeneous annual IRF index of the whole country. The IRF time series exhibits small oscillatory fluctuations superimposed on apparently long term decadal and inter-decadal variations, which can be revealed in detailed spectral analyses. One of the best available records of

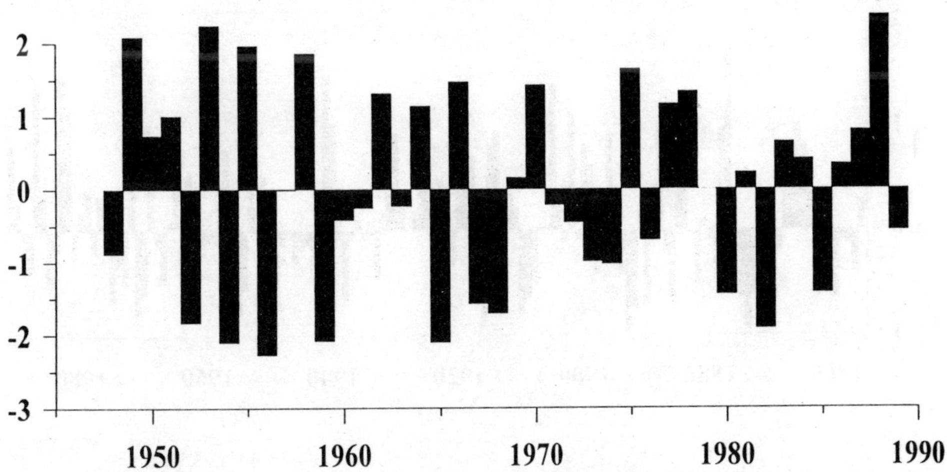

Figure 1: Coral Growth Rate Time Series

temperature variability $NINO_3$ (proxy for ENSO) variability is presented by Kaplan *et al.* (1998) and widely analysed by several workers (Figure 2) (Felis *et al.*, 2000).

Spectral Methods

We perform here multiple spectral analyses (*e.g.* wavelets & MTM) to isolate statistically significant harmonics, if any, in IRF and coral growth rate records. There are two main problems: 1) the presence of deceptive signal due to red noise and 2) non-stationarity of geophysical records besides several others in the analysis and interpretation of geophysical records. We analysed and invoked the typical climate null hypothesis of 'red noise' by generating robust statistical model (Mann and Lees, 1996). The MTM spectral analysis has been used for the analyses of geophysical/ geochemical and environmental signals (Mann and Lees, 1996; Cole *et al.*, 2000). In addition to the MTM analysis, we also use wavelet spectral analyses to examine the stability and stationarity of the spectral components. We briefly describe the main features of these methods:

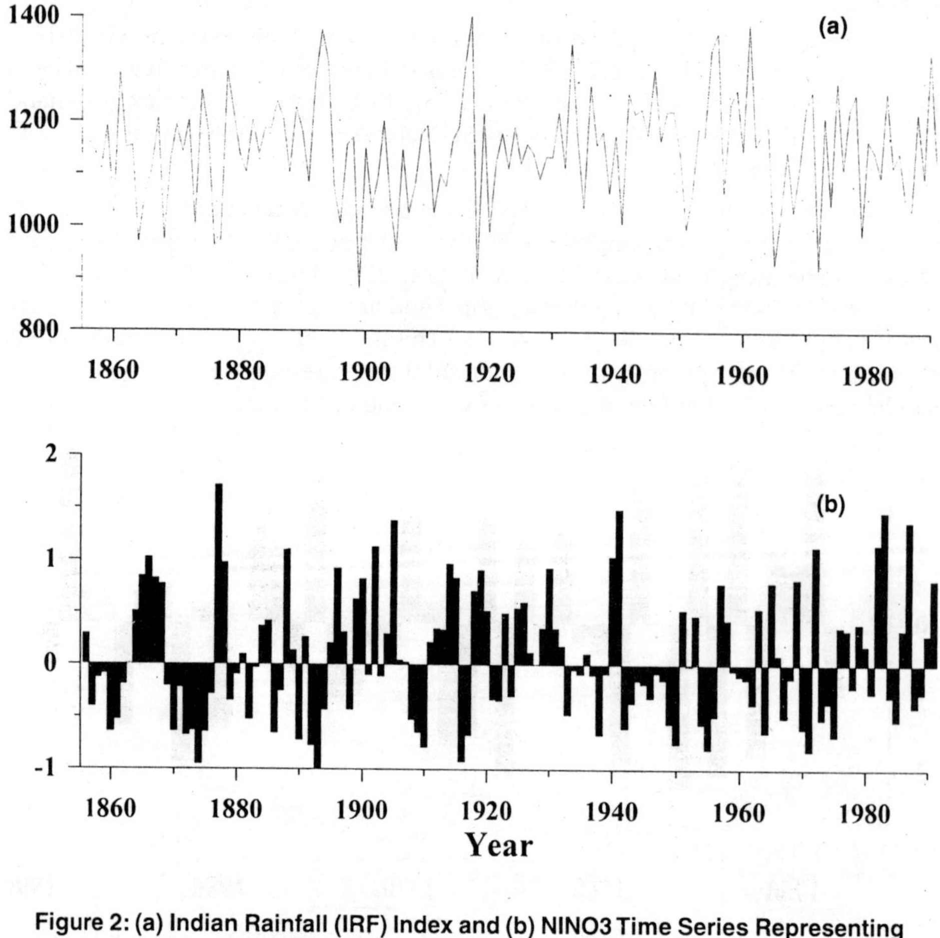

Figure 2: (a) Indian Rainfall (IRF) Index and (b) NINO3 Time Series Representing ENSO Related Temperature Variability

MTM method is a technique to isolate climate signals in time series having robust "red noise" background, which arises from temporal persistence. In this method, a set of optimal taper 'k' is calculated to optimise the spectral leakage due to outside a prescribed bandwidth 'W' for a periodic signal (Thomson, 1982). The number of relevant tapers is then proportional to the bandwidth so that a cutoff between resolution (small W) and confidence (large number of tapers) has to be found by trial and error (Thomson, 1982). Independent spectral estimates with a set of K tapers (with a given bandwidth W) are computed for a time series X product of X and each taper. The average of these spectra gives the Multitaper spectral estimate having good statistical properties. The MTM is appropriate for monitoring the significant modes in such distinct variability because it has low variance, high spectral resolution and accurate statistical significance for the detected spectral peaks (Thomson, 1982; Mann and Lees, 1996). It is important, however, to vary the bandwidth parameter W and number of tapers to ensure the stability of the frequency module estimates. The harmonic analysis provides a robust statistical test, which allows rejection of null hypothesis against red noise (Mann and Lees, 1996).

Wavelet analysis is used on non-stationary signals because the wavelet used here can provide exceptional time-frequency localisation. It is an increasingly used tool for detecting the oscillations of paleoclimatic signals in both time and frequency domains. This method decomposes a given time series into scale components for identifying oscillations occurring at short period and others at a long period (Holschneider, 1995). Mathematically, the continuous wavelets transform of a time series f (t) can be given as:

$$W_{\psi}(a,b) = \frac{1}{\sqrt{a}} \int_{-\infty}^{\infty} f(t)\psi\left(\frac{t-b}{a}\right)dt \tag{1}$$

Here Ψ is the base wavelets function (in this case, Morlet function), with a length that is much shorter than the time series f (t). W stands for wavelet coefficients. The variable 'a' is a scale factor that determines the frequency (or scale) so that varying 'a' gives rise to spectrum. 'b' is shift of the analysis window in time so that varying b represents the sliding method of the wavelet over f(t). Logarithmic scale axis allows for better resolution of small-scale components, *i.e.*, higher frequencies. The complex-valued Morlet wavelet can be represented by a periodic sinusoidal function which is defined as (Morlet *et al.*, 1982):

$$\psi(t) = \pi^{-1/4} e^{i\omega_0 t} e^{-t^2/2} \tag{2}$$

where,

ω_0 is the frequency parameter that allows one to shift the frequency range for investigation. We use the morlet wavelet to calculate the wavelet power spectra to identify large-scaled features in the selected frequency bands with respect to time.

Results and Discussion

MTM Spectra

MTM analysis exhibits significant peaks (at >90% confidence level according to F- test) that occur around 66.66 yrs, 20-22 yrs and 13-14 yrs (Figure 3). The possible sources for the 66.66 years rainfall cycle could be either due to random forcing or to some physical processes such as external solar-ocean–atmospheric system. This statistically significant cycle at 66-70 years in the IRF time series is interesting because it is similar to the well known inter-decadal periodicity of 50- 70 years reported in the global mean temperature record (Schiesinger and Ramankutti, 1994; Minobe, 1997; Tiwari and Rao, 2004). The 12-14 year cycle may be related to the decadal climate–temperature cycle.

The MTM analysis also revealed statistically significant peaks (at >90% C.I) centred at 7.5-5.7, 3.4-3.2, and 2.8-2.1 years. (Figure 3) matching with modern ENSO related climate variability.

Similar analysis of relatively shorter coral record (Figure 3) reveals peaks at 4.2, 2.8 and 2.2 years, which are also statistically significant according to the F-test (Mann and Lees, 1996). A smaller peak of order of 12 yrs also appears, but in view of smaller time span of coral record, we will restrict our discussion only to the main ENSO band. Similar power spectral analysis of SST averaged over the east central Pacific at the equator for 1950-1997 and normalised surface pressure difference between Tahiti, in the Mid- Pacific, and Darwin Australia (a measure of the pressure gradient across the tropical Pacific) exhibit a broad but robust peak centred at approximately 4 yrs and 2 yrs period (Hanson *et al.*, 1989; Enfield, 1989). This suggests that the coral record analysed here, although smaller, matches well with results of global events.

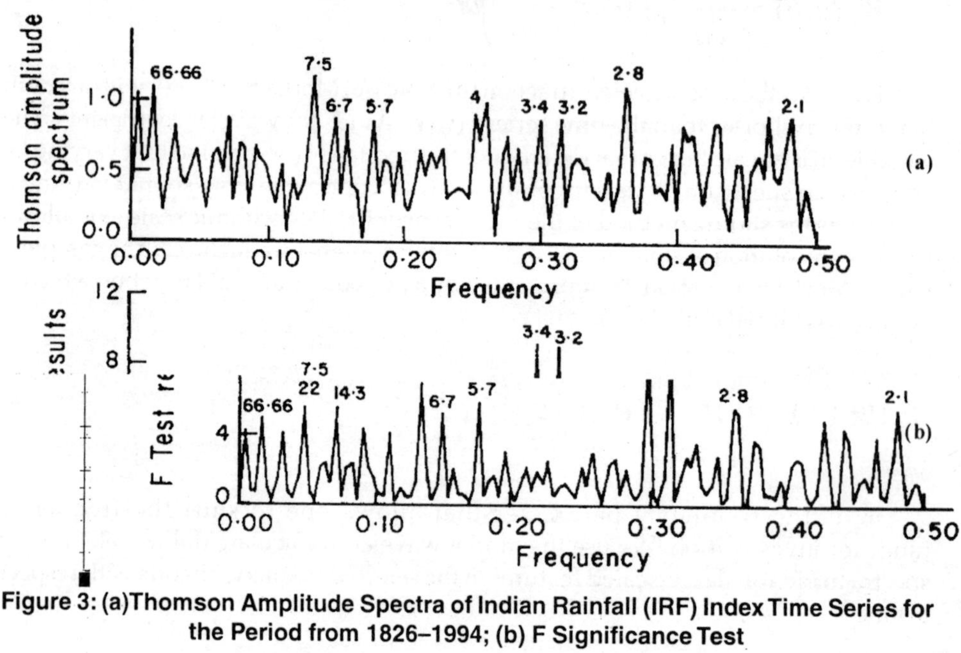

Figure 3: (a)Thomson Amplitude Spectra of Indian Rainfall (IRF) Index Time Series for the Period from 1826–1994; (b) F Significance Test

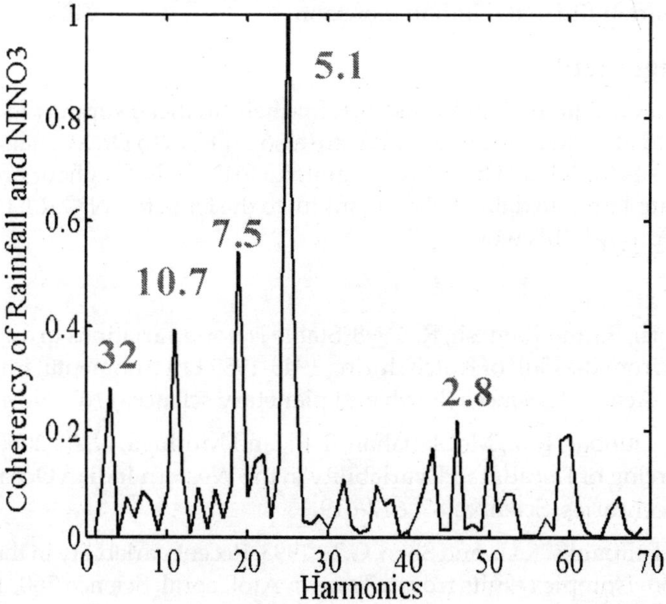

Figure 6: Coherency Calculated Between the IRF and NINO3 Records

corresponding to 5.2 and 2.3 yrs, the two signals are in phase. However, there is some exception during 1935-1965 when the rainfall indices representing Indian monsoon intensity show more variable relation with NINO3 due to weak ENSO activity during this period (Cole *et al.*, 1993).

Conclusion

Our results indicate that MTM and wavelet analyses are promising tools for the optimal detection of periodic and quasi-periodic signals buried in a time series.

- The multiple spectral analyses of a new IRF time series for the whole Indian sub-continent indicate a robust multidecadal cycle of order of 65-70 years which may possibly be related to the well known time scale of internal ocean-atmospheric system dynamics.
- The spectral analyses also reveal apparent peaks in a period range of 2-7 yrs similar to ENSO modes suggesting the role of ENSO signal in Indian monsoon only at these frequencies.
- Frequency characteristics of the coral record from Kutch (India) and instrumental rainfall data index over all India based on the MTM and Wavelet Spectra show that the interannual and decadal variability in Arabian Sea (Kutch region) is related directly to the Indian monsoon and other global change phenomena of the equatorial region.

These results may provide constraints for modelling of climatic variability over the Indian region and ENSO phenomena associated with the redistribution of SST;

thereby suggesting that ENSO phenomena may have played subtle role in triggering inter-annual variability in the Indian monsoon.

Acknowledgements

We are thankful to the INSA and CSIR for their financial support to attend the roundtable held at Jakarta, Indonesia. We are also grateful to Dr. Michael Evans for suggesting the site for NINO3 data. We are grateful to Dr. N.N. Singh for providing us the new/updated rainfall data. We are thankful to the Director, N.G.R.I. for his kind permission to publish this work.

References

1. Chakraborti, S., and Ramesh, R., 1998. Stable isotope variations in a coral (Favia Speciosa) from the Gulf of Kutch during 1948-1989 Environmental implications. Proc. Ind. Acad. of sciences (Earth and planetary sciences) 107, No 4, 331-341.
2. Cole, J.E., Dunbar, R.B., McClanahan, T.R., and Muthiga, N.A., 2000. Tropical Pacific forcing of Decadal SST variability in the Western Indian Ocean over the past two centuries. Science 287, 617-619.
3. Cole, J.E., Fairbanks, R.G., and Shen. G.T., 1993. Recent variability in the Southern Oscillation: Isotopic results from a Tarawa Atoll coral. Science 260, 1790-1793.
4. Enfield, D.B., 1989. Is El Nino becoming more common? Oceanography 1, 23-27. Also, D.B. Enfield Luis Cid.s Toga Notes No.1, Fall 1990.
5. Felis, T., Patzold, J., Loya, Y., Fine, M., Nawar, A.H., and Wefer, G., 2000. A coral oxygen isotope record from the northern Red Sea documenting NAO, ENSO, and North Pacific teleconnections on Middle East climate variability since the year 1750. Paleoceanography 15, No. 6, 679-694.
6. Hanson, K., Brier, G.W., and Maul, G.A., 1989. Evidence of significant non-random behaviour in the recurrence of strong El Nino between 1525 and 1988. Geophysical Research Letters 16, 1181-1184.
7. Holschneider, M., 1995. Wavelets: An analysis tool, Oxford University Press, Oxford, 455 pp.
8. Kailash, S.V., and Narasimha, R., 2000. Quasi-cycles in monsoon rainfall by wavelet analysis. Current Science 78(5), 592-595.
9. Kaplan, A., Cane, M., Kushnir, Y., Clement, A., Blumenthal, M., and Rajgopalan, B., 1998. Analysis of global sea surface temperature. Journal of Geophysical Research 103, 18567-18589.
10. Mann, M.E., and Lees, J.M., 1996. Robust estimation of background noise and signal detection in climate time series. Climate change 33, 409-445.
11. Minobe, S., 1997. A 50-70 years climate oscillation over the North Pacific and North America. Geophysical Research Letters 24, 683-686.
12. Morlet, J., Arens, G., Fourgeau, E. and Girard, D., 1982. Wave propagation and sampling theory, Sampling theory and complex waves. Geophysics 47, 203-221.

13. Schiesinger, M.E., and Ramankutti, N., 1994. An oscillation in the global climate system of period 65-70 years. Nature 367, 723-726.

14. Singh, N., and Sontake, N.A., 1996. The instrumental period rainfall series of the Indian region: documentation. Contribution from Indian Institute of Tropical Meteorology, Pune, Research Report No. PR-067 ISSN 0252-1075

15. Thomson, D.J., 1982. Spectrum estimation and harmonic analysis. Proc. of the IEEE 70, 1044-1096.

16. Tiwari, R.K., and Rao, K.N.N., 2004. Signature of global ENSO dynamics in the Arabian Sea coral growth rate (Feviaspeciosa) record and Indian monsoon. Pure and Applied Geophysics 161, No. 2, 413-427.

11

Influence of Eurasian and Tibetan Snow on Indian Summer Monsoon

S.K. Dash*, P. Parth Sarthi and M.S. Shekhar

Centre for Atmospheric Sciences,
Indian Institute of Technology, New Delhi – 110 016, India
Phone: +91-11-26591307; Fax: +91-11-26591386
**E-mail: skdash@cas.iitd.ernet.in*

ABSTRACT

It is well known that there is an inverse relationship between the strength of the Indian summer monsoon and the extent of Eurasian snow cover in the preceding season. Since the Tibetan plateau acts as the heat source/sink, it seems that Tibetan snow cover also affects the Indian Summer Monsoon Rainfall (ISMR). In this paper, a modest attempt has been made to use the actual observed snow depth values over Eurasia and Tibet in a General Circulation Model (GCM) and Regional Climate Model (RegCM3) respectively. The spectral GCM of IITD at resolution T80L18 has been integrated for six months starting from 5th April to 30th September in order to examine the influence of Eurasian snow on the monsoon wind and associated rainfall. The Historical Soviet Daily Snow Depth (HSDSD) version II data set has been used for these GCM experiments. Model simulations demonstrate that high (low) Eurasian snow depth in spring is followed by deficient (excess) monsoon rainfall over India. Model simulations also show weak (strong) lower level monsoon westerlies and upper level easterlies in response to high (low) April snow over Eurasia.

The Regional Climate Model version 3 (RegCM3) has also been integrated from 1st April to 30th September in four years starting from 1993. Monthly snow depth data based on NIMBUS-7 SMMR satellite are used for conducting sensitivity experiments with RegCM3. Model simulations reveal that excess Tibetan snow in April decreases the rainfall over India in the following monsoon season. Simulations also show that lower level westerlies and upper level easterlies are weakened in the snow experiment than in the no-snow experiment.

Keywords: *Spectral GCM, Regional climate model, Snow depth, Indian summer monsoon rainfall, Inverse relationship, Sensitivity experiments.*

Introduction

Earlier studies by several authors (Hahn and Shukla 1976, Kripalani and Kulkarni 1999, Bamzai and Shukla 1999) based on observed data show the inverse relationship between the Indian Summer Monsoon Rainfall (ISMR) and the Eurasian snow cover/depth in the preceding season. By using General Circulation Models (GCMs), sensitivity experiments were done by several authors such as Barnett *et al.* (1989), Vernekar *et al.* (1995) etc. Their results clearly indicate that positive snow anomalies over Eurasia in winter/spring do affect the monsoon circulation in the following summer in terms of weaker monsoon. Dash *et al.* (2006a) confirmed the inverse snow-ISMR relationship by using the actual observed values of snow depth of Historical Soviet Daily Snow Depth (HSDSD) version II data set in the spectral GCM of Indian Institute of Technology Delhi (IITD).

The positive correlation between Tibetan sensible heat flux and southeast Asian rainfall suggests an inverse relationship between Tibetan snow cover and southeast Asian rainfall (Zwiers, 1993). GCM experiments conducted by Ose (1996) also show that the anomalous cooling due to the positive snow mass anomalies in early spring over Tibet tend to produce a weak Asian monsoon. The recent developments in regional models suggest that the effect of Tibetan snow on the Indian summer monsoon can be best studied by using a regional model. Dash *et al.* (2006b) have used RegCM3 (Girogi, 1990) to simulate the characteristics of Indian Summer monsoon circulation and rainfall reasonably well. They have also demonstrated the inverse relationship between Tibetan snow and Indian summer monsoon rainfall.

The Models

The original version of IITD spectral GCM belongs to the European Centre for Medium range Weather Forecasts (ECMWF) at horizontal resolution T21L05. Here the letter T followed by the numeral stands for the maximum truncation limit in the triangular truncation scheme in the horizontal direction and the letter L followed by the number represents the number of sigma levels in the vertical. Earlier, T21 model was successfully used for simulating circulation patterns over India (Dash and Chakrapani 1989) and its higher resolution version T42L09 was used successfully for several sensitivity studies (Dash 1995, 1999). The earlier model has currently been modified to higher resolution T80L18. It has 256x128 equivalent grids in the horizontal, where surface fields such as, orography, SST, soil temperature, soil moisture, albedo, roughness parameter and snow depth are prescribed. The mean orography based on US Navy data has been prescribed in the model along with 2-dimensional Lanczos filter (Navarra *et al.* 1994) in order to take care of the sharp discontinuities of the mountains, specially to represent the Himalayas and the Western Ghats realistically. The physics packages in the model include dry and moist adiabatic adjustment, large-scale condensation, radiation and surface processes of Geophysical Fluid Dynamics Laboratory (GFDL).

RegCM3, an upgraded version of the Abdus Salam International Centre for Theoretical Physics (ICTP) regional climate model RegCM2 (Giorgi *et al.*, 1993a, b), is a compressible, grid point model with 14 vertical layers and hydrostatic balance. There are two categories of land use such as MM4 vegetation and Global Land Cover Characterisation (GLCC) which determine surface properties like albedo, roughness, moisture etc. at each grid point. MM4 vegetation has 13 different types and GLCC has similarly 20 types of lands. The model dynamical code is essentially the same as that of the hydrostatic version of the mesoscale model MM5 (Grell *et al.* 1994). The model includes cumulus parameterisation schemes, large scale precipitation scheme, Planetary Boundary Layer (PBL) parameterisation, state-of-the-art surface vegetation/soil hydrology package, the Biosphere-Atmosphere Transfer Scheme (BATS), Ocean flux parameterisation, pressure gradient scheme, explicit moisture scheme, the radiative transfer scheme and the ocean-atmosphere flux scheme.

Initial Data and Experimental Design

The HSDSD version II data set and rainfall data of IMD have been used to select two cases; a high snow year (exp1) followed by deficient ISMR and a low snow year (exp2) followed by excess ISMR. It is found that the snow depths of the years 1979 and 1975 suit the above cases respectively and hence these are used as surface conditions in the IITD spectral GCM experiments. The HSDSD version II snow depth data prescribed in the model experiments pertain to the domain 52-66^{0}N and 52-66^0 E. Beyond this domain the observed snow depth values are very small and hence are not included. The difference of snow depths between the high snow depth year (1979) and low snow depth year (1975) used in the GCM over the Eurasian region is shown in Figure 1.

IITD spectral GCM has been integrated upto 30th September starting from 5th April 1996 using the NCMRWF analysis of atmospheric and surface fields as initial conditions. In both the model runs 'exp1' and 'exp2', daily climatological values of NCEP/NCAR Sea Surface Temperature (SST) are used with a view to establish that the changes in the simulations are due to the variations in Eurasian snow prescribed to the model in the two years concerned.

For simulating the monsoon circulation features and rainfall in RegCM3, the central grid point is chosen at 80° E and 20° N with 101 grid points along the latitude circle and 115 points along the longitudinal direction. The domain chosen is 55° E to 105° E and 5° S to 45° N with horizontal grid distance of 55km. The original monthly averaged optimum interpolation SST available from NCEP for the whole year is horizontally interpolated into the specified domain and also in each time step for the model integration. The RegCM3 has been integrated from 1st April to 30th September

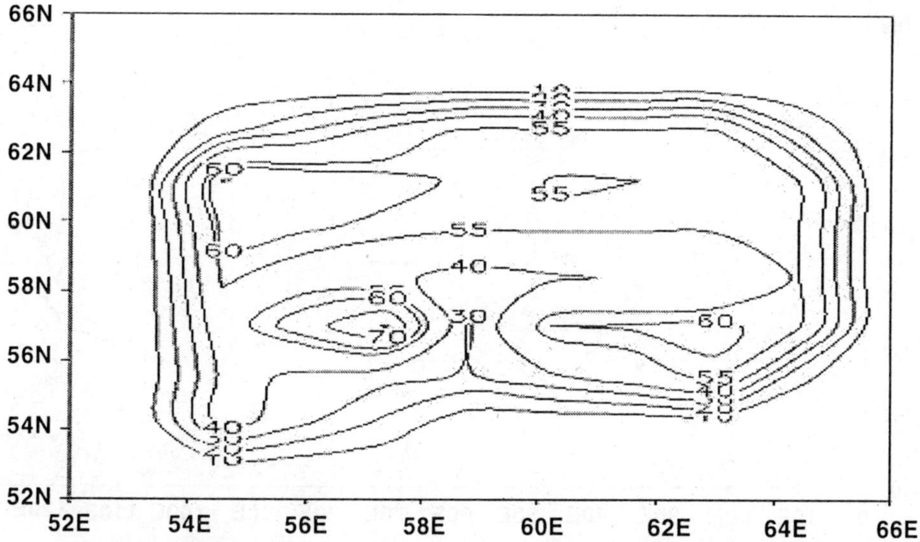

Figure 1: Difference (Exp1–Exp2) of Depth (cm) Between the High Snow Depth Year 1979 and Low Snow Depth Year 1975 in the Month of April Based on HSDSD Version II Data Set (1966–1994) Prescribed to the Model as surface boundary conditions

in the years 1993 to 1996 using reanalysed data. In one set of experiments called the 'no-snow experiment', there is zero snow depth over the Tibetan domain. In another set of experiments called the 'snow experiments' 10cm of snow depth has been uniformly prescribed over the Tibet.

Results and Discussions

GCM Results

The difference in the circulation characteristics in high snow depth (1979) and low snow depth (1975) years are studied in detail by analysing mean wind of four months from June to September (JJAS).

Figure 2 shows the difference (exp1-exp2) in the seasonal wind field at 850 hPa as simulated in the model in response to the snow depth anomaly. The model simulated lower level wind shows a well organised anomalous cyclonic circulation over central Eurasia. Also the model simulates anomalous westerly to the south of Caspian Sea, which implies that westerly is stronger in high snow depth case than in low snow depth case. Comparative study reveals (Dash *et al.* 2006a) that similar anomalous circulation spreading over larger area persists in the mid-latitude belt between 40^0 N to 70^0 N in NCEP/NCAR reanalysis. Both in the model simulation and NCEP/NCAR reanalysis, an anomalous anticyclonic circulation to the north of Arabian Sea exists, which leads to anomalous easterlies over the Arabian Sea during monsoon season. This implies that Asian summer monsoon lower level westerlies are weaker in exp1

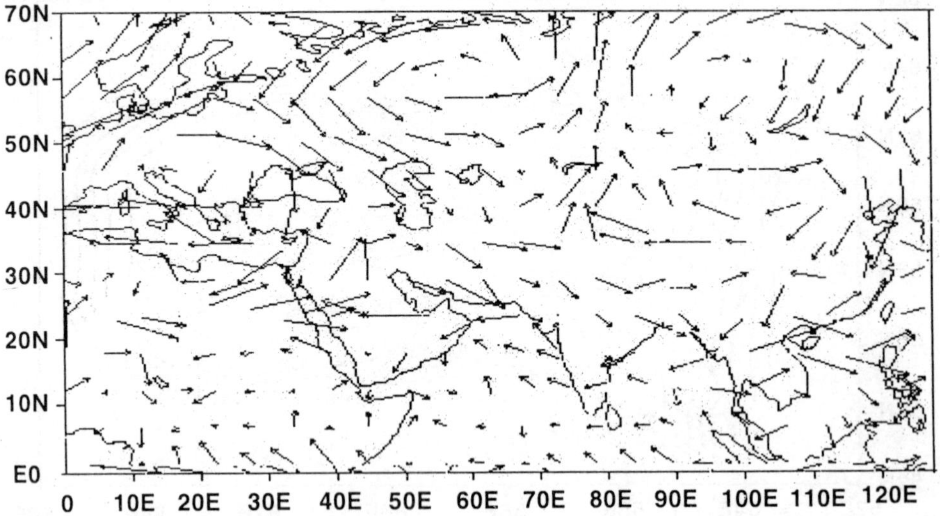

Figure 2: Difference (Exp1–Exp2) in the Seasonal (JJAS) Mean Wind (m/s) at 850 hPa Simulated by the Model in Response to Snow Depth Anomaly Given in Figure 1

in response to high Eurasian snow depth than in exp2 where there is low snow depth.

Figure 3 shows the difference (exp1-exp2) in upper level monsoon mean wind fields simulated by the model. An anomalous cyclonic circulation is simulated by the model over central Eurasia and another anomalous weak anticyclonic circulation is simulated over Bay of Bengal and South East Asia. The NCEP/NCAR reanalysis also reveals anomalous cyclonic circulation over central Eurasia, but it is spread over larger area compared to the model simulated circulation. The anomalous westerlies over Arabian Sea are similar in both NCEP/NCAR reanalyses and model simulations. Both from model results and analysed fields it seems that such anomalous features suppress the development of upper tropospheric anticyclones and hence the monsoon circulations over India. These results indicate that Asian summer monsoon easterlies are weaker in exp1 in response to high snow depth than in exp2 where the snow depths are less.

Figure 4 shows the difference (exp2-exp1) in Asian summer monsoon rainfall simulated by the model in response to snow depth anomaly as indicated in Fig.1. The model simulated difference of rainfall shows positive anomaly meaning there by increase in rainfall in response to less snow depth. The anomalies in the Indian summer monsoon circulation may be responsible for the variation in associated monsoon rainfall. It appears that the anomalous circulation patterns over central and west Asia in response to snow anomaly over Eurasia might have caused the weakening of monsoon flows over India. The accurate magnitude of the rainfall difference and its spatial distribution are beyond the scope of the present paper.

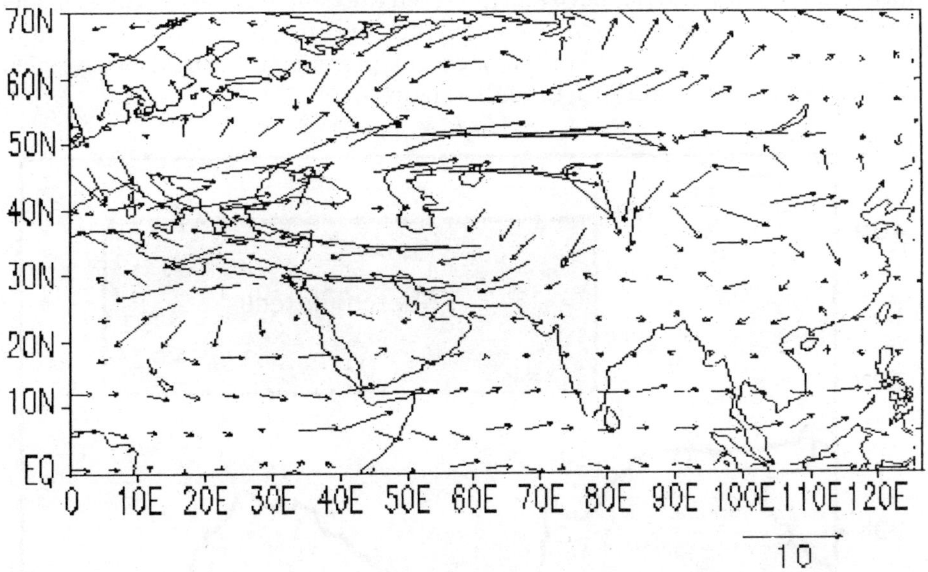

Figure 3: Same as in Figure 2 Except for Wind (m/s) at 200 hPa

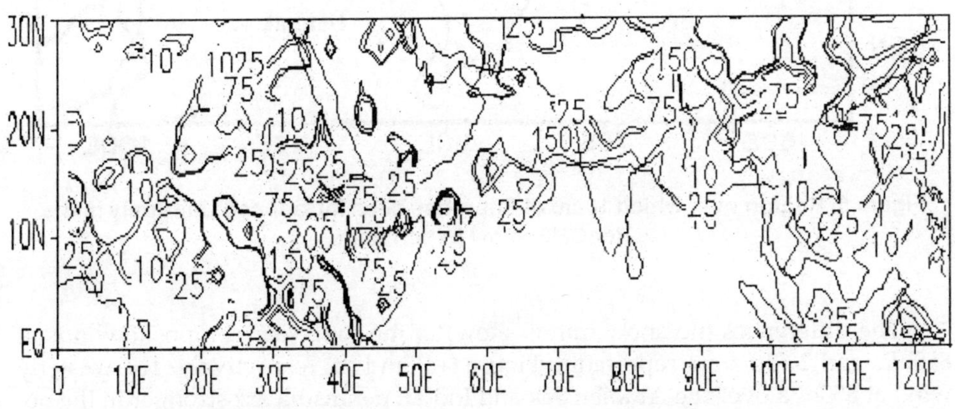

Figure 4: Differences (Exp2–Exp1) in the Seasonal (JJAS) Mean Rainfall (cm) as Simulated by the Model in Response to Snow Depth Anomaly Given in Figure 1

RegCM3 Results

Results of Dash *et al.* (2006b) indicate that RegCM3 successfully simulates some of the important characteristics of Indian summer monsoon circulation such as 850hPa westerly and 200hPa easterly flow when Grell convection scheme is used with Arakawa-Schubert as the closure assumption compared to the Kuo scheme. Also, the seasonal mean summer monsoon rainfall simulated by RegCM3 is close to the corresponding GPCC values when the Grell convection scheme is used. Thus, the Grell scheme, which shows a generally good performance in reproducing the basic monsoon circulation and rainfall features, is used to examine the sensitivity of model simulated Indian summer monsoon circulation and precipitation to changes in Tibetan snow depth. An initial April snow cover is prescribed over the Tibetan region covering 28° N to 40° N and 70° E to 100° E (Figure 5).

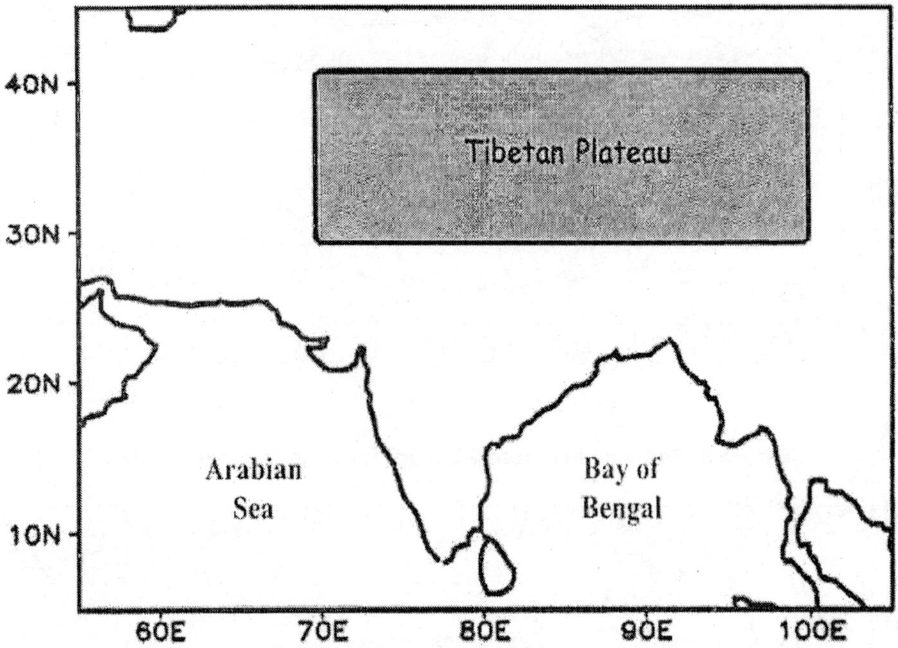

Figure 5: Region over which 10cm of Snow has been Introduced Uniformly in the RegCM3 Snow Experiment

The differences (no-snow minus snow) in the four-year composite winds at 850hPa and 200hPa are reported in Figure 6(a) and (b) respectively. The westerly wind at 850hPa over the Arabian Sea and Indian peninsula are stronger in the no-snow experiment than in the snow experiment (Figure 6a) by 0.6m/s. Similarly, differences of wind at 200hPa (Figure 6b) show stronger easterlies over the Arabian Sea, Indian Peninsula and the northern part of the country in the no-snow experiment. Therefore we find that Tibetan snow during spring induces relatively weak lower level monsoon westerlies and higher level monsoon easterlies. Figure 6(c) depicts the differences of the four year composites of JJAS mean rainfall simulated by the model over India. Greater rainfall amounts are mostly simulated in the no-snow experiment than in the snow experiment. More specifically, in the no-snow experiment more rainfall is found over the Western Ghats, the foothills of the Himalayas, North West India, Central Northeast India and North East India. Conversely increased precipitation is found in the snow experiment over the Arabian Sea and the Bay of Bengal.

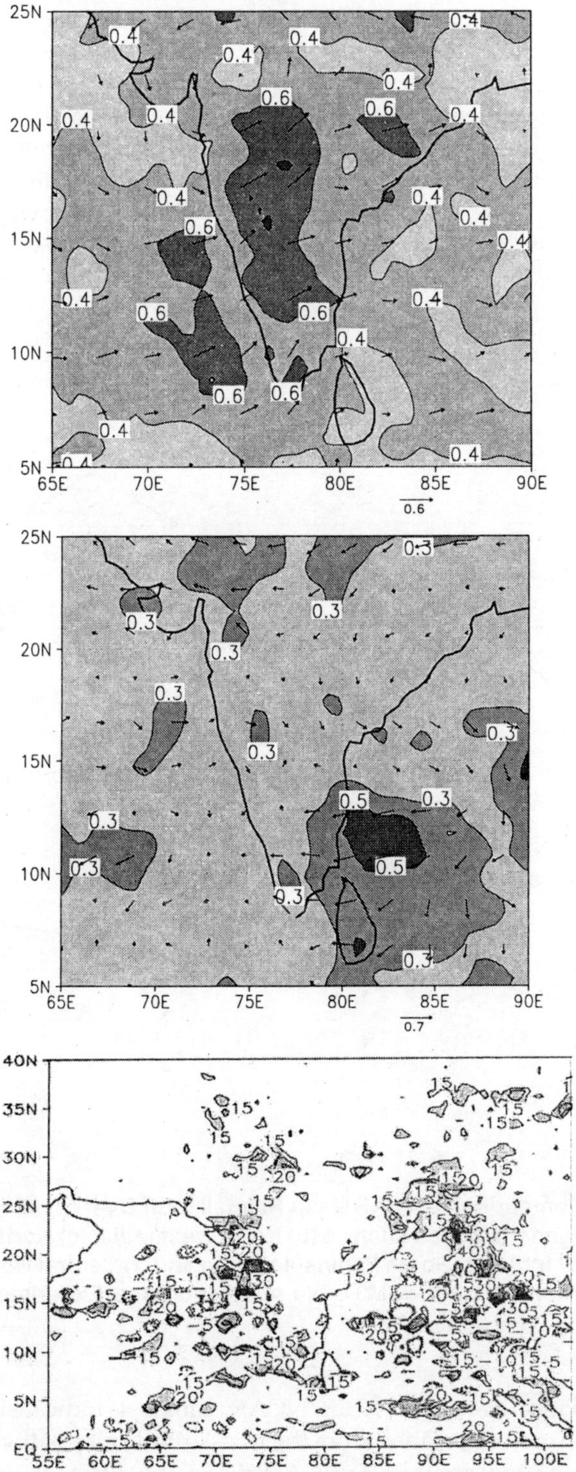

(a)

(b)

(c)

Figure 6: JJAS Difference (No-snow Minus Snow) of Wind (m/s) at (a) 850hPa, (b) 200hPa and (c) Rainfall (cm) Simulated by RegCM3

Monsoon rain over all India as well as five homogeneous zones of India in no-snow and snow experiments for each of the years 1993, 1994, 1995 and 1996 and the composite of the above four years are shown in Figure 7. Quantitatively, it is found that, in the snow experiment, Indian summer monsoon rainfall decreases by about 37%, 38%, 20% and 25% for 1993, 1994, 1995 and 1996, respectively (Figure 7a). On an average, ISMR indicates a decrease by 30% for the whole of India, 23% for NWI, 20% for WCI, 25% for CNI, 30% for NEI and 15% for SPI. In general, RegCM3 simulates weaker monsoon winds and lower associated rainfall in response to the prescribed spring snow depth over the Tibetan area.

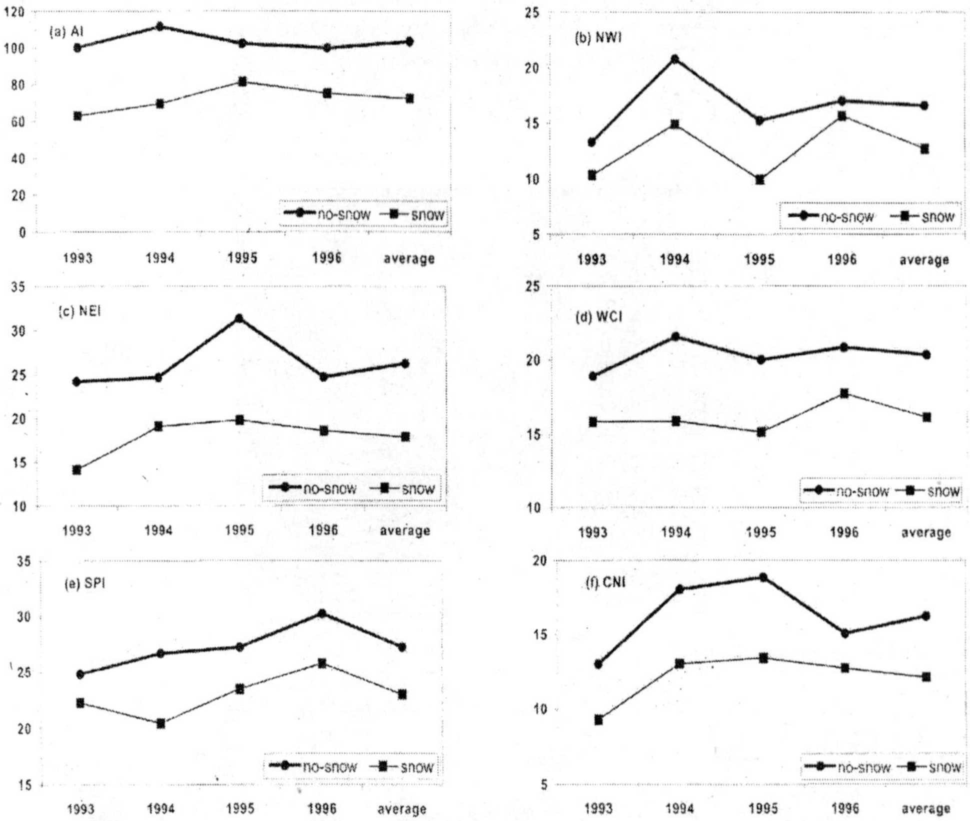

Figure 7: Comparison of JJAS Mean Rainfall (cm) Over (a) All India and its Five Homogenous Zones such as (b) North West India, (c) North East India, (d) West Central India, (e) South Peninsular India and (f) Central Northeast India as Simulated by RegCM3 in No-snow and Snow Experiments

Conclusions

Model simulation as well as NCEP/NCAR reanalysis indicate the evolution of weak/strong monsoon circulation from the mid-latitude circulation in response to high/low Eurasian snow depth in April. At 850hPa, the difference in wind fields in high and low snow depth years shows an anomalous anticyclonic circulation to the north of Arabian Sea and western sector of India which is responsible for weak easterlies over Indian subcontinent. The difference of wind fields at 200hPa shows anomalous cyclonic circulation over south of the Caspian Sea, which might have contributed to the anomalous easterlies over the Arabian Sea and Indian subcontinent. Results show that excess of summer monsoon rainfall over the Indian region corresponds to low April snow depth over Eurasia region. The reverse happens in case of high Eurasian snow depth.

In the sensitivity (snow) experiment using RegCM3, the prescription of 10 cm initial April snow depth over Tibet leads to a reduction of All India monsoon rainfall of about 30% in the subsequent monsoon season. Simulations also show that lower level westerlies and upper level easterlies are weakened in the snow experiment than in the no-snow experiment.

Acknowledgements

The results reported in this paper are the outcome of a project sponsored by the Department of Science and Technology, Government of India to Prof. S. K. Dash as Principal Investigator. The snow depth data are obtained from HSDSD CD of National Snow and Ice Data Centre (NSIDC) and the observed rainfall data are obtained from the India Meteorological Department.

The RegCM3 installed at IIT Delhi belongs to the Abdus Salam ICTP, Trieste, Italy. The Tibetan snow depths used in RegCM3 are based on NIMBUS-7 SMMR data obtained from Dr. R. H. Kripalani, IITM, Pune.

References

1. Bamzai and Shukla, 1999: "Relation between Eurasian snow cover, SD and the Indian summer monsoon: An observational study", J. Climate, 12, 3117-3132.
2. Barnett, T. P., Dumenil, L., Schlese, U., Roeckner, E. and Latif, M., 1989: "The effect of Eurasian snow over on regional and global climate variations", J. Atmos. Sci., 46, 661-685.
3. Dash, S. K., 1995: "Impact of orographic representation on Indian summer monsoon simulation". Proc. Fifth WMO/IMD Regional workshop on Asian/ African monsoon, IMD, New Delhi, 30 Jan-3 Feb 1995. Published in TMRP Report No. 52, WMO/TD-No., 698, 165-174.
4. Dash, S. K., 1999: "Realistic representation of the Himalayas in numerical models", Proc. DST sponsored brain storming seminar on Himalayan experiment, IIT Delhi, Dec. 1995. Published in the book "The Himalayan Environment", Eds. S. K. Dash & J. Bahadur, New Age International, 79-91.
5. Dash, S. K. and B. Chakrapani, 1989: "Simulation of a winter circulation over India using a global spectral model", Proc. Indian Acad Sci. (Earth Planet Sci.), 98, 189-205.
6. Dash, S. K., Parth Sarthi, P. & Panda,S. K., 2006a: "A Study on the Effect of Eurasian Snow on the Summer Monsoon Circulation and Rainfall using a Spectral GCM", Int. J. Climatol, 26, 1017-1025.

7. Dash, S., K., M. S. Shekhar and G. P. Singh, 2006b: "Simulation of Indian summer monsoon circulation and rainfall using RegCM3", Theor. Appl. Climatol, 86,1-4,161-172

8. Giorgi, F., 1990: Simulation of regional climate using a limited area model nested in a general circulation model. J. Climate, 3: 941-963.

9. Giorgi, F., M. R. Marinucci and G. T. Bates, 1993a: "Development of a second generation regional climate model (RegCM2). Part I: boundary-layer and radiative transfer processes", *Mon. Wea. Rev.*, 121, 2794-2813.

10. Giorgi, F., M. R. Marinucci, G. T. Bates and G. De Canio, 1993b: "Development of a second-generation regional climate model (RegCM2). Part II: convective processes and assimilation of lateral boundary conditions", *Mon. Wea. Rev.*, 121, 2814-2832.

11. Grell, G., A., J. Dudhia and D. Stauffer, 1994: "A description of the fifth-generation Penn-State/NCAR mesoscale model", *NCAR technical report note TN-398*, National Centre for Atmospheric Research, Boulder, Colorado, USA.

12. Hahn, D. J. and Shukla, J., 1976: "An apparent relation between Eurasian snow cover and Indian monsoon rainfall", J. Atmos. Sci., 33, 2461-2462.

13. Kripalani, R. H. and Kulkarni, A., 1999: "Climatology and variability of historical Soviet snow depth data: some new perspectives in snow – Indian monsoon tele-connection" Climate Dynamics, 15, 475-489.

14. Ose, T., 1996: The comparison of the simulated response to the regional snow mass anomalies over Tibet, Eastern Europe and Siberia. J. Meteor. Soc. Japan, 74: 845-866.

15. Navarra, N, Stern, W.F. and Miyakoda, K, 1994: "Reduction of Gibbs Oscillation in Spectral Model Simulations", Journal of Climate, 7, 1169-1183.

16. Vernekar, A. D., Zhou, J. and Shukla, J., 1995: "The effect of Eurasian snow cover on the Indian monsoon", J. Clim., 8, 248-266.

17. Zwiers, F. W, 1993: Simulation of the Asian summer monsoon with CCC GCM-I. J. Clim., 6, 470-486.

12

Influence of Enso on the Southwest Monsoon Rainfall Over Pakistan: A Review

Tariq Masood Ali Khan*, Arif Mahmood, M.M. Rabbani*, S. Moazzam Ali* and Nadeem Faisal****

**National Institute of Oceanography, Pakistan*
Phone: 92-21-9251172-78; Fax: 92-21-9251179
E-mail: tariqmak@yahoo.com
***Pakistan Meteorological Department, Pakistan*

ABSTRACT

The climatic changes and ENSO events affect weather, climate, marine and terrestrial ecosystems and economies worldwide. Recent studies have brought the relationships between ENSO and rainfall in different areas of the world, which vary from season to season. The response of the Indian Ocean to ENSO also varies with the variations in the walker circulation in the Pacific.

The impact of ENSO on the monsoon rainfall of Pakistan, which is prone to the impulse of summer monsoon, is discussed in this review paper. The correlation between monthly rainfall of summer monsoon season and bi-Monthly Multivariate ENSO Index (MEI) has been calculated to investigate the influence of El Nino on the summer monsoon rainfall. MEI is bimonthly ENSO Index pertaining to the period from first week of previous month to first week of the month under consideration. The MEI is more appropriate than other indices like Southern Oscillation Index (SOI) to study the correlation's with the ENSO events out side the Pacific Ocean.

There is a tendency of reduction in summer monsoon rainfall over Pakistan during El Nino years. The deficiency in % rainfall is statistically significant up to 90 % level during July and September months. It is interesting to note that Pakistan receives more than normal rainfall during summer monsoon season in the immediately following year after the El Nino event. Since topography plays an important role in the frequency, intensity and distribution of rainfall, correlation analysis is also performed for northern and southern Pakistan region.

Introduction

The response of the Indian Ocean to ENSO varies from season to season (Singh and Rout, 1999, Kumar *et al.*, 1999). According to Singh *et al.* (2002), the frequency of monsoon depressions over the Bay of Bengal in July and August is higher during El Nino Years. This gives some indication of the type of relation between ENSO and monsoon depressions. It is well known that Indian summer monsoon is adversely affected by ENSO and Indian subcontinent receive less than normal rainfall during ENSO monsoon years (Shukla and Paolino, 1983). However, when we consider the rainfall on sub-seasonal and smaller spatial scales different relationships emerge. For instance, ENSO does not seem to have any significant impact on the monsoon rainfall of eastern region of India and Bangladesh (SMRC, 1999). The enhanced frequency of depressions dampens the adverse impact of ENSO on the rainfall of eastern coastal region of India and Bangladesh which falls in the track of monsoon depressions. Therefore, the general impression that the ENSO adversely affects the monsoon rainfall of entire Indian subcontinent is perhaps not correct and the correlation between ENSO and rainfall during different seasons must to be studied on regional basis.

The ENSO system is a semi-periodic oscillator whose major parameters include sea surface temperature, pressure, the surface wind and upper layer thickness over the Pacific. The Southern Oscillation Index (SOI), various sea surface temperatures anomalies and different weather anomalies over the Pacific are generally taken as measure of ENSO while linking different oceanic and meteorological parameters with ENSO. SOI gives a simple measure of the status of the Walker circulation, a major wind pattern of the Asia/Pacific region. The variability in Walker circulation not only affects rain fall in eastern and western pacific but also other parts of the world. However, studies show that the index such as SOI (Tahiti-Darwin pressure) may be more suitable for the study of weather anomalies over the Australia, Indonesia and the areas located in the Pacific Rim region. For other parts of the world, the correlation's with the ENSO events, the Multivariate ENSO Index (MEI), which integrates complete information of six oceanic and meteorological variables over the tropical pacific would be more appropriate. The studies (SMRC, 1999; Singh *et al.*, 2000) showed that the MEI and summer monsoon rainfall for Bangladesh and eastern coastal belt of India are very much correlated and can be used for other parts of the subcontinent as well.

Pakistan is also prone to the impulse of summer monsoon. There have been some qualitative studies on the relationships between the EL Nino years and the rainfall over Pakistan (Mahmood *et al.* 1994; Chaudhary *et al.*, 1998). There have been attempts to find out the impact of warm phase of ENSO on the monsoon rainfall of Pakistan on monthly scale basis (Mahmood *et al.*, 1994, 2004, 2006). In these studies the relationship between MEI and summer monsoon rainfall over Pakistan in the individual monsoon months have been examined. Due to the typical nature of the topography, geographical position, and the meteorological conditions, there is a great variation in the precipitation over Pakistan. The whole area was therefore divided into two regions, called Northern Pakistan and Southern Pakistan. Furthermore, the correlation between MEI and rainfall was also determined separately in these two regions. In this review paper, the relationship between ENSO and summer monsoon rainfall of Pakistan on a monthly scale and quantitative basis have been discussed.

Data and Methodology

Summer monsoon rainfall data was obtained from Pakistan Meteorological Department. Time series' of rainfall at about 56 stations are used in the analysis. Stations are located in both hilly and flat areas of Pakistan. Monthly rainfall departure over Pakistan has been computed for July, August and September for the period of 50 years 1950-2003. It may be noted that since in Pakistan monsoon rain starts from the last week of June or from the 1st week of July, June rainfall data is not used in this study.

The MEI is calculated as the first principal component of six variables over the tropical Pacific namely sea surface temperature, sea level pressure, zonal and meridional components of the surface wind, air temperature and total cloudiness fraction. The MEI values are computed for every month based on the two preceding calendar months. Thus MEI values are bimonthly and correspond to 1st week of pervious month to 1st week of the next month. The computation details of Multivariate ENSO Index may be seen in Wolter and Timlin (1997, 1993, 1998) work. The data pertaining to MEI values and El Nino (warm) and La Nina (cold) episodes for the last 50 years are obtained from NOAA/CIRES Climate Diagnostics Centre, Boulder, USA and Climate Prediction Centre, Washington D. C., USA. The standardized departure of MEI values since 1950 is shown in Figure 1. The MEI and Percent rainfall departure over Pakistan during monsoon months are given in Table 1. Monthly correlations of percentage departure of summer monsoon rainfall with MEI values pertaining to the period from the first week of previous month to the 1st week of the month under consideration have been computed. Regarding the mode of computation of the long-term trends, statistical analysis is performed by using the well known least squares method.

Results and Discussion

The correlation coefficients (CC) between the MEI and % monthly rainfall departure during summer monsoon season over Pakistan are computed here. Due to the typical nature of the topography, geographical position and as well as the climatic nature of Pakistan, the whole area is divided into two regions, called Northern

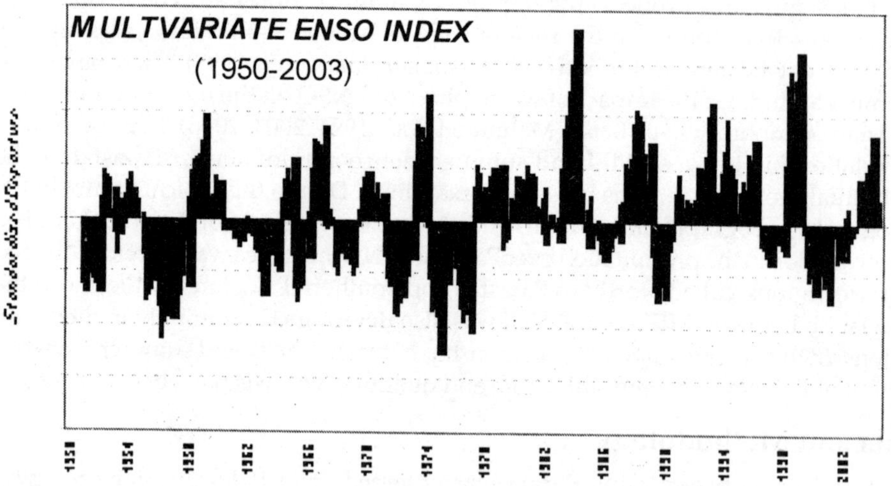

Figure 1: Standardised Departure of MEI Since 1950

Pakistan and Southern Pakistan. Therefore, statistical analysis is also performed for both regions so as to get region- wise analysis. The correlation coefficients between monthly summer rainfall and corresponding MEI values for Northern Pakistan, Southern Pakistan and for all Pakistan are presented in Table 2. It may be noted that due to the nature of MEI values all CCs are lagging from monthly % rainfall. Moreover, while doing the different studies for Indian Ocean region, it is was found that ENSO does have influence on the atmospheric and oceanographic processes in this region with some lag (Singh *et al.*, 2000, Khan *et al.*, 2002, Singh *et al.*, 2002).

Table 1: MEI and Percent Rainfall Departure Pver Pakistan during Monsoon Months

Year	*MEI_{jj} (1st Week of Jun to 1st Week of Jul)*	*July % Rainfall Departure*	*MEI_{ja} (1st Week of Jul to 1st Week of Aug)*	*August % Rainfall Departure*	*MEI_{as} (1st Week of Aug to 1st Week of Sept)*	*September % Rainfall departure*
1950	-1.303	-10.1	-1.057	-13.6	-0.644	-11.9
1951	0.769	-52.5	0.876	-30.3	0.807	-96.7
1952	-0.191	11.9	-0.153	-51.7	0.348	-90.7
1953*	0.433	-24.0	0.251	16.4	0.547	-17.4
1954	-1.406	-48.1	-1.433	-55.1	-1.190	155.2
1955	-1.888	-68.6	-1.986	129.5	-1.788	149.5
1956	-1.182	177.2	-1.118	30.5	-1.345	-38.2
1957*	0.978	-64.7	1.115	-24.0	1.147	-76.5
1958	0.679	23.3	0.382	-56.9	0.077	125.8
1959	-0.209	103.9	0.071	-8.3	-0.015	314.2
1960	-0.311	8.2	-0.246	-38.2	-0.511	-44.9
1961	-0.262	63.4	-0.353	-11.5	-0.351	133.1
1962	-0.801	-15.6	-0.550	-12.1	-0.517	103.7

Contd...

Table 1–Contd...

Year	MEI_{jj} (1st Week of Jun to 1st Week of Jul)	July % Rainfall Departure	MEI_{ja} (1st Week of Jul to 1st Week of Aug)	August % Rainfall Departure	MEI_{as} (1st Week of Aug to 1st Week of Sept)	September % Rainfall departure
1963	0.379	-60.6	0.656	-44.1	0.752	-41.2
1964	-1.368	20.0	-1.539	-3.3	-1.301	-6.7
1965*	1.429	-29.8	1.514	-45.7	1.447	-80.0
1966	-0.118	-34.3	0.157	-53.9	-0.121	-32.6
1967	-0.615	6.6	-0.504	7.9	-0.698	-36.7
1968	-0.495	-55.4	-0.150	-42.8	0.186	-95.1
1969	0.419	-21.2	0.277	-56.7	0.222	-40.1
1970	-1.100	-42.3	-1.005	33.0	-1.237	118.6
1971	-1.232	-28.1	-1.260	-29.2	-1.463	-32.8
1972*	1.814	-46.9	1.764	-39.7	1.582	-33.1
1973	-1.076	56.9	-1.356	88.2	-1.693	-11.0
1974	-0.784	-22.1	-0.703	-55.7	-0.622	-30.1
1975	-1.504	17.7	-1.678	75.7	-1.812	76.4
1976	0.621	28.6	0.724	86.4	1.024	206.4
1977	0.847	33.1	0.698	-21.6	0.776	46.5
1978	-0.365	160.8	-0.217	11.6	-0.351	3.3
1979	0.360	-37.8	0.622	32.7	0.807	0.8
1980	0.786	-6.4	0.369	-44.1	0.265	-3.6
1981	-0.045	72.3	-0.152	2.2	0.127	-61.4
1982*	1.600	-46.1	1.749	21.9	1.794	-80.5
1983	1.788	1.4	1.232	119.5	0.527	102.8
1984	-0.200	-1.6	-0.233	68.7	-0.098	45.8
1985	-0.205	10.0	-0.422	-22.1	-0.542	-65.2
1986	0.384	-29.6	0.709	45.2	1.089	-51.1
1987*	1.824	-53.5	2.018	-43.4	1.905	-76.3
1988	-1.213	79.7	-1.307	23.4	-1.516	-23.6
1989	-0.489	81.3	-0.558	3.2	-0.268	-58.9
1990	0.094	-39.8	0.100	59.0	0.421	76.0
1991*	1.022	-62.9	1.041	-36.9	0.748	50.2
1992	1.020	30.0	0.596	84.1	0.480	159.5
1993	1.117	38.7	1.056	-70.2	1.006	-5.7
1994	0.814	98.4	0.610	79.3	0.658	268.0
1995	0.272	119.8	0.055	-11.9	-0.341	-54.2
1996	-0.175	-44.4	-0.262	8.4	-0.309	-46.1
1997*	2.633	-4.5	2.869	36.6	2.840	-27.8
1998	0.343	-27.2	-0.172	-35.1	-0.551	74.7
1999	-0.532	-30.4	-0.735	-21.9	-0.877	-8.5
2000	-0.226	-11.3	-0.165	-29.4	-0.232	-12.7
2001	0.133	33.9	0.274	-41.2	-0.222	-27.1
2002	0.544	-75.2	0.843	-43.6	0.787	-10.2
2003	0.022	94.9	0.265	18.7	0.455	7.2

* Strongest El Nino years since 1950.

Table 2: Correlation Coefficients Between MEI and % Summer Monsoon Rainfall Departure (Mahmood *et al.*, 2004)

	Correlation Coefficient (CCs)		
	MEI_{jj} - July % Rainfall	MEI_{ja} - August % Rainfall	MEI_{as} - September % Rainfall
Pakistan	-0.183*	-0.157	-0.167*
Northern Pakistan	-0.188*	-0.118	-0.193*
Southern Pakistan	-0.170*	-0.175*	-0.110

* Significant up to 90%level.

The negative CCs indicates less than normal rainfall, where as the positive CCs show the higher than normal rainfall.

During summer monsoon, for all Pakistan basis, the July, August and September % rainfall are deficient having negative correlation -0.183, -0.157 and –0.167 respectively (Table-1). However, deficiency in rainfall during July is significant upto 90% during El Nino Years. In all selected El Nino years Pakistan received deficient rainfall during month of July. The rainfall over Pakistan during July of 1957, 1987 and 1991 were very much deficient *i.e.* –64.7%, -62.9% and -53.5% respectively. July rainfall was also below normal during other El Nino years. Same is true for the months of August and September also. However, relatively week correlation in these months suggest that it is not always true as in case of 1997 El Nino years.

During September of severe El Nino years such as 1957, 1965, 1982 and 1987, Pakistan received much below rainfall than the normal. This type of trend during El Nino Years shows that there is a tendency of reduction in monsoon rainfall during the September of El Nino years. It may be interesting to note that deficient rainfall (-95.1) was also observed during some non-ENSO years such as 1968. However, during statistical analysis it would not be correct to expect always one-to-one relationship between ENSO and rainfall departure.

The correlation between MEI and August % rainfall departure over Pakistan during El Nino years is not significant statistically (-0.157). Thus the Impact of El Nino on August rainfall of El Nino years is not significant. But it is evident from Table-1 that, there is a tendency of subdued rainfall over Pakistan during August of El Nino years. Maximum deficiency of August rainfall *i.e.* –70.2 was observed during the period of long ENSO epochs 1991-1993 in the year 1993. Similarly highest excessive rainfall, which is about +119.5 was also observed during the period of ENSO event 1982-1983 in the year of 1983. This simply shows that ENSO does not have any significant adverse impact on August rainfall over Pakistan.

Careful analysis of rainfall departure over Pakistan and corresponding MEI values indicates that Pakistan receives more than normal rainfall during summer monsoon season in the immediate following year after the El Nino event. During all months of summer monsoon season (July, August and September) of 1983 and 1992, which are the following years of El Nino events 1982 and 1983, Pakistan receives higher than normal rainfall. However, in some cases it is not true for all summer monsoon months, but the over all total summer rainfall is always excessive in the following year just after the El Nino events (year).

The topography of Pakistan is very complex. Northern Pakistan consists of mainly hilly areas and plateau including famous mountain ranges such as Himalayan, Koh Hindukash and Karakrum ranges whereas southern Pakistan is mainly plain land with some hilly areas in the northwestern side. The orographic effect and wind pattern in the mountainous areas play important role in the frequency, intensity and distribution of rainfall in the northern and southern Pakistan. Therefore, to see the correlation pattern between MEI and % summer monsoon rainfall departure area wise, the selected meteorological stations were divided into two parts, northern Pakistan and southern Pakistan.

From the correlation between MEI and % departure of rainfall, it is evident that July rainfall in both regions during El Nino years are less than normal and reduction in rainfall is significant. Statistically, the correlation between MEI and % July rainfall departure for Northern Pakistan and Southern Pakistan are –0.188 and –0.170 respectively. Therefore, it is clear that there is a strong tendency of reduced rainfall during July of El Nino years regardless of the region.

Very interesting results are noted when correlation was made for August and September months for both regions. In northern areas very week negative correlation (-0.118) indicate that the reduction in the August rainfall during monsoon years is not significant. Whereas for southern region it is September, when very weak and not significant correlation exists (-0.11). In other words, over northern areas the reduction in % rainfall departure is significant during July and September during El Nino years, whereas in case of southern Pakistan, July and August rainfall show significant reduction during El Nino years.

Conclusion

In view of the above analysis it is clear that there is an adverse impact of ENSO on the summer monsoon rainfall over Pakistan. Though in this complex system of atmosphere and ocean one to one relationship does not exist always, it is certain that ENSO imply a bad monsoon over Pakistan and receives deficient rainfall during monsoon months. The reason may be the low intensity cyclogenesis over Bay of Bengal and they dissipate without reaching to Northern India or Pakistan.

References

1. Chaudhary, Q. Z., Farooqi, A. B., Rasul, G. (1998). "Tendency of Pakistan's Current Climate and Climate Change Scenarios: Climate Change Impact Assessment and Adaptation Strategies in Pakistan", UNDP.
2. Khan, T. M. A., Amjad, S. Ishaq, S. (2002). "EL Niño Southern Oscillation (ENSO) and its relationship with Fish Catch along the Pakistan Coast, In the proceedings of the International Seminar on "Utilisation of Marine Resources", ISESCO/ NIO, 20-22 December, 2002, Karachi, Pakistan.
3. Kumar, K. K., B. Rajagopalan, Cane, M. A. (1999). "On the weakening relationship between the Indian monsoon and ENSO". Science, 284, 2156-2159.

4. Mahmood, A., Khan, T.M. A., Faisal, N. (2004) "Correlation between Multivariate ENSO Index (MEI) and Pakistan's Summer Rainfall. Pakistan Journal of Meteorology, Vol. 1, 2, 53-64.

5. Mahmood, A., Khan, T.M. A., Faisal, N. (2006). "Relationship between El Nino and Summer Monsoon Rainfall over Pakistan", Pakistan Journal of Marine Sciences, 15, 1, (in press)

6. Mahmood, A., Askari, M., H., Rashid, A. (1994). "Influence of El Nino on Pakistan Rainfall", Pakistan Meteorological Department, Karachi.

7. Shukla, J., Paolino, D. A. (1983). "The southern oscillation and long range forecasting of summer monsoon rainfall over India", Mon.Wea.Rev.111, 1830-837.

8. Singh, O. P., Khan, T.A.M., Rahman, M. S., Uddin, S. (2002). "Impact of southern oscillation on the frequency of monsoon depressions in the Bay of Bengal", Natural Hazards, 25,101-115.

9. Singh, O. P., Rout, R. K. (1999). "Frequency of cyclonic disturbances over the North Indian Ocean during ENSO years", In the Proceedings of TROPMET-99, Chennai, India.

10. Singh, O. P., Khan, T. A. M., Rahman, M. S., Uddin, S. (2000). "Summer Monsoon Rainfall over Bangladesh in relation to Multivariate ENSO Index", Mausam, 51, 3, 255-260.

11. SMRC, (1999). Changes in the frequencies of cyclonic storms and depressions over the Bay of Bengal and the Arabian Sea. SMRC Report No. 2, SAARC Meteorological Research Centre (SMRC), Dhaka, Bangladesh.

12. Wolter, K. (1987), "The Southern Oscillation in surface circulation and climate over the tropical Atlantic, Eastern Pacific, and Indian Oceans as Captured by cluster analysis",J. *Climate. Appl. Meteor.*, 26, 540-558.

13. Wolter, K., and M. S. Timlin, (1998), "Measuring the strength of ENSO - how does 1997/98 rank?" *Weather*, 53, 315-324.

14. Wolter, K., Timlin, S. (1993), "Monitoring ENSO in COADS with a seasonally adjusted principal component index", *Proc. of the 17th Climate Diagnostics Workshop*, Norman OK, NOAA/NMG/CAC, NSSL, Oklahomes Clim. Survey, CIMMS and the School of Meteor., University of Oklahoma, 52-57.

13

The Monsoonal Climatic Profile of Sri Lanka

Chandima Gomes
Department of Physics, University of Colombo,
Colombo – 03, Sri Lanka
Phone: +94-0-777396438; Fax: +94-11-2683755
E-mail: gomes@phys.cmb.ac.lk

ABSTRACT

In this paper we review the information on the general climatic profile of Sri Lanka giving emphasis on the monsoon pattern. The two monsoonal and two inter-monsoonal periods in the country are more dominant than the well defined 4-seasons in temperate regions. The topography of the country plays a vital role in the rainfall characteristics in different regions. The onset of the southwest monsoon is 26th of May with a standard deviation of 6 days. The date of onset of the north-east monsoon is not determined. However, the first week of December is treated as the period of onset of the north-east monsoon. The strength and onset characteristics of the monsoon periods may be altered by the global effects such as El Niño and La Nina. The variations of onset, period of activation and intensity of monsoons have direct impact on the agriculture in Sri Lanka. The surface wind patterns of the country are also governed by the monsoon regimes. Finally, we discuss the occurrence of severe weather conditions such as cyclones and the relation of their occurrence pattern to the monsoon periods. The cyclonic and severe cyclonic conditions are closely related to the onset of the northeast monsoon.

***Keywords**: Lanka, Monsoon, Tropic, Oceanic, Colombo, Indian, Ocean, SST.*

Introduction

Sri Lanka is a tropical oceanic country with latitude between 5° 55 ′ & 9° 51′ N and longitude between 79° 42' & 83° 53° E Meteorologically, Sri Lanka is regarded as a part of the Indian sub-continent, thus many climatic variations experienced by the southern parts of India is felt by Sri Lanka as well. The country is having a basic climatic pattern of two monsoonal and two tropical convective periods. The west of the country faces the Arabian Sea while the eastern part is exposed to the Bay of Bengal which breeds frequent atmospheric disturbances. The topography of the country plays an important role in climatic variations, especially in the rainfall characteristics. Except for few locations, the coastal belt is lowland with 103 river basins. The topography of the North central parts and central highlands is highly complex, characterised by sharp and blunt peaks, valleys, plateaus, escarpments, ridges and isolated rocks etc. The spatial distribution of wind, rainfall, temperature, humidity and other climatic phenomena are strongly influenced by these complex topographical variations (Gregory,1965; Ayoade, 1972; Puvaneswaran and Smithson, 1991). The effects of the topography on climate are observed both during the monsoon and inter-monsoon periods.

In the low country (up to 600 m above msl), the annual average minimum and maximum temperatures are 20°C and 31°C respectively while in upcountry (beyond 600 m above msl) the two values are 11°C and 25°C respectively. The average mean temperatures are 27°C in the lowlands and 20°C in the highlands. The above data is obtained from the Meteorological Department of Sri Lanka.

The rainfall variation of the country is basically due to the movement of Inter Tropical Convergence Zone (ITCZ), tropical cyclones over Indian Ocean, orographic ascend and thermodynamic instability over the neighbouring land and water masses. In addition, the global effects, such as El Nino, La Niña etc. also have significant effects on the climatic variation of the country. The average annual rainfall of the country varies between 1000 mm and 5700 mm. The island has been divided into 3 areas based on the rainfall data (Cook, 1951; De Silva, 1952), namely the wet zone (above 1900 mm), dry zone (between 1270 mm and 1900 mm), and arid zone (below 1270 mm). Later, another zone known as the intermediate zone has been defined between the dry and arid zones (Study Report, Canada Hunting Soil Survey Company, 1965; Zubair and Somasundera, 2000). Figure 1 depicts the zonal classification of the country.

Basic Climate Pattern in Sri Lanka

The four rainfall seasons in Sri Lanka are:

- North-east Monsoon period (December to February)
- South-west Monsoon period (May to September)
- First inter-monsoon convective period (March to April)
- Second inter-monsoon convective period (October to November)

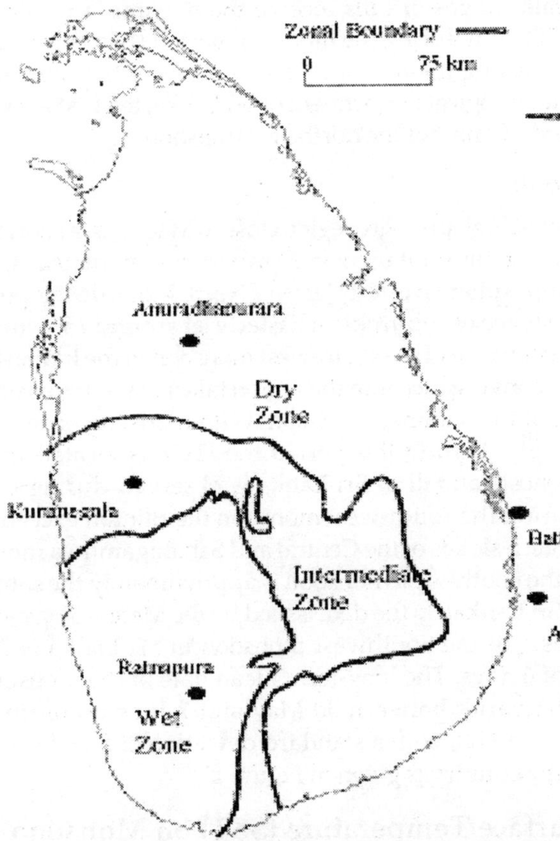

Figure 1: The Climatic Zones of Sri Lanka
[Adopted from Zubair and Somasundara, 2000]

Northeast Monsoon

The basic mechanism that drives monsoonal wind cycles is the cross equatorial pressure gradients resulting from differential level of heating of land and ocean and subsequent modifications caused by the rotation of the earth. In the southern parts of the Indian subcontinent, the north-east monsoon is caused by the occurrence of easterly waves caused by the development of high pressure cells in the region close to the north and north-east parts of India (Alles, 1971; Suppiah and Yoshino, 1984). The ITCZ is located in the Southern hemisphere during this period. The easterlies moving westward across the Tibetan Plateau or Bay of Bengal, brings rain, mostly to the northern and northeastern parts of Sri Lanka. If the high-pressure cells are developed in the Tibetan Plateaus in the mid latitudes, the north-east monsoon brings cold and dry wind masses that deprive Sri Lanka from getting expected rainfall. If the wind streams pass over Pacific and the Bay of Bengal, the monsoon will be moist and cause heavy rainfall to east and northeast of the country. In such cases, the eastern slopes of

Rakwana and Rangala ranges of hills receive the maximum rainfall that will be around 500 mm to 2500 mm during the monsoon period (Nishanthi, 2004). There is no data available regarding the average date of onset of the northeast monsoon. According to the Meteorological Department of Sri Lanka, the first week of December is treated as the period of onset of the northeast monsoon.

Southwest Monsoon

The development of high pressure region close to Madagascar and in the Arabian sea, the low pressure regions built up over Northern Indian plateaus, change of the position of the mid troposphere westerly jet over North India, development of Somali jet (a westerly), persistence of sub-tropical Easterly jet around 15° North etc., causes the generation and sustenance of the south-west monsoon in the Indian Subcontinent. Large-scale moisture convergence into the region takes place at this time, laying the ground for the onset of the summer monsoon. With monsoon onset, the SST in the warm pool falls sharply. During this period the ITCZ is located in the northern hemisphere. The highest rainfall in Sri Lanka is observed during the south-west monsoon period. During the south-west monsoon the rainfall exceeds 3000 mm in the southern and western slopes of the Central and Sabaragamuwa mountain ranges. The time of onset of the south-west monsoon is approximately the same in southern parts of India and in Sri Lanka. By the data issued by the Meteorological Department, the mean date of onset of the Southwest monsoon in Sri Lanka is 26th May with standard deviation of 6 days. The long-term mean date of the monsoon onset over Kerala in South India varies between 30 May and 2 June according to different estimates (Joseph *et al.*, 1992), with a standard deviation of 8–9 days. The monthly rainfall variation in the country is given in Figure 2.

Impact of Sea Surface Temperature (SST) on Monsoon

Sri Lanka is surrounded by the Indian ocean, and convection over this ocean plays a major role in the monsoon rainfall over Sri Lanka. Oceanic convection depends on the SST and global effects, such as El Niño and La Niña of various strengths, and local and regional effects, change the SST of the Indian Ocean. The change of SST significantly affects the climatic pattern in the sub-continent and in turn the agriculture-based Sri Lankan economy, as observed during the last half a century. The relationship between El Niño and La Niña events and the variability of rainfall in Sri Lanka and in the other parts of sub-continent have been investigated in several studies (Shukla 1975; Shukla and Misra, 1977; Rasmussen and Carpenter, 1983; Ropelewski and Halpert, 1989; Rowell, 1991; Suppiah, 1997; Kane, 1998 and Zubair and Somasundera, 2000; Zubair, 2002b). The analysis of rainfall data of a large number of collecting stations in the country reveals that a significantly greater amount of Second Inter-monsoon precipitation (on average, 70 mm/month greater than that for other years) has been resulted during El Niño years. A few stations, in the eastern and northern coastal area, receive increased South-west Monsoon precipitation during La Nina years compared to that during El Niño years (14 to 20 mm/month greater) (Malmgren *et al.*, 2003).

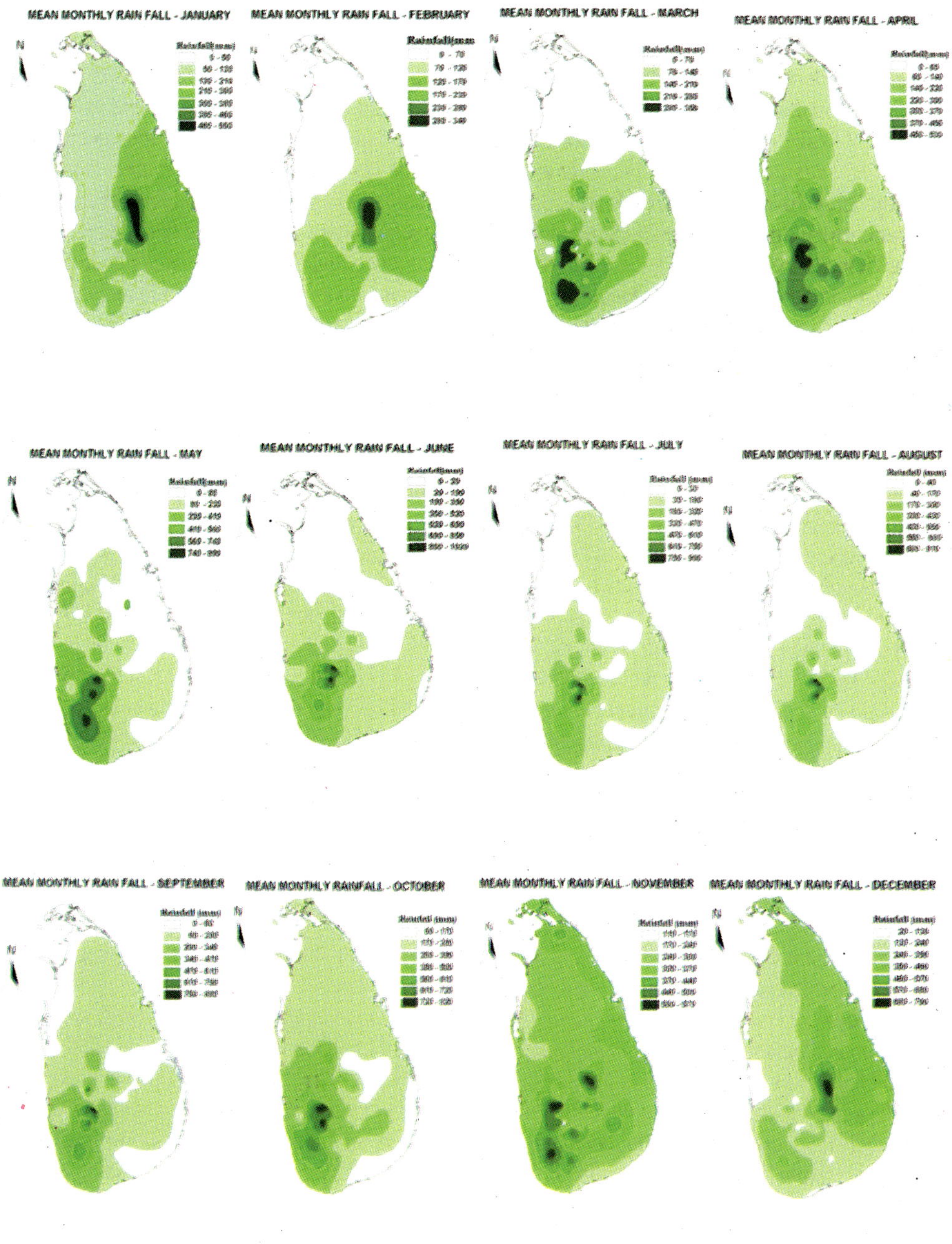

Figure 2: Monthly Variation of Rainfall in Sri Lanka (Information published by The International Research Institute for Climate and Society)

Analysis of the SST field by Joseph *et al.* (1992) have shown that delayed southwest monsoon in Kerala, South India is associated with warm SST anomalies south of the equator in the Indian and Pacific oceans and cold SST anomalies in the tropical and subtropical oceans to the north during the season prior to the monsoon onset (*i.e.,* March to May). Shukla and Misra, 1977 have analysed sixty years (1901–60) of mean monthly sea surface temperature and surface wind speed observed over the central Arabian Sea. The two variables have been correlated with the observed mean monthly rainfall over India during the peak monsoon months of July and August. They have found that correlation coefficients between SST during July and rainfall over central and western India during August are positive and significant. Correlation coefficients between surface wind speed during July and rainfall during July are also found to be positive, but correlation coefficients between surface wind speed during July and rainfall during August are either negative or insignificant. Spatial homogeneity and statistical significance of correlation coefficients lends support to the hypothesis of a possible relationship between SST over central Arabian Sea and rainfall over central and western India. According to their observations the SST during July may be a useful parameter to estimate monsoon rainfall during August.

The impact of the El Nino and La Nina on the agricultural sector in Sri Lanka is clearly outlined by Zubair and Somasundera, 2000; and Zubair, 2002a. The principal cultivation season in Sri Lanka, known as "Maha", is from October to March. During this season, there is usually enough water to sustain the cultivation of all rice fields. The subsidiary cultivation season, known as "Yala", is from April to September. Usually, there is only enough water for cultivation of half of the land extent during Yala. In El Niño years, the Maha rainfall in Sri Lanka is increased and Yala rainfall declines. In La Niña years, there is a rise in Maha rainfall and a decline in Yala rainfall. Therefore the overall impact of an El Niño event is to increase the Maha production and to decrease that of Yala. Similarly, the impact of a La Niña is to increase the Maha production and decrease that of Yala.

Impact of Low Level Jet Stream on Monsoon

The strong cross-equatorial low level jet stream (LLJ) of the Asian summer monsoon (June–September), with its core around 850 hPa, is found to have large intra-seasonal variability. During the monsoon onset over Kerala, and during break monsoon periods, when the convective heating of the atmosphere is over the low latitudes of the Indian Ocean, the axis of the LLJ is oriented southeastward over the eastern Arabian Sea and it flows east between Sri Lanka and the equator and there is no LLJ through peninsular India Joseph and Sijikumar, 2003). In contrast, during active monsoon periods when there is an east–west band of strong convective heating in the latitudes 10°–20°N from about longitude 70° to about 120°E, the LLJ axis passes from the central Arabian Sea eastward through peninsular India. These variations of the LLJ affect the transport of moisture produced over the Indian Ocean to peninsular India and the Bay of Bengal.

Strengths of the convective heat source (OLR) over the Bay of Bengal and the strength of the LLJ (zonal component of wind) at 850 hPa over peninsular India and also the Bay of Bengal between latitudes 10° and 20°N have the highest linear correlation coefficient at a lag of 2–3 days, with OLR leading (Joseph and Sijikumar, 2003). The LLJ crossing the equator close to the coast of East Africa will pass through India only if there is active monsoon convection in the latitude belt 10°–20°N over south Asia. The position in latitude of the LLJ axis between longitudes 70° and 100°E is decided by the south–north movement of the east–west convective cloud band of the monsoon in its 30–50-day oscillation. When there is little convection over south Asia in the latitude belt 10°–20°N, the LLJ crossing the equator curves clockwise over the Arabian Sea under conservation of potential vorticity and bypassing India passes east close to the equator. It is speculated that the cyclonic vorticity associated with this low-latitude LLJ causes convergence in the boundary layer and consequent upward motion in the atmosphere resulting in the formation of a convective cloud band there that later moves into the Bay of Bengal as part of the monsoon's 30–50-day oscillation. Since LLJ is very important in monsoon dynamics, monsoon modelers should take adequate care to see that LLJ and the associated deep convection and their intraseasonal variability are properly simulated in their models (Joseph and Sijikumar, 2003).

Surface Wind

In Sri Lanka, the surface winds are dominated by the monsoon regimes, with North-easterlies from November to January, South-westerlies from February to May and Westerlies and North-westerlies from June to October. Except from June to August, during the whole year, the average wind speed is around 6-8 m/s. From June to August, it is around 10-14 m/s. Wind in June is gusty due the location of the low-level Easterly jet over Sri Lanka. The wind undergoes a reversal in both zonal and meridional directions in March and November coincident with the migration of the Inter-Tropical Convergence Zone. Notwithstanding the period from May to September being designated as the Southwest monsoon, the wind is from West, South-West-West and North-North-West. During the South-west monsoon, wind speed during the night is nearly as high as that during the day (Zubair, 2002b). However, the periodic wind pattern anomalies can be resulted by the emergence of El Niño (Luther and Harrison, 1983). However, studies are yet to be done in Sri Lanka to fully understand the effect of El Niño and La Niña on the wind pattern

Severe Weather Conditions

The typical monsoonal pattern of Sri Lanka is abruptly changed by the movement of cyclonic depressions over the country. During the period from year 1901 and 2000, seventeen cyclonic and severe cyclonic storms have crossed the island (data from the Meteorology department, Sri Lanka). Out of that 10 cyclones have occurred during the northeast monsoon period. Eight of those cyclones have entered the country in December coincident with the onset of the north-east monsoon. Five cyclones have occurred in November, immediately preceding the north-east monsoon. In two cases the cyclones have crossed the country in March during the Inter Monsoon Convective period. This long lasting trend was broken in the year 2003, as a severe cyclonic condition developed in May, after the onset of the south-west monsoon. To elaborate the severity of impacts of cyclonic conditions in Sri Lanka, the reports of two recently occurred cyclones are given below:

According to the Preliminary Appeal, no: 36/00 (Sri Lanka: Cyclone) by the International Federation of Red Cross and Red Crescent Societies, 28 December, 2000, The cyclone 04B swept across central Sri Lanka on Tuesday, December 26, 2000 bringing 48 hours of heavy rains and winds gusting up to 120 km per hour. The cyclone hit land on the eastern coast in a 150 km wide band from Tirukkovil to Trincomalee. The cyclone moved north-west leaving Sri Lanka's western coast between Mannar and Puttalam on Wednesday, 27 December. The Sri Lanka Red Cross has received reports from Trincomalee, Batticaloa, Puttalam, Manmar, Polonaruwa and Amparai districts indicating 42,000 families affected, many with their houses destroyed in the cyclone or by floods. Tidal surges swept 100 meters inland on the eastern coast causing severe damage to many villages. The final effect as being reported on the 4th of January 2001, there were 75,000 families left homeless and 8 people were killed (ACT Alert, Sri Lanka-1/01, Powerful Cyclone hits Sri Lanka, Geneva, 4 January, 2001)

During the period May 15-19, 2003, the tropical Cyclone 01B developed in the Indian Ocean and achieved hurricane status. The storm produced heavy rainfall in Sri Lanka, leading to flash flooding and a large loss of life and property. The event was treated as the worst disaster in 50 years in the island up to 2003. Floods and landslides claimed 260 lives. The total rain accumulation exceeded nine inches during this period (NASA Earth Observatory report 2003). The World Meteorological Organisation cited it as evidence for the increase of anomalous climatic extremes in recent years (Zubair, 2004).

Summary

The basic climatic pattern of Sri Lanka is discussed giving special attention to the monsoon periods. The studies on the occurrence characteristics of monsoon periods and the effects of global effects and the sea surface temperature on the strength and outbreak of monsoon have been investigated. The country is having a topographic structure with low-level coastal belt and mid-country mountain ranges. This topography is very significant in the special distribution of the rainfall and other meteorological characteristics in different regions. The strength and onset characteristics of the monsoon periods are also altered by the sea surface temperature changes that are usually caused by global effects such as El Niño and La Niña. The surface wind pattern of the country is determined by the strength and onset of the monsoon regimes as well as the movement of the Inter-Tropical Convergence Zone. The El Niño and La Niña effects may also affect the surface wind profile in the same way that they affect the other meteorological phenomena. The monsoon characteristics may markedly vary from their usual behaviour in the presence of severe weather conditions such as cyclones. It is noted that, the occurrence of cyclonic and severe cyclonic conditions are remarkably coincidental with the early stages or the period just prior to the onset of the north-east monsoon.

Acknowledgements

The author would like to thank the Head, Department of Physics, University of Colombo and the staff of the Meteorological Department, Sri Lanka, for providing required facilities and information to complete this study successfully.

Reference

1. Alles, W.S., 1971: Rainfall data of Ceylon, Tropical Agriculture, 127, pp 11-21
2. Ayoade, J.O., 1971: A Statistical Analysis of rainfall over Nigeria, Journal of Tropical Geography, 39, pp 11-23
3. Bhat, G. S., S. Gadgil, P. V. Hareeshkumar, S. R. Kalsi, P. Madusoodanan, V. S. N. Murty, C. V. K. Prasada Rao, V. Ramesh Babu, L. V. G. Rao, M. Ravichandran, K. G. Reddy, P. Sanjeeva Rao, D. Sengupta, D. R. Sikka, J. Swain, and P. N. Vinayachandran, 2001: BOBMEX - the Bay of Bengal Monsoon Experiment. Bull. American Meteorological Society.
4. Gadgil S., P. V., Joseph and N. V. Joshi, 1984: Ocean-atmosphere coupling over monsoonal regions. Nature, 312, 141-143.
5. Graham, N. E and Barnett, T. P., 1987: Sea surface temperature, surface wind divergence, and convection over tropical oceans. Science, 238, 657-659.
6. Gregory, S., 1965, Rainfall over Sierra Leone, Monograph, No.2, Department of Geography, University of Liverpool, pp 58
7. Joseph, P.V., Eischeid, J.K., and Pyle R. J., 1992: Interannual Variability of the Onset of the Indian Summer Monsoon and its Association with Atmospheric Features, El Niño, and Sea Surface Temperature Anomalies Journal of Climate: Vol. 7, No. 1, pp 81–105.
8. Joseph, P. V. and Sijikumar, S., 2003: Intraseasonal Variability of the Low-Level Jet Stream of the Asian Summer Monsoon, Journal of Climate: Vol. 17, No. 7, pp. 1449–1458.
9. Kane, R. P., 1998: ENSO relationship to the rainfall of Sri Lanka, International Journal of Climatology, 18 (8), pp 859-872.
10. Luther D.S. and Harrison D.E., 1983: Observing Long-Period Fluctuations of Surface Winds in the Tropical Pacific: Initial Results from Island Data, Monthly Weather Review: Vol. 112, No. 2, pp 285–302.
11. Malmgren, B.A., Hulugalla, R., Hayashi, Y., and Mikami, T., 2003: Precipitation trends in Sri Lanka since 1870 and relationships to El Nino-Southern Oscillation, International Journal on Climatology, 23, pp 1235-1252
12. Nishanthi, D. D., 2004, Effect of topography on rainfall during southwest monsoon, MSc Thesis, University of Colombo.
13. Puvaneswaran, K.M., and Smithson, P.A., 1991: Precipitation elevation relationships over Sri Lanka, Theor. Appl. Climatology, 43, pp113-122.
14. Rasmusson, E. M. and Carpenter, T. H., 1983: The relationship between eastern equatorial Pacific sea surface temperature and rainfall over India and Sri Lanka, Monthly Weather Review, 110, pp 354-383.
15. Ropelewski, C. F., and Halpert, M. S., 1989: Precipitation patterns associated with the high index phase of the Southern Oscillation, Journal of Climate, 2, (3), pp 268-284.

16. Rowell, D.P., 1991: The impact of SST forcing on simulation of the Indian and African Monsoons, WMO / WCRP, 68, pp2145-2151.
17. Shukla, J., 1975: Effects of Arabian SST anomaly on Indian Summer Monsoon: A numerical experiment with GFDL model, Journal of Atmospheric Science, 32, pp 503-511.
18. Shukla, J., and Misra, B.M., 1977: Relationships Between Sea Surface Temperature and Wind Speed Over the Central Arabian Sea, and Monsoon Rainfall Over India, Monthly Weather Review: Vol. 105, No. 8, pp 998–1002.
19. Suppiah, R.,1997: Extremes of the southern oscillation and the rainfall of Sri Lanka, International Journal of Climatology, 17 (1): 87-101.
20. Suppiah, R., and Yoshino, M.M., 1984: Rainfall variations of Sri Lanka, Part 1: Spatial and temporal pattern. Arch. Met. Geoph. Bioclim. Ser B, 34, pp329-340
21. P.N. Vinayachandran and T. Yamagata, 1998: Monsoon response of the sea around Sri Lanka: Generation of thermal domes and anticyclonic vortices, J. Phys. Oceanogr., 28, 1946-1960.
22. Waliser, D. A., N. E. Graham and C. Gautier, 1993: Comparison of the highly reflective cloud and outgoing longwave radiation datasets for use in estimating tropical deep convection. J. Climate, 6, 331-353.
23. Zubair, L., 2002a: El-Niño-Southern Oscillation influences on Rice Production in Sri Lanka, International Journal of Climatology. 22(2) pp 249-260.
24. Zubair, L., 2002b: Diurnal and seasonal variation in surface wind at Sita Eliya, Sri Lanka, Theoretical and Applied Climatology, pp 119 – 127, Volume 71, Numbers 1-2.
25. Zubair, L., 2004, May 2003: Disaster in Sri Lanka and Cyclone 01-B in the Bay of Bengal, Natural Hazards, pp 303 – 318, Volume 33, Number 3.
26. Zubair, L and Somasundera, S., 2000: ENSO influences on Rice Production in Sri Lanka, Proceedings of the IRI Forum on Agriculture, Climate Prediction, Agriculture and Development.

14

Impact of Monsoons to Tanzania

E. Matari
Tanzania Meteorological Agency,
Dar es salaam, Tanzania
Email: ematari@meteo.go.tz

ABSTRACT

This paper deals with the impact of monsoons to Tanzania by analysing several factors. Annual rainfall for different stations in Tanzania is standardised and plotted in a linear graph in order to pick extreme rainfall events which are associated with El- Nino or La Nina years. Zoning of the country climatologically has been carried out and seasonal rains which are influenced by monsoons are discussed. Impact of monsoons such as floods, droughts, tropical cyclones, landslides and lightning strikes are discussed. The analysis shows that monsoons play a key role in the livelihood and economy of the people of Tanzania because most of the rains associated with monsoons are used for agriculture which accounts for 50% of the GDP of Tanzania. When monsoons are associated with large scale circulation factors such as ENSO, the rainfall is increased or decreased and thus causing either floods or droughts.

Introduction

Tanzania is located in east Africa between latitude 1.5ºS to 12ºS and longitude 29º E to 40º E. It is bounded by Indian Ocean to the east, Kenya and Uganda to the north, Rwanda, Burundi, Democratic Republic of Congo (DRC), Zambia and Malawi to the west and Mozambique to the south (Figure 1). The principal physical features include Mt. Kilimanjaro, the highest (5895m) mountain in Africa in the north, Mt.

Meru (4585m), southwestern highlands where there are Poroto Mts. (2961m), Rubeho Mts. (2397m), Olmoti crater (3099m), Loolmalasin Mts. (3648m), Mbizi Mts. (2418m) and the rift valley running from north across the central areas to southern Tanzania.

Tanzania also has several fresh water lakes, namely; Victoria, Tanganyika, Nyasa and Eyasi. Figure 2 below shows the topography of the country.

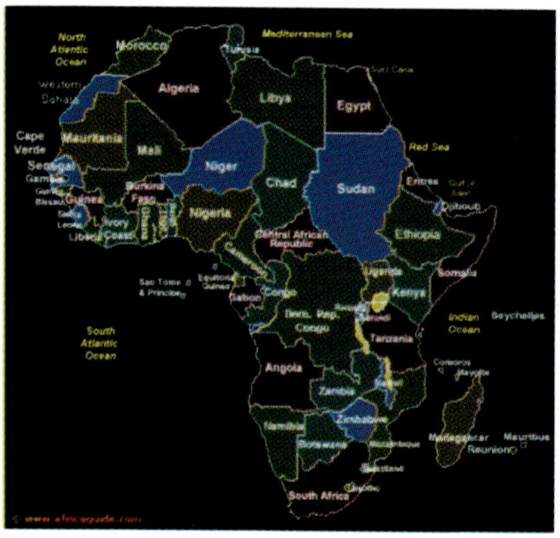

Figure 1: The Position of Tanzania on the Map of Africa

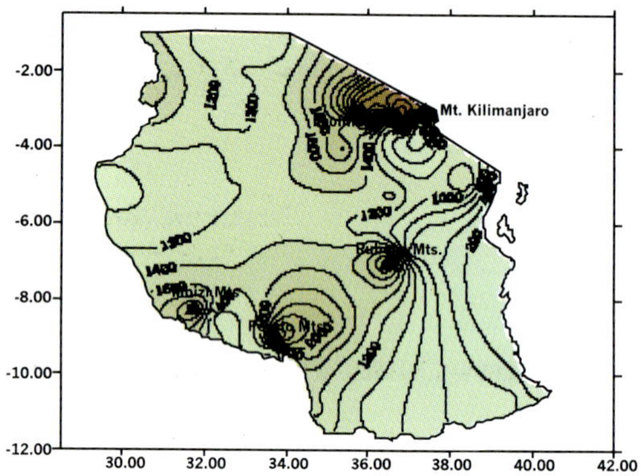

Figure 2: Topography of Tanzania in (m)

Climatology of Rainfall

The country is divided into two areas with different rainfall patterns. The northern part which lies between 0 to 6 $^{\circ}$S of latitude receives bimodal rainfall and between 6° to 11° the area receives unimodal rainfall. The area between the unimodal and bimodal areas is a transition zone where some of the stations alternate from one year to another in terms of their rainfall pattern. The country is divided into six homogeneous regions which are southern coast, northern coast, northeastern highlands, lake zone, western & southwestern area and central & southern areas. The bimodal areas receive their rains in the months of October to December and these rains are called Vuli rains (or short rains). These rains are generally unreliable and erratic. These rains are experienced during the north east monsoon. The Masika rains normally fall in the months of March to May, during the period of south east monsoon. These rains are reliable and most farmers rely on these rains. The main rain generating mechanisms are, the movement of zonal arm of Intertropical Convergence Zone (ITCZ) during the period of southeast and northeast monsoons, the meridional arm of the ITCZ which is aligned in a north to south direction is created by the convergence of the Congo airmass and the monsoon air mass, the strengthening and weakening of both the Arabian and Mascarene high and tropical cyclones in the Indian Ocean.

The areas which are mainly affected by the monsoons are confined over the coastal and north eastern areas which receive 800 to 1000mm of annual rainfall as seen in Figure 3.

The main factors that influence the rainfall in Tanzania are;

- The position and intensity of the Inter-Tropical Convergence Zone (ITCZ) that follows the movement of the sun closely.
- Sub-tropical high pressure systems in the southwest Indian Ocean (Mascarene High), the St Helena High in the southeast Atlantic Ocean, Azores/Sahara High in the North Atlantic Ocean and Arabian High to the northeast, Inter Hemispherical monsoonal wind systems
- Tropical Cyclone activities in Southwest Indian Ocean.
- Easterly and westerly waves
- Teleconnections with El-Nino/Southern Oscillation (ENSO), Intra seasonal (Madden-Julian) waves, Quasi-biennial oscillations (QBO) and hPa 200 winds.

The regional factors, which modify rainfall over parts of Tanzania, include the lakes and the terrain like mountains.

Rainfall Pattern during South East Monsoon

During the period of south east monsoon which commences in March and continues up to July, the region receives its dependable rainfall in the months of March to May (Figure 3). These rains are mainly experienced over bimodal areas which cover the coastal belt, north east highlands and the lake Victoria basin. These rains account for 70% of the annual rainfall in this sector. During northeast monsoon the bimodal area receives rains in the months of September to December and these

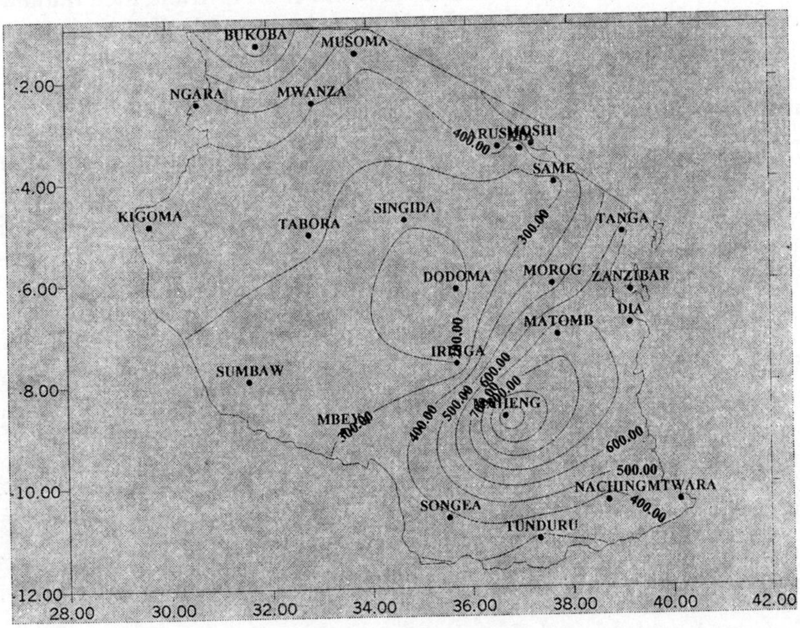

Figure 3: Mean Rainfall (mm) Distribution in Tanzania During MAM

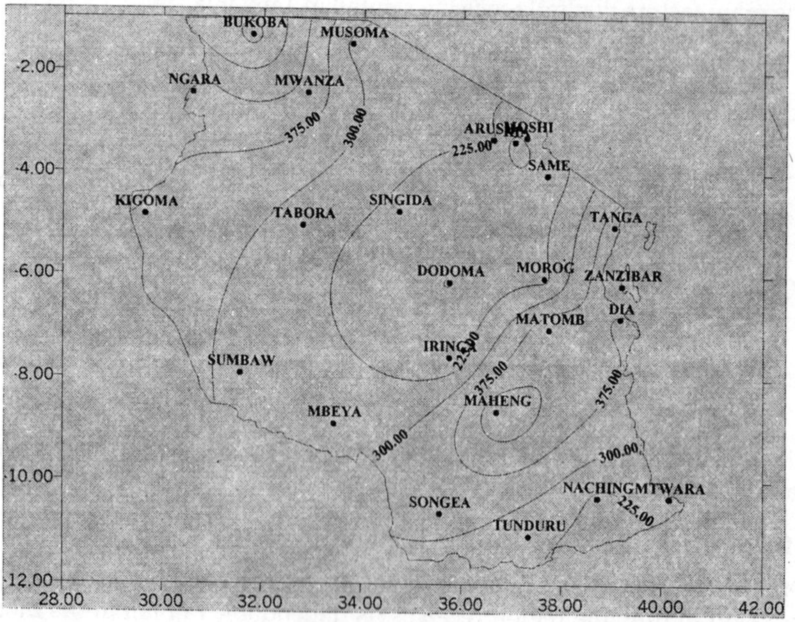

Figure 4: Mean Rainfall (mm) Distribution in Tanzania During SOND

rains are erratic and not quite dependable (Figure 4). Other parts of the country to the south of 6°S receive uimodal rainfall from November to April and their rainfall due to the monsoons in combination with other factors for example the influx of moisture from the Congo forest.

Homogeneous Climatological Zoning of Tanzania

Using PCA analysis Mutoni (2000) divided the country into zones in order to look for the cause of rainfall in each area. Using March to May seasonal rainfall data from 49 stations for the period 1960–1990, Tanzania was demarcated into 10 homogeneous climatological zones as given in Figure 5 below. Similar zones were obtained when the rainfall data for September to December season was used.

The cause for rainfall for each zone is as follows.

Zone I: This is the northern coastal area experiencing two rainy seasons in a year, from March to May and from September to December. Rainfall is generated by ITCZ, sea breeze and easterly waves. Moisture influx is from Indian Ocean.

Zone 2: Rainfall generated by ITCZ and orographic lifting due to the topography of the region.

Zone 3: This is a coastal region with a unimodal rainfall pattern, rainfall is generated by the ITCZ, easterly waves and sea breeze. Moisture influx is from Indian Ocean.

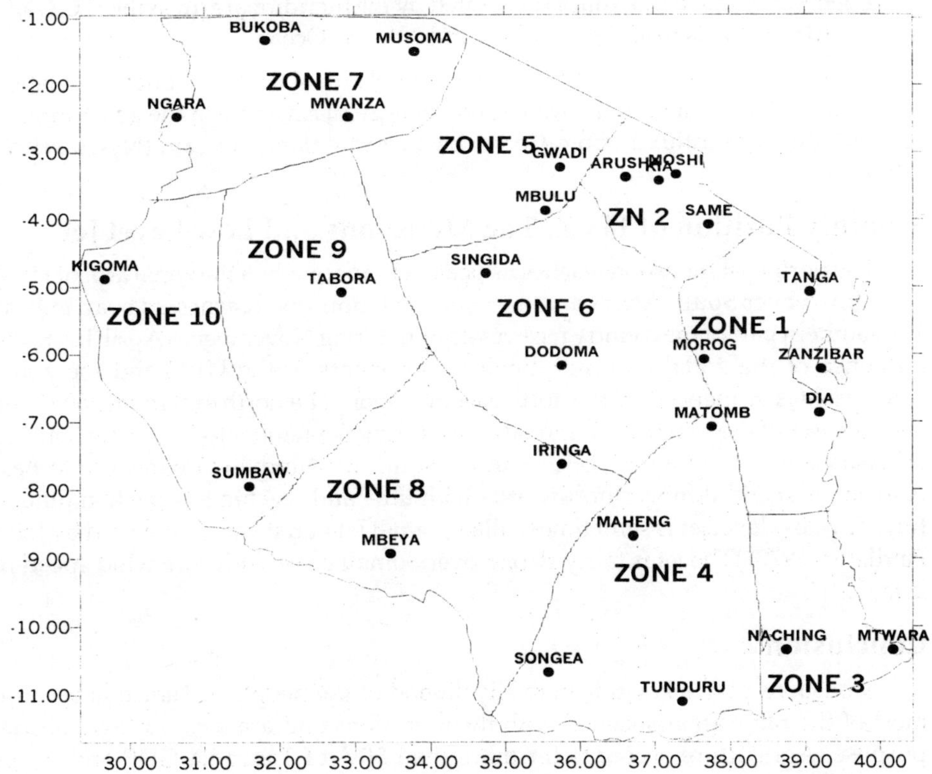

Figure 5: Climatological Homogeneous Zones Over Tanzania

Zone 4: This is the southern region. Moisture influx is from both Congo basin and Indian ocean. Rainfall in generated by ITCZ and westerly waves, modified by the existing highgrounds.

Zone 5: This zone lies within the rift valley and on the windward side of northeastern highlands. These factors play a role on the rainfall generated by the ITCZ.

Zone 6: Central areas are basically lowland and inland areas. They are quite distant from major moisture source bodies like Indian Ocean and Congo basin. Rainfall is generated by meridional arm of the ITCZ and moisture influx is from Congo basin.

Zone 7: This zone is within lake Victoria basin. Rainfall generation mechanism by the ITCZ is modified by local circulation enhanced by the lake. This is an area with the highest frequency of thunderstorms in the country (Chaggar, 1977).

Zone 8: This zone is a highground area. The highgrounds modify the rainfall generated by the meridional arm of the ITCZ and the westerly waves. Moisture influx is from Congo basin and Atlantic Ocean.

Zone 9: Rainfall in this zone is generated by the meridional arm of the ITCZ, and the moisture influx is from Congo basin and Atlantic Ocean.

Zone 10: Rainfall generated by the meridional arm of the ITCZ. Local circulation enhanced by Lake Tanganyika water body energy plays a role in the generation of rainfall. Moisture influx is from Congo basin and Atlantic Ocean. (Nyenzi *et al.*, 1997).

Monthly Position of ITCZ, The Monsoons and Low Level Jet

The northeast monsoon reaches its peak in January when the zonal arm of ITCZ is confined over South Africa and the southeast monsoon reaches its peak in July. The southern part of the country receives its rain during November to April due to the influence of the zonal and meridional components of the ITCZ and the zonal component is influenced by the north east monsoon. The north east monsoon is one of the causes of the rains over bimodal areas during September to December. During February a low level Jet establishes in the south west Indian Ocean close to East African coast and it moves northwards with time and reaching its peak in June to July. This low level jet is sometimes called Somali Jet and it was discovered by John Findlater (1977). The jet is fairly strong over Somali coast with core wind speed of 25m/s.

Conclusion

Monsoons play a key role in the livelihood of the people of Tanzania because most of the rains are associated with the monsoons and are used for agricultural purpose. Agriculture accounts for more than 50% of Tanzania GDP and hence monsoons have a role to play in the process of the country development. On few occasions monsoons have a disadvantage to us when they are associated with large-scale circulation factors such as Nyenzi and Matari (1997) whereby rainfall is increased or decreased and thus causing floods or droughts.

References

1. Chaggar, T.S., 1977: Geographical distribution of monthly and annual mean frequency of thunderstorm days over East Africa, East Africa Tech. Dept. Memo. No.26, East African Community, Nairobi.

2. Findlater, J., 1977: Observational aspects of the low level cross equatorial jet stream over the western Indian Ocean, *Pure. Appl. Geophys.*, 115, 1251-1262.

3. Nyenzi, B.S. and Matari, E., 1997: Indices and Indicators of Climate extremes in Tanzania. Presented at the climate extremes meeting held in North Carolina USA June 1997.

4. Mutoni, E.J., 2000: Climatological Atlas for Tanzania.

5. Nyenzi, B.S., Kavishe, M.M., Tibaijuka, P.F., Kululetera, V., Nassib, I.R., Tillya, F.F., May, 1997: A study on long range weather forecasting in Tanzania.

15

Prediction of Extreme Weather and Climate in the Indonesian Maritime Continent Based on Sunspot Numbers

The Houw Liong* and Plato Martuani Siregar**

**Department of Physics,*

***Department of Geophysics and Meteorology,*

FIKTM-ITB, Bandung, Indonesia

ABSTRACT

From various geographical stations in the Indonesian Archipelago, anomalies of yearly rainfall were collected and plotted against the anomalies of yearly sunspot numbers between 1948 and 2003. It is seen that there is a strong correlation between sunspot numbers and the various geophysical variables, such as the mean temperature of Earth, the cloud cover, the sea surface temperature and the rainfall throughout the regions. The ability of cosmic ray particles to penetrate the earth's atmosphere is limited by the earth's magnetic field. In addition, during sunspot maximum the magnetic field of the solar wind increases and this in turn strongly reduces the flux of cosmic rays that reach the earth.

A correlation exists between cosmic rays, formation of clouds and climate as some researchers suggest. This paper shows that the knowledge of sunspot numbers can be used to predict extreme climate and weather in Indonesia.

Introduction

The relative positions of the sun in the sky during the seasons, as well as the cycles of solar activity influence the weather and climate throughout the Indonesian archipelago. Solar irradiance increases with higher solar activity. This in turn increases the solar wind which consists of charged particles emitted by the sun which could alter the interplanetary magnetic field, and hence the intensity of cosmic rays reaching the earth. The cosmic ray intensity increases with higher solar activity. Thus the solar activity is often considered as the dominant factor that determines the dynamics of climate[1,2]. The dynamics of earth's atmosphere and oceans, evaporation, clouds formation and rainfall, are influenced by the solar energy entering the earth. Several studies indicate that strong correlations exist between the cloud cover and the intensity of cosmic rays.[3]

Both phenomena may affect the climate, for example during 1645–1715 exceptionally low solar activity (also known as the Maunder minimum) led to low temperatures causing what is known as the little ice age.

The present study shows that there is a strong correlation between rainfall in the Archipelago and sunspot numbers.

The Effect of Solar Activity to Weather and Climate

The cosmic rays interact in the upper atmosphere and produce secondary particles. Generally the charged particles so produced can not penetrate to lower layers of the atmosphere, except the neutrons and the muons (below 6 km heights). When the neutrons or the muons interact with the air molecules or water molecules, they become charged and act as condensation nuclei for the formation of clouds. The cosmic ray becomes the source of ions in the air besides radiation coming from earth originated by the radio isotope radon.

During the sunspot minimum, the intensity of the cosmic ray becomes maximum which in turn increase the coverage of clouds. This implies that solar radiation reaching the earth will be minimized. Conversely, during sunspot maximum, the intensity of cosmic ray reaching lower levels of the atmosphere reduces, the cloud cover decreases, furthermore extra energy received from flares during prominent eruptions, maximises the amount of solar energy received on earth.

The global cloud cover produces global warming (the greenhouse effect) which amounts to 13%, but it also causes a cooling effect as much as 20% due to reflections against direct solar radiation[1]. The total energy derived from the sun is thus the solar constant averaging to 6.3×10^{20} joules/hour which is equal to the energy of 40 tropical cyclones or 60 times the energy released by a major earthquake in Indonesia.

From the 21st solar cycle the irradiance received on earth shifted between 1367.0 W/m^2 and 1368.5 W/m^2 - it varies by 0.15 % only[5]. However, the large quantity of energy derived from the sun together with the forcing of atmosphere and oceans and the variation of the irradiance contribute considerably to the weather and climate.

Landscheidt[4] has shown that between years 1950 to 1975 very strong correlations existed between the events of El Nino and sunspot minimum SMin and its harmonics to SMin/2 or sunspot maximum SMax. The occurrences of La Nina correspond to maximum eruption ME and its harmonics ME/2. Then around the year 1975, a phase reversal occurred, and this continued from year 1976 up to the present, there the ME and its harmonics correlated well to El Nino, while SMax and its harmonics correspond to La Nina. Therefore, in this way, one can predict that the year 2006 will be the year of La Nina.

Starting from year 1950 to 1976, during the occurrences of El Nino, the sea temperature in the eastern region of the archipelago was low, and conversely during La Nina, the sea temperature was high, which means that low sea temperature in the archipelago correlates positively to sunspot minimum SMin and its harmonics, while the high sea temperature correlates positively to maximum eruptions ME and its harmonics. In 1976 phase reversal occurred, SM and SM/2 or sunspot maximum SMax correlate positively with high sea surface temperature in eastern Indonesia and as a result precipitations increased.

The Correlation of Sunspot to Rainfall in the Indonesian Archipelago

With the equator crossing Indonesia, the sensible heat flux plays an important role in global circulations. The latent heat which originates mainly from the release of latent heat when water vapour condenses into clouds droplets(a number of large clouds form through convections in the Inter Tropical Convergence Zone (ITCZ) which is above Indonesia). The cold monsoon season in northern hemisphere (Asian monsoon) and in the southern hemisphere (Australian monsoon) are influenced by the heat source distribution or the release of latent heat above Asia and in the neighbourhood regions[13]. At present it seems that the Indonesian zone holds the key to southern oscillation system which determines the forcing of El Nino-Southern Oscillation (ENSO)[14]. Therefore, Indonesia, through which the equator crosses has the maximum sensible heat flux, high rainfall, and monsoon circulations. Consequently, it is one of the most primal zones for convection processes, an equatorial-tropical zone where Coriolis effects are practically nullified, where atmospheric circulations are very different compared to the extra-tropical zones[15].

The observations and studies on Indonesian climate are limited, and the mathematical formulations of tropical dynamics are far more complex relative to those in the extra-tropical zones. For decades the awareness of the importance of climates in Indonesia have been neglected by international research community[16]. The distinct daily convection variability induced by land-sea wind circulations over some islands in Indonesia characterises the aspect of rainfall throughout the Indonesian Archipelago which are very different from other regions on the earth[17]. The studies mentioned above, show that rainfall is an important quantity in the Indonesian Archipelago and sunspot is believed to be the major predictor.

Although there is an indirect physical link between sunspot and rainfall, the correlations which existed in general are weak. In other words, these signify that the dynamics of the atmosphere is being viewed as the cause of the small correlations. However, in the case of static model atmosphere, determination of correlations based on data-averaging of anomalies of sunspot on a monthly basis against the average anomaly of rainfall for various stations in Indonesia, one comes to time series as shown in Figures 1a, 1b, and 1c at various regions for the period 1948-2003.

From Figure 1 and Figure 2 we can conclude that eastern Indonesia (Jayapura region) which represent Eastern Indonesian Maritime Continent is strongly influenced by ENSO. After 1976 sunspot maximum SMax and sunspot minimum SMin correspond to precipitations above normal also to La Nina and maximum eruptions ME corresponding to precipitations below normal and also to El Nino. In Pontianak region which represent western Indonesian Maritime Continent, the yearly precipitation is mainly determined by sunspot cycles. Precipitations above normal occur at sunspot maximum SMax, and precipitations below normal at sunspot minimum SMin. Precipitations in middle and east Java which represent North Australia Indonesian Monsoon are influenced by ENSO similar to those observed in Jayapura region. Precipitations in Jakarta region are weakly influenced by ENSO.

The fuzzy c-means clustering shows that the west Indonesian regions are influenced by IOD, the east Indonesian regions are influenced by ENSO and the middle region is mainly influenced by sunspot numbers.

Acknowledgement

This research is sponsored by RUT XI.2, LIPI.

References

1. Bryant, E., 1977. Climate Process and Change, Cambridge University Press.
2. Landscheidt, T., 1988. Solar Activity: A Dominant Factor in Climate Dynamics, Schroeter Institute for Research in Cycles of Solar Activity, http://www.johndaly.com/solar/solar.htm.
3. Carlslaw, K.S., R.G. Harrison, J. Kirkby, 2002. Cosmic Rays, Clouds, and Climate, Science's Compass, Vol. 298.
4. Landscheidt, T., 2003. New ENSO Forecast Based on Solar Model, Schroeter Institute for Research in Cycles of Solar Activity.
5. Foucal, P. and J. Lean, 1990. An Empirical Model of Total Solar Irradiance Variation between 1874 and 1988, Science, 247, 556-558.
6. Friis-Cristensen,E. and Lassen, K., 1991: Length of The Solar Cycle :an Indicator of Solar Activity Closely Associated with Climate, J. Science, 254, 698.
7. Baliunas, S. and W. Soon, 1996: The Sun-Climate Connection. Sky & Telescope, Dec., 38-41.
8. Reid, G.C., 1987: Nature. Vol. 329, hal.142.
9. Ratag, M.A., 999: Dampak Variabilitas Matahari terhadap Vegetasi:Cincin-cincin Kayu, Prosiding lokakarya program Iklim Nasional, 126-132, Jakarta.

10. Ratag, M.A., 1999: Fraktal Variabilitas Matahari dan Kaitannya dengan Dinamika Variabilitas iklim,Prosiding lokakarya program Iklim Nasional, 133-144, Jakarta.
11. Ratag, M.A., 1999: Dinamika Sistem Matahari-Bumi dan Perubahan Iklim Global, Prosiding lokakarya program Iklim Nasional, 150-160, Jakarta.
12. Ratag, M.A., 1994: Perubahan iklim global dan hubungan matahari-bumi, Proc.Media dirgantara LAPAN, 101-115.
13. Arief,S., 1999: Analisis aktivitas konveksi di benua maritim Indonesia dan sekitarnya pada perioda monsun Asia 1990-1997, Lokakarya Program Iklim Nasional Terpadu, 174-187.
14. Trenberth, K.E. and T.J. Hoar, 1996: The 1990-1995 El-Nino/Southern-Oscillation Event: Longest on Record, Geophys. Res. Lett., 23, 57-60.
15. McBride, J., 1992: The Meteorology of Indonesia and The Maritime Continet. The Fourth International Symposium on Equatorial Atmosphere Observation over Indonesia, Nov., 10-11, Jakarta.
16. Salby, M.L. and D.J. Sheaq, 1991: Correlation Between Solar Activity and the Atmosphere:An Unphysical Explanation.,J.Geophys.Res.,96,22,579-22,595.
17. Johnson, R.A. and D.W. Wichem, 1992: Applied Multivariate Statistical Analysis, third edition,Prectice Hall,New Jersey.
18. Ziegler, J.F: 1998. Terrestrial Cosmic Ray Intensities, IBM Journal of Research and Development, Vol. 42, No. 1

16

Characteristics of Indian Summer Monsoon in the Warming Scenario

S.K. Patwardhan*, K. Krishna Kumar, K. Kamala, Preethi Bhaskar, J.V. Revadekar and K. Rupa Kumar

Indian Institute of Tropical Meteorology,
Dr. Homi Bhabha Road, Pune, India
Phone: +91-20-25893600 ; Fax: +91-20-25893825
**E-mail: patwar@tropmet.res.in*

ABSTRACT

Regional climate models (RCMs) are comprehensive tools to develop physically consistent climate change scenarios on regional/local space scales. A state-of-the-art regional climate modeling system, known as PRECIS (Providing Regional Climates for Impacts Studies) developed by the Hadley Centre for Climate Prediction and Research, U.K. is applied over the Indian domain to develop high-resolution climate change scenarios. The PRECIS simulations at ~50 km resolution are made for two time slices, present (1961-1990) and the future (2071-2100) and analysed. The model simulations under scenarios of increasing greenhouse gas concentrations and sulphate aerosols indicate marked increase in both rainfall and temperature towards the end of the 21st century. The characteristics of two very important features of the southwest monsoon, viz. the onset date and the frequency and intensity of cyclonic disturbances have been examined as simulated by PRECIS in the baseline simulations. Likely future changes in these two aspects in the increased GHG scenario runs are discussed. The analysis of daily rainfall data indicates no significant change in the mean onset date in future though the variability of onset date will be more in warming scenario. The cyclonic disturbances in the monsoon season are likely to be more intense though less frequent towards the end of the 21st century.

Introduction

The changes in the climate of the earth during the past few decades have become the focus of scientific and social attention. Some evidences have also been gathered in favour of a definite change in the earth's climate system. Several studies have been undertaken with the observed data as well as General Circulation Model (GCM) integrations to project different scenarios of the climate change (IPCC, 2001). According to the Third Assessment Report of the Inter Governmental Panel on Climate Change (IPCC), average global temperature may rise by 1.4° to 5.8° C by 2100. The physical evidences of climate change are more specific to regions and hence it is necessary to concentrate more on the change in the regional scale climate.

For a country like India, where the economy of the country mainly depends on agriculture, the performance of monsoon both in space and time is very crucial and important. Onset of monsoon over the southernmost state of Kerala is the prime event in the meteorological calendar of India. Every year, summer monsoon arrives over Kerala coast around the end of May/beginning of June. Although no objective criterion exists for fixing the date of onset, the primary indicator from the early days of Indian Meteorology has been a sharp and sustained increase in rainfall at a group of adjacent stations. (Ananthkrishnan, 1967). The mean onset date over Kerala, according to India Meteorological Department, is 1st June with a std. dev. of 7.28 days. Ananthkrishnan and Soman (1988) have used a dense network of rain guages to find the mean onset date over south Kerala to be 30th May and for north Kerala 1st June with the standard deviation of about 9 days for both. In view of the importance of the onset in the Indian context, the likely effect of global warming on the onset of southwest monsoon is evaluated in the present study.

As the southwest monsoon progresses over India, the space-time variation of rainfall often occurs in association with the genesis and movement of synoptic scale systems, such as cyclonic disturbances (storms/depressions). The influence of greenhouse gas-induced warming on tropical cyclone activity, over different ocean basins, has been investigated by many researchers in recent years (Haarsma *et al.*, 1993; Bengtsson *et al.*, 1996; Walsh and Ryan, 2000; Sugi *et al.*, 2002). The analysis of the cyclonic disturbances over the Indian region for the period 1891-1998 indicates decreasing trend in the frequency of monsoon season cyclonic disturbances (Patwardhan and Bhalme, 2001). Analysis of the HadRM2 simulations show a decrease in the frequency of cyclonic storms over Indian region in 2041-2060 due to the global warming (Krishna Kumar *et al.*, 2005).

The effect of global warming on these two important components of southwest monsoon, viz onset of monsoon and cyclonic disturbances is studied using HadRM3H (PRECIS) model simulations.

Data

The Regional Climate Model PRECIS

PRECIS is an atmospheric and land surface model of limited area and high resolution which can be configured for any part of the globe. Dynamical flow, the atmospheric sulphur cycle, clouds and precipitation, radiative processes, the land surface and the deep soil are all formulated in the model and boundary conditions are required to be specified at the limits of the model's domain. Information about every aspect can be diagnosed from the model. The basic aspects explicitly handled by the model are briefly outlined in Noguer *et al.* (2002). For the present study, PRECIS has been configured for a domain extending from about 1.5°N to 38°N and 56°E to 103°E with a horizontal resolution of 0.44° in latitude and 0.44° in longitude

Lateral boundary conditions, namely surface pressure, winds, temperature and humidity, provide the necessary dynamical atmospheric information at the latitudinal and longitudinal edges of the model domain. PRECIS is forced at its lateral boundaries by a GCM of 150 km horizontal resolution called HadAM3H in so-called time slice experiments. HadAM3H is an atmosphere-only model which has been derived from the atmospheric component of HadCM3, the Hadley Centre's state-of-the-art coupled model which has a horizontal resolution of 3.75° latitude by 2.5° longitude. HadAM3H has been favoured over HadCM3 for driving the RCMs, since it has a higher resolution and exhibits an improved control climate, especially with respect to the positioning of the storm tracks of the Northern Hemisphere (Jones *et al.*, 1999). HadAM3H has thus been used to drive PRECIS for India over the two time slice periods. An ensemble of three HadAM3H runs for the period 1961-1990, three simulations for the A2 future scenario (2071-2100) and one simulation for the B2 future scenario (2071-2100) have been run and assessed by Hudson and Jones (2002).

Simulations using PRECIS have been performed to generate the climate for the present (1961-1990) and a future period (2071-2100) for two different socio-economic scenarios both characterised by regionally focused development but with priority to economic issues in one (A2 scenario) and to environmental issues in the other (B2 scenario). The IPCC published a new set of scenarios in 2000 for use in the Third Assessment Report (Special Report on Emissions Scenarios - SRES). The SRES scenarios were constructed to explore future developments in the global environment with special reference to the production of greenhouse gases and aerosol precursor emissions. The detailed description of SRES scenarios are reported in Nakicenovic N. A. *et al.* (2000). The results obtained for A2 and B2 scenarios are quite similar, though differ slightly in magnitude. Hence in the present study the climate change impacts are assessed and presented with respect to A2 scenario only.

Observed Data

The observed frequencies of cyclonic disturbances over the Indian region for the period 1961-1990 are taken from the Journal 'Mausam'. The regional mean rainfall and surface temperature series from the homogeneous monthly data sets developed by the Indian Institute of Tropical Meteorology (IITM; http://www.tropmet.res.in) have been used. Details of these data sets are discussed by Pant and Rupa Kumar (1997).

Discussion

The high-resolution regional simulations generated using PRECIS have been studied in detail to evaluate the model skill in representing the regional climatological features, especially the summer monsoon characteristics. The RCMs have shown

(Figure 3). This may be due to the fact that PRECIS simulated May rainfall for baseline (9.78 mm/day) is greater than A2 scenario (8.24 mm/day).

Table 1: Onset Dates of Southwest Monsoon Over Kerala Simulated by PRECIS

	Mean Onset Date over Kerala	*Std. Dev. (days)*
Observed	1st June	7.28
Baseline	27th May	7.2
A2 scenario	29th May	14.1

The model simulated OLR fields have been analysed in relation to the onset of monsoon. After the onset, the convective activity over Arabian sea decreases slowly and increases over northeast Bay of Bengal in model simulations. These results are matching well with the earlier study by Soman *et al.* (1993). But the convection is deeper in baseline (OLR < 140 W/m^2) as compared to the A2 scenario (OLR < 160 W/m^2).

Earlier studies have shown that the kinetic energy of zonal winds at 850 hPa over Arabian Sea rises steadily after the onset (Krishnamurthy *et al.*, 1981 and Raju *et al.*, 2005). Analysis of the model-simulated winds at 850 hPa over southeast Arabian sea captures this increase in zonal kinetic energy. It increases from 31 m^2/s^2 (onset – 5 days) to 67 m^2/s^2 (onset) for the baseline run. After the onset it rises steadily upto 118 $m^2/s.^2$ The rise is slightly less in future scenario as compared to baseline. In the warming scenario it rises from 33 m^2/s^2 (onset – 5 days) to 54 m^2/s^2 (onset) and shows steady rise upto 113 m^2/s^2 thereafter.

The cyclonic disturbances are identified from the PRECIS outputs using the following criteria: i). The centre of cyclonic disturbances is a grid point at which the sea level pressure over the region of cyclogenesis is minimum. ii) The centre of cyclonic disturbance is a grid point at which the sea level pressure departure from the daily mean should be less than -5 hPa. iii) Maximum wind speed at 10m level near the centre of the disturbance should be more than 17 knots and iv) The system should persist for at least two days. The cyclonic disturbances identified using the above criteria are studied to find out the effect of global warming on their frequency and intensity. The model overestimates the frequency and the intensity of the cyclonic disturbances in baseline simulation. The frequency of the cyclonic disturbances during monsoon season appears to decrease in the future due to the increase in the concentration of greenhouse gases. In addition the analysis indicates that the systems may be more intense in the warming scenario (Table 2).

Table 2: Monthly Frequency of Cyclonic Disturbances (Per Year) Simulated by PRECIS. The values in the parenthesis indicate the mean maximum intensity (knots).

	June	*July*	*Aug.*	*Sept.*	*Monsoon*
Observed	1.5(27)	1.4(23)	2.1(24)	2(29)	7(26)
Baseline	1.6(34)	2.2(32)	1.7(29)	2.7(31)	8.2(31)
A2 scenario	1.7(37)	1.7(34)	1.4(30)	2.6(34)	7.4(34)

Summary

The high resolution regional climate model simulations are analysed to study the model skills in evaluating the monsoon characteristics. PRECIS shows good skill in depicting the monsoon climatology over Indian region. Model simulations under scenarios of increasing greenhouse gas concentrations and sulphate aerosols indicate marked increase in both rainfall (20%) and temperature (2.5° to 5° C) into the 21st century. Following are the major conclusions based on the analysis of model outputs

- The model simulates early onset of Indian monsoon over Kerala (27 May) as compared to the normal onset on 1st June. Future scenarios also show higher variability for the date of onset.
- The intensity of the cyclonic disturbances during monsoon appears to be higher in the warming scenario. However, the disturbances may be less frequent in the future.

Acknowledgments

This work is part of a Joint Indo-UK collaborative programme on climate change impacts in India. The authors are grateful to the Department for Environment, Food and Rural Affairs (DEFRA), Government of United Kingdom, for sponsoring this project and the Ministry of Environment and Forest (MoEF), Government of India, for coordinating its implementation. The project team is grateful to the Hadley Centre for Climate Prediction and Research, UK Meteorological Office, for making the regional models and their data products available for this study.

References

1. Ananthkrishnan R., Acharya, U.R. and Rama Krishna, A.R., 1967: On the criteria for declaring the onset of the southwest monsoon over Kerala. Forecasting Manual, FMU. Rep. No. IV- 18.1, India Meteorological Department, Pune, India, 52pp.
2. Ananthkrishnan R. and Soman M. K., 1988: The onset of south-west monsoon over Kerala: 1901-1980. J. Climatol. 8. 283-296.
3. Bengtsson L., Botzet M. and Esch M., 1996: Will greenhouse gas-induced warming over the next 50 years lead to higher frequency and greater intensity of hurricanes? Tellus 48A, 57-73.
4. Haarsma R. J., Mitchell, J. F. B. and Senior, C. A., 1993: Tropical Disturbances in a GCM, Clim Dyn. 8, 247-257.
5. Hudson, D.A. and Jones, R.G., 2002: Regional climate model simulations of present-day and future climates of Southern Africa. Technical Note No. 39, Hadley Centre for Climate Prediction and Research, Exeter, UK, 42pp.
6. IPCC, 2001: Climate Change 2001: The Scientific Basis. Contribution of Working Group I to the Third Assessment Report of the Intergovernmental Panel on Climate Change (J. T. Houghton, Y. Ding, D. J. Griggs, M. Noguer, P. J. Vander Linden, X. Dai, K. Maskell and C. A. Johnson Eds.), Cambridge University Press, Cambridge, UK, 881pp.

7. Jones, R. G., *et al.*, 1999: Configuring new climate models for Europe with improved climatologies via better representation of physical processes. UKMO second year report for MERCURE. EC contract ENV4.CT97.0485.

8. Krishna Kumar K. Mishra P. K., Patwardhan S. K., Revadekar J. V. and Rupa Kumar K., 2005: Impact of Global warming on the Cyclonic storms in the Bay of Bengal and the Arabian sea. Predicting Meteorological Events : Mathematical Approach, Ed.N. C. Mahanti. 114-125.

9. Krishnamurthy, T.N., Ardanuy, P., Ramanathan Y. and Pasch, R., 1981: On the onset vortex of summer monsoon, Mon. Wea. Rev., 109(2), 344-363.

10. Naguer M., Jones R., Hessel D, Hudson D, Wilson S. Jenkins J, and Mitchell J., 2002: Workbook on generating high resolution climate change scenarios using PRECIS, Hadley Centre for Climate Prediction and Research, Met Office, Bracknell, UK., 43pp.

11. Nakicenovic N. A. et. al., 2000: Special Report on Emission Scenarios. A special report of working Group III of the International Panel on Climate Change, Cambridge University Press, Cambridge, U. K., 599pp.

12. Pant, G.B. and Rupa Kumar, K., 1997: Climates of South Asia. John Wiley & Sons, Chichester, 320pp. (ISBN 0-471-94948-5).

13. Patwardhan S. K. and Bhalme H. N., 2001: A study of cyclonic disturbances over India and the adjacent Ocean. Int. J. Climatol., vol 21 527-534.

14. Raju, P.V. S., Mohanty, U. C. and Bhatla R., 2005: Onset characteristics of the southwest monsoon over India., Int. J. Climatol., vol. 25, no. 2, 167-182.

15. Rupa Kumar K., A.K. Sahai, K. Krishna Kumar, S.K. Patwardhan, P.K. Mishra, J.V. Revadekar, K. Kamala and G.B. Pant, 2006 : High-resolution climate change scenarios for India, Current Science, vol. 90, no. 3, 334-345..

16. Soman M. K. and Krishna Kumar K., 1993: Space-time evolution of Meteorological features associated with the onset of Indian summer monsoon. Monthly Weather Review. Vol 121, 4, 1177-11

17. Suji M., Noda A. and Sato N., 2002: Influence of the global warming on tropical cyclone Climatology : An experiment with the JMA Global model J. Met. Soc. Japan, vol. 80, No. 2 249-272.

18. Walsh K. and Ryan B.F., 2000: Tropical cyclonic intensity increase near Australia as a result of Climate Change, J. Climate, 13, 3029-3036.